Informality

For most of the twentieth century, modernity has been characterised by the formalisation of social relations as face to face interactions are replaced by impersonal bureaucracy and finance. As we enter the new millennium, however, it becomes increasingly clear that it is only by stepping outside these formal structures that trust and cooperation can be created and social change achieved. In a brilliant theoretical tour de force, illustrated with sustained case studies of changing societies in the former eastern Europe and of changing forms of interaction within so-called 'virtual communities', Barbara Misztal argues that only the society that achieves an appropriate balance between the informality and formality of interaction will find itself in a position to move forward to further democratisation and an improved quality of life.

Barbara A. Misztal is Senior Lecturer in the Faculty of Arts at Griffith University, Brisbane. She is the author of *Trust in Modern Society*, Polity, 1996.

International Library of Sociology

Founded by Karl Mannheim

Editor: John Urry
University of Lancaster

Informality

Social theory and
contemporary practice

Barbara A. Misztal

London and New York

First published 2000
by Routledge
11 New Fetter Lane, London EC4P 4EE

Simultaneously published in the USA and Canada
by Routledge
29 West 35th Street, New York, NY 10001

Routledge is an imprint of the Taylor & Francis Group

© 2000 Barbara A. Misztal

Typeset in Baskerville by Bookcraft Ltd, Stroud
Printed and bound in Great Britain by Biddles Ltd, Guildford and King's Lynn

British Library Cataloguing in Publication Data
A catalogue record for this book is available from the British Library

Library of Congress Cataloging in Publication Data
Misztal, Barbara A.
  Informality: social theory and contemporary practice/
  Barbara A. Misztal
      p.   cm. — (International library of sociology)
   Includes bibliographical references (p.   )
   1. Social interaction. I. Title. II. Series.
HM1111.M57   1999
302—dc21   99-16271
                                              CIP

ISBN 0-415-15673-4 (hbk)
ISBN 0-415-15674-2 (pbk)

For David, who knows we need formality

Contents

Introduction: What use is the concept of informality?

In all differentiated societies, as in many simpler ones, there are categories of social situation in which the social code demands from members raised in the society that they behave in formal ways – or, to use a noun, it demands *formality* of behaviour; and there are other categories of social situation where, according to the code, informal behaviour, – that is, a more or less high degree of *informality* is appropriate (Elias 1996:28).

WHY ARE MANAGERS STILL TRAVELLING?

Despite modern communications technologies (teleconferencing, video-conferencing, faxes, electronic mail, telephones, etc), senior managers still spend the majority of their time in face-to-face encounters (Rice 1991). In order to meet their business partners, bosses of the biggest corporate giants travel up to five days a week (*The Economist,* 16 December, 1995:16). So, why are they travelling? The answer to this question will illustrate why people, despite the fact that the essence of modern social life is the replacement of informal obligations and interaction by impersonal and formal rules, still value informality.

Generally, it can be said that managers do travel because they value face-to-face contacts as having the potential to draw individuals deeper into relationships with one another and thereby offer a fuller sense of individual recognition and trust.

Managers' well-documented preference for face-to-face communication (Minzberg 1973; Kurke and Aldrich 1983; McKenney, Zack and Doherty 1992; Nohria and Eccles 1992) is based on their belief that co-present communication can reduce the risk of uncooperative behaviour due to its capacity to build an understanding and to enact solutions to disputable problems (McKenney, Zack and Doherty 1992). Managers 'forsake the convenience of e-mail for the discomfort of air travel' because they presume that nothing succeeds in creating trust better than 'eyeball to eyeball' contact (*The Economist,* 16 December, 1995:16). Modern organizations and their managers operate under the new conditions of the growing division of labour, the enlarging dependence on employees' judgement and commitment and the expanding importance of cooperative networks, which all contribute to the increase in demand for negotiation and trust (Fukuyama 1995; Misztal 1996; Seligman 1997). In a world where so many issues look so complex and unpredictable, to recreate the condition of trust often requires to overstep the frontiers of formal divisions, boundaries and rules since, as Unger (1987:139) convincingly argues, the possibility of change and improvement of societal conditions depends on 'the replacement of the impersonal by the personal'. Consequently, as the need for trust is spreading and as cooperative networks and innovative approaches are becoming important sources of economic success, many companies try to reconcile the 'twin claims of trust and flexibility' (*The Economist*, 16 December, 1995:16) by reducing formal control, limiting the role of traditional monitoring systems and increasing informal engagements of employees. Furthermore, managers' main task, which is to secure beneficial deals, and their not totally formalized and regulated conduct, necessitate negotiation. The more negotiation, the more the need to secure some kind of pre-commitment or, as Ring and Van de Ven (1992) argue, the more the need to be concerned with the trustworthiness of the other party.

Managers' intuitive appreciation of the importance of informality is supported by a substantial body of social psychological research indicating that the medium and conditions of conversation do affect ratings of the conversation and the conversation partner (Reid 1977). These experiments not only suggest that visual clues, such as facial expression, gesture and posture, are associated in regular and predictable ways with particular types of face-to-face conversation and with types of communicators, but also that face-to-face contact gives participants the feeling that the other can be influenced more, thus making it appear more worthwhile to act cooperatively (Wichman 1970). New media of communications are not a substitute for face-to-face interaction because co-present interaction offers an unusual capacity for repair, negotiation, feedback, interruption and learning as well as a wide range of information and impressions that partners want to give to one another. Secondly, this group of experiments on people's perception has found that in face-to-face discussion participants reach agreement sooner than in any negotiation taking place not in the face-to-face condition (Dorris, Gentry and Kelly 1971). In face-to-face interaction 'differences in initial positions held by negotiators converge more rapidly' (Nohria and Eccles 1992:296). Thirdly, these studies have also discovered that the absence of 'vision' produces a more 'formal discussion', so that discussions at a distance tend to become more a negotiation between two organizations than between two people, while face-to-face contact accentuates the interpersonal and social aspects of the conversation (Morley and Stephenson 1970). 'The less formal face-to-face negotiation will thus produce more emphasis on the human and reciprocal processes of interpersonal communication; this results in greater generosity and yielding by the side with the stronger case' (Reid 1977:401). Furthermore, participants in face-to-face negotiations express significantly higher confidence in their judgements than participants in other types of negotiation, for instance, in bargaining carried out on the telephone (Reid 1977). Finally, co-present interaction is especially valued in the situation of uncertainty and ambiguity, where non-verbal clues (such as facial expressions or gestures) can clarify the meaning of messages. Summarizing, it can be said that 'face-to-face communication plays an essential role in establishing and maintaining the kind of multidimensional and robust relationships necessary for effective interaction and coordinated action in situations of uncertainty, ambiguity and risk' (Nohria and Eccles 1992: 299).

So, managers are still travelling because they value information about the trustworthiness of their business partners and they assume that the informality of face-to-face interaction is the best and a relatively inexpensive way of gathering such information. In other words, they appreciate the usefulness of informal strategies to secure the predictability of the system and, consequently, to achieve their organizational goals. Managers' appreciation of informal encounters and tacit understanding shows that, although the process of formalization is the dominant trend in modern social life, informality is the essential element in constructing trust relationships and, therefore, in any cooperative arrangement aimed at improving the quality of life. Nonetheless, despite their understanding of the importance of informality in securing their organizational goals, managers would not like to abandon the formal guarantees provided by the contract for the advantages of more personalized arrangements. This recognition of the importance and the necessity of formal contracts and rules is a result of managers' awareness of negative consequences of informality, such as favouritism, nepotism and patronage. So, it can be said that the positive value of informality is only ensured in the context of the process of formalization of individual rights and public rules.

INFORMALITY AND FORMALITY

The realization that informality may be a threat to fair and just treatment contributes to the appreciation of an impersonal order of hierarchical rules, which, as Weber noted, offers forms of protection both for the individual and wider organizations. Evidence such as the fact that white graduates are almost twice as likely to be offered jobs by top British companies as their black and Asian counterparts (*Guardian Weekly*, 18 January, 1998:10) shows that informal factors are a vital component of indirect discrimination. So we cannot rely solely on informality to create a more trustworthy, cooperative and just society. This message has also been brought to our attention by the recent Asian economic crisis, usually portrayed as the failure of a capitalism based on 'informal connections' such as nepotism, clientelism and corruption. Crony capitalism, with its institutional weaknesses, its lack of transparency of informal links and its inability to move beyond the informal and the personal in its ways of doing business (Rohwer 1996:57), is presented as responsible for the recent economic problems of the region. Hence it can be said that informal bonds, networking and dealings, while crucial for cooperative, quick and flexible arrangements, need to be supported and need to operate within formal structures securing transparency, accountability and partners' rights.

Formal procedural democracy and rational universal administration are modern societies' essential instruments to facilitate societal cooperation. In Western democracies the universalism and openness of formal procedural ruling are intended to ensure that the role of personalized ties, such as patriomonialism or clientelism, is limited. While the impersonality of formalized public rules reduces personal dependency, the impersonality in the exercise of power fails, however, to 'dispose of the practical costs and the social discontents of dependence' (Unger 1987:109). This failure exposes a weakness of liberal democratic structures: that is, their inability to inspire in people positive and strong emotions in support of existing political institutions. The increasingly visible shortcoming of liberal systems seems to suggest that impersonality and formalization enhance people's feeling of emptiness and their resistance to both the standardizing potential of the market and the totalitarian trends of a fully administrated society. Many recent changes, which have eroded the democratic order's grounds for the universally applied rules, point to the need for a strategy combining impersonal and procedural rules with more particularistic and local standards, thereby ensuring equality without undermining individual uniqueness.

This growing awareness that further democratization requires recognition of the importance of not only the public sphere and its formal rules but also of many informal debates, has been assisted by the erosion of the demarcation between the personal domain of the primary groups and the impersonal domain of formal institutions. With both formal relations of the political and economic system and informal ties linking civil society into a single system of relations, informal bonds, debates and associations are valid platforms for exploring social problems, conflicts and disagreements. They allow people to associate freely with each other and undertake cooperative actions outside established formal institutions. Such actions require mutual trust and respect, the cultivation of which is the essence of civil society. However, while seeing in civil society's informal ties a ready remedy for our major problems, we have to be aware that such ties and actions can also restrict individual freedoms and bar outsiders from gaining access to societal resources. So, in order to revitalize the idea of civil society, we have to recognize the importance of particular affiliations without rejecting the formal rationality of our highly differentiated and complex societies.

The question about the links between formal and informal is also brought to our attention by the expanding scope and the practical importance of various non-hierarchical, voluntarily negotiated forms of self-coordination, which are a result of the growing division of labour, shifts of boundaries between private and public and the development of new means of communication. The process of the growing division of labour, together with an increase in the number of roles we fulfil in society, expands the demand for negotiation because the boundaries and content of specific role expectations are no longer entirely explained according to rigid or formalized codes (Seligman 1997). Consequently, with roles open to negotiation and interpretation, with the processes of the pluralization of contexts of action, diversification of authorities and the growing variety of lifestyles, people are faced with indeterminacy and unpredictability, which require a closer look at the potential of various tactics, especially informality, for the constitution of order. We should not, however, forget that the recent movement towards the loosening of formal hierarchies and de-conventionalization of organized practices still occurs in the context of the continuous process of formalization and within the persistent importance of institutions, where the explicit rationality of bureaucratic rules and conventions is still the dominant mood of control and organization.

With the demarcation between the personal domain of the primary groups and the impersonal sphere of formal institutions being now eroded, there is a growing awareness that further democratization requires recognition of the importance of not only the public sphere and its formal rules but also of many informal debates as valid platforms for exploring social problems, conflicts and disagreements. Since not only the formal relations of the political and economic system, but also the informal ties link civil society into a single system of relations, both of them are essential. In their continuous practical attempts to constitute the orderliness of social life, people now more than ever try to avoid sharply dichotomized and exclusive alternatives and try to mediate between the particularism of personalized relations and the impersonality of formal structures. Furthermore, with the complexity of the relationships between informal and formal being increased by new means of communication, which induce less formal modes of interaction and bring new fluidity to human relationships, the usefulness of informality – as a tactic to alleviate the growing contingency and ambiguity of the globalized world – has been expanded.

Today, this search for balance between informality and formality becomes especially significant because globalization, helped by new electronic means of communication, enhances the importance of cooperative relationships and the innovative use of knowledge as sources of productivity gains (Madrick 1998). What becomes increasingly valuable is the imaginative use of information, which – in turn – requires open, unrestricted, reciprocal communication, based on an understanding that expands beyond instrumental concerns and beyond formal hierarchy. However, while all these new developments require us to reinvent the relationships between formal and informal interactional practices, the task of re-thinking strategies of negotiation of order is not a simple assignment.

The search for balance between informality and formality is a difficult task because each phenomenon differently alters societal demand for trust and the level of social trust. For instance, the process of informalization increases the unpredictability of the social world by making irrelevant all previously known codes of behaviour, hence increasing social demand for negotiation and trust. On the other hand, the process of formalization, by taking the responsibilities for negotiation from the participants, may reduce their mutual trust and understanding. How this growing reliance on the formal rules and rights to regulate interaction reduces our responsibility for negotiating the boundaries of acceptable behaviour is well illustrated by Seligman's description of his reaction to the banning of smoking from public spaces: 'I stopped asking the people around me if it bothered them. From my perspective the matter had been taken out of my hands: it was no longer something to be negotiated by the partners to the interaction but was solely the function of legal and abstract dicta ... . Freed from the burden of concern, indeed, of civility, the field of smoking was henceforth ruled by law, that is, by system, rather than by negotiation and by trust' (1997:173).

The relationships between informality and formality are further complicated by the fact that the trends towards formalization and informalization reciprocally fuel each other and by the paradoxical nature of these processes' long-term consequences. For example, the atrophy of informal control leads to the expansion of bureaucratic controls which, in turn, 'weakens trust, undermines the willingness both to assume responsibility for oneself and to hold others accountable for their actions' (Lasch 1995:98). Moreover, in a similar way to that in which the expansion of bureaucratic control leads to the erosion of partners' consideration for each other's trust and respect, the extension of less hierarchical and less formal control may also contribute in the long term to the erosion of cooperative spirit and trust. The flexible exercise of power can undermine trust, which tends to 'develop informally in the cracks and crevices of bureaucracies as people learn on whom they can depend' (Sennett 1998:141), because such organizations, instead of promoting employees' reliance on others in crises, inspire vulnerability and make people mistrustful of others. For instance, the new flexible mood of production, while expanding the demand for trust, at the same time erodes the bases of trust relationships by contributing to downsizing, short-line production, the disappearance of permanent jobs, the reduction of opportunities for well-structured career paths and on-the-job training as well as contributing to the increase in casual and part time jobs. Consequently, as the reduced stability and duration of interpersonal relations and bonds at work undermine the importance of informal groups at the workplace, workers' ability to experience commitment, loyalty and trust is corroded.

While, on one hand, the short time-frame, unpredictability and flexibility of modern institutions limit 'the ripening of informal trust' (Sennett 1998: 24), on the other hand, organizational rigidity and inability to tolerate any degree of unpredictability are incompatible with the environment's request for innovation and change. So, 'the project of creating a wholly or largely predictable organisation committed to creating wholly or largely predictable society is doomed and doomed by the facts about social life' (MacIntyre 1981:101). At the same time, society, for its long-term functioning, requires predictability because predictability enables us to plan and engage in long-term projects and, therefore, 'it is a necessary condition of being able to find life meaningful' (MacIntyre 1981:98). A quest for meaning in life, as a life project, is both the result and the antecedent of our actions. In MacIntyre's approach, the construction of a definition of 'a good life' is a process that never ends. Its unpredictability, however, does not imply inexplicability, just as 'predictability does not entail explicability' (*ibid*:97). Consequently, it can be said that, as many of the central features of human life 'derive from the particular and peculiar ways in which predictability and unpredictability interlock' (*ibid*:98), a life dedicated to a quest for a good life presents a balance between the predictable and unpredictable elements in social life. Because of the connections between unpredictability and informality and between predictability and formality, the relationships between informality and formality can be seen as a special case of the more general relations between predictability and unpredictability. They are therefore also responsible for the quality of social life.

To sum up, the trends towards formalization, seen as contributing to an expansion of predictability of social life, and informalization, seen as contributing to the demise of predictability, are essential parts of modern life. When their effects, such as expanding the need for trust and introducing new formal ways of regulating interaction, are well balanced, these two processes taken together can improve the quality of social life. As the uncertainty and unpredictability of the modern context increase, the creation of conditions for cooperation and integration requires both the structural preconditions and the familiarity of informal relations. Only the balanced relationship between informality and formality of interactional practices can secure a potentially more imaginative solution to today's problems of coordination, solidarity and innovation.

AIMS OF THE BOOK

My broadest aim in this book is to construct a synthetic approach to the issue of informality and to develop a sociological perspective on the relationship between formality and informality of interactional practices. Assuming that the reduction of uncertainty and the establishment of reciprocal expectations is essential for societal trust, I argue that, just as it was necessary in the past to invent ways of combining formal and informal rules that go into social order, so it is necessary today to construct such a balance between informality and informality which will help to facilitate people's cooperative and creative conduct. Modern systems are seen not only as incorporating formal rules and informal practices but also as being shaped by the dynamics of these relations, which itself is determined by the system's orientation towards predictability. I argue that since society requires predictability and orderliness for its long-term functioning, there is a need to rethink the relationships between formality and informality in such a way that would allow us to take full advantage of the expanded opportunities to shift frames, without, however, undermining the basic structures of society.

While the goal of the book is to initiate discussion on the relationships between informal and formal interactional practices, its main focus will be on the notion of informality as it is a less theoretically developed and appreciated concept. The current literature on the issue of informality, as the review of the main perspectives addressing the problem of informality illustrates (Chapter 1), is fragmented into separate areas, each with its own concepts and theories and each dealing with its own specific topics (community studies, organizational studies, ethnomethodology, network analysis, interactionism and so on). This empirical and theoretical fragmentation of the field, as well as the growing number of calls to construct a plausible synthetic approach, suggests the need for a more integrated sociological approach to the issue of informality. Seeing informality as an essential element of interactional practice requires us to pay special attention to an interactionist perspective as the most helpful approach in the understanding of social intercourses whose ends are fluid, changeable and undetermined. However, to portray a style of interaction that successfully balances freedom and reflexivity (as the features of informality) and restrictions of scripts (as the aspects of formality) calls for the enrichment of an interactionist perspective by an institutional approach.

Although none of the sociological theories addresses the issues of informality in a direct and entirely satisfactory way, their examination permits us to conclude that informality cannot be limited to face-to-face interaction and to a local context where there is a relative absence of asymmetries of power. Following a growing number of sociological studies, which are trying to overcome the dichotomous formal–informal distinction, and which are beginning to show that in many spheres of life both formal and informal aspects co-exist and that these multiple relations become too dynamic to be expressed by the rigidity of the dualism, I argue that informality does not necessarily imply an exclusive focus on the micro level or on solely non-instrumental and particularistic-oriented interaction. Instead of looking at informality as only referring to small talk, tacit behaviour or gossiping, it can be understood as a form of interaction among partners enjoying relative freedom in interpretation of their roles' requirements. Such a definition of informality allows us to capture the shape of the 'formality-informality span', which refers to 'the extent and strictness of the social rituals which bind the behaviour of people in their dealings with each other' (Elias 1996:70). Since the expanding scope for informality is matched by an increase in the number of rules and in the formalization of rights in the public sphere (Elias 1996), the process of informalization is seen in the context of the persisting tendency towards the depersonalization of social relations in the public realm.

Following the line of argument that the shape of the 'informality-formality span' is the main factor responsible for the type and nature of social relationships, it can be assumed that the balanced relationships between informality and formality are essential to an integrated and cooperative society. Because the dynamics of these relations have shaped the system's orientation towards predictability, informalization and formalization are the key to reinventing and sustaining meaningful social relationships in modern societies. Hence, the essential issue is how to synchronize these two processes so they would contribute to the improvement of the quality of social life. I argue that constituting a new balance between formal and informal styles of behaviour is a process that depends on the piecing together of new modes of social control, new institutions and new means of communication.

In the context of the diversity of lifestyles, the advanced division of labour, the active presence of the mass media and with the growing popularity of electronic means of communication, it is very likely that people receive conflicting signals and that they perceive social order as being relatively unpredictable (Chapter 2). In order to recreate the condition of trust, in the context of the absence of a shared meaning, people attempt, on one hand, to introduce procedural, impersonal universalistic rules and, on the other hand, to construct a common understanding in the course of informal interaction. In other words, while confronting the problem of the unpredictability of order, we try to do both: to construct clear-cut formal rules and to recreate a shared meaning. Furthermore, these solutions are not totally disassociated. It is within these informal personalized networks on which people rely in ambiguous circumstances where the collective interest is constructed, which may then translate itself into new rights, formal rules and institutionalized privileges (Barnes 1995). Informality and formality are thus not to be regarded as mutually exclusive options but rather as two tactics, each providing a partial solution to the unpredictability of the system.

The importance of both informal and formal interactional practices for coping with the unpredictability of the social system means that the relationship between formality and informality is one of the main factors responsible for the quality of social life. Hence, the issue of how to synchronize the processes of informalization and formalization can be reformulated as the question: into what style of interaction should we now be socialized in order to achieve a better quality of individual and social life?

I argue that it should be a style of interaction which would prevent informalization from becoming synonymous with the notion of 'the permissive society' and which would not allow attempts at overcoming contingencies of the social order to become nothing more than the expansion of personal loyalties, parochialism and corruption. Secondly, it should be a style of interaction able to enhance partners' mutual respect, their mutual responsibility and reciprocity. How actors strike the optimal balance between informal and formal interactional practices or, in other words, how they manage to treat others with tact or 'the right touch', depends upon particularities of a given type of interaction. It means that a different tactful behaviour is essential for different types of interaction. By analyzing such optimal styles of interactional practices (civility, sociability and intimacy) in three social realms of interaction (encounters, exchange and pure relationships), the conditions for the construction of trustworthy and cooperative relations can be identified.

Civility, sociability and intimacy, as kinds of context-specific tact, are seen as the essential steps in achieving a better quality of individual and social life because these interactional practices open a door to more inspiring solutions to the problems of cooperation, integration and innovation. On one hand, they allow us to preserve distance, to avoid offensive and intrusive violations of the private sphere of the person, and to suppress socially unacceptable levels of spontaneity and particularism within their respective realms. On the other hand, they mitigate the unnecessary formalism and abstractness of universalism and help to train receptivity and sensitivity towards others. Consequently, these three styles of interaction, as the manifestations of the fine tuning of informality and formality in different social settings, are seen as being central to the creation of social trust, while the concept of 'the formality-informality span', seen as a useful way of looking at the changing world of global communication and shifting boundaries, is also a suitable tool for explaining the nature of different political systems.

To sum up, the main assumption holds that only a society that achieves an optimal balance between the informality and formality of interactional practices is in the position to create conditions for cooperation, cohesion and innovation. By arguing that the fine tuning of informality and formality is central to the creation of social trust, this approach offers not only a potentially more imaginative approach to the problems of cooperation, integration and innovation, but also a more comprehensive perspective which combines different levels of analysis of some of the major transformations in modern societies. Furthermore, by providing a theoretical framework for understanding people's creative and flexible responses to situational complexity and ambiguity, it overcomes the shortcomings of approaches concentrating on the content of the relationships between the individual and society, and allows for the reconceptualization of levels of inquiry and the elimination of the contrast between a macro-institutional order and micro-interaction order.

OUTLINE OF THE BOOK

The book is divided into three parts. The first part consists of three chapters and is devoted to the further elaboration of our understanding of the concept of informality and its assets. In order to identify the principal arguments employed within the discipline to discuss the phenomenon of informality, Chapter 1 looks at sociological theories that go beyond the definition of human agency as habitual, repetitive and taken for granted. An interactionist approach, Goffman's perspective and empirically oriented studies of ordinary conversations are discussed in the search for a definition of informality. Informality, defined as a style of interaction among partners enjoying relative freedom in interpreting their formal roles' requirements, is seen in the context of the persisting tendency towards the depersonalization of social relations in the public realm.

Because a full explanation of how actors strike the optimal balance between informal and formal styles of interaction requires a more careful examination of social contexts in which interaction takes place, Chapter 2 looks at the structural changes that demand a rethinking of the relationship between formality and informality. While analysing the processes of de-conventionalization, the blurring of the boundaries between public and private regulation and between the frontstage and backstage regions, it is argued that the growth of unpredictability and formlessness of the contemporary social world creates new opportunities to escape role obligation, while at the same time increasing the demand for trust.

Chapter 3 is the summary presentation of civility, sociability and intimacy as three styles of interaction, characteristic of three different types of being together: encounters, exchange and pure relationships. The argument that civility, sociability and intimacy represent the essential basis for any meaningful reinvention of the individualized and deconventionalized modern society is based on the supposition that only a society that finds an optimal balance between the informality and formality of interactional practices is in the position to create conditions for cooperative, integrated and innovative society.

The second part of the book, *Revealing the significance of informality*, tries to uncover implicit assumptions about the role of informality in theories of social cooperation, integration and innovation. Chapter 4 examines rational theory, the normative perspective and Tocqueville-like approach's explanations of the phenomenon of cooperation. While debating the links between informality and cooperation, it is argued that the production of public good is a contingent process depending on people's perception of one another as trustworthy or their ability to predict other's behaviour. The higher likelihood of cooperation is seen as coupled with the strength of group identity and with the existence of a more predictable context, which – in turn – is linked to the broader scope of institutionalization and wider social networks as well as a dense system of conventions.

Chapter 5, while looking at the process of integration, examines connections between informality and proximity and the role assigned to informality in theories stressing the structural and hierarchical integration between actors in their specific roles. It proposes that in order to explain the process of the construction of networks of cohesive relations we should incorporate the strategic side of interaction, a factor neglected by communicative action theories, as well as the communicative nature of collective action, which is ignored by the rational choice approach. Bringing interest and solidarity together allows us to conceptualize sociability as contributing to socio-cultural constraints on self-interested behaviour and as playing an important part in open, widespread networks connecting people in their formal as well as informal roles.

Chapter 6, which is devoted to an examination of the dynamics of innovation, provides more arguments for and proof of the growing appreciation of informal networks, seen as essential in maintaining the flow of tacit knowledge. Because innovation is 'about taming uncertainty' and because of the growing importance of knowledge in the process of production, a new productive challenge depends more and more on enlarging the chance of communication and commitment among partners enjoying relative freedom of interpretation of their formal roles' requirements. To ensure that all participants in complex innovative endeavours have good reasons to cooperate in trustworthy exchange, they need to be a part of social networks, able to facilitate the collective process of learning.

The third and last part of the book looks at the empirical evidence of the role of informality in the contemporary world. Chapter 7 examines the impact of new means of communication and describes the nature of informality in cyberspace. Chapter 8 tries to show that the nature of the political regime can be seen as responsible for the scope of informality and the role of the informal realm in shaping solutions to the system's problems. By looking at both communist and post-communist societies, with Poland being the main case study, we will be able to evaluate how the liberation of the private sphere has changed the nature of society and how the postcommunist future may be affected by the overlapping relationships between the private and public.

Finally, in the Conclusion some earlier themes are revisited and the role of informality in the process of democratization is discussed. Internal to this discussion is a warning about the danger of idealizing the potential of informality. It is argued that the idea of informality as the main factor responsible for the quality of social life and for productivity gains should not be overstated, yet the contribution of informality to the creation of the opportunity to achieve a more flexible society should not be ignored. Rethinking the bases of obligations and responsibilities in such a way as to increase awareness of mutual interdependence requires such an institutional design, which – without solely relying on co-presence, yet protecting communication free from formal control and sanctions – would improve the cooperative links between people.

In summary, the following chapters explore the issue of informality and its relationships with formality in order to enhance the competence of our social theory and extend our understanding of people's creative and flexible responses to situational complexity and ambiguity. They provide fresh insights into styles of interaction essential for further democratization by stressing the importance of links between informal, discursive sources of democracy and its decision-making institutions.

Part I

Informality and its assets

1   Defining informality

... above and beyond the instituted forms that still exist and sometimes pre-
dominate, there is an informal underground centrality that assures the
perdurability of life in society. It is to this reality we should turn: we are not
used to it and our analytical tools may be rather rusty (Maffesoli 1996:4).

PROBLEMS WITH THE CONCEPT OF INFORMALITY

In social theory the ambiguous nature of concepts is nothing new. They are
used, despite their vagueness, because they, as products of 'imagination,
vision, intuition' (Nisbet 1970:18), may show some phenomena in a new
light and, therefore, they may contribute to the further development of
social theories. They can be seen as 'sensitizing concepts' which, while 'lacking the precise specification of attributes and events of definitive concepts,
do provide clues and suggestions about where to look for certain classes of
phenomena' (Turner 1982:336). Instead of seeking a false sense of scientific
security through rigid definitions, the use of these kinds of sensitizing concepts can provide, by encouraging flexible approaches and continuous investigation of new territories, a more adequate perspective on our changing
world. However, it needs to be admitted that our uncertainty as to what we
are referring to can obstruct us 'from asking pertinent questions and setting
relevant problems for research' (Blumer 1954:150). Therefore, while the
nature of the social world necessitates working with not always clearly
defined concepts, our task should be to overcome this deficiency by trying to
redefine them so they more explicitly communicate and reflect the empirical reality.

The problem with the concept of informality is that it is a mundane term,
difficult to define not only in sociological theories but also in everyday language. In everyday talk, this difficulty is reflected in the employment of the
concept of informality in a variety of situations and actions. In some contexts,
'informality' is used to describe a relaxed, casual or non-ceremonial
approach to conformity with formal rules, dress codes and procedures,
while, in other situations, it can refer to actions taking place behind the

official scene and which – because they are not in accordance with prescribed regulation – are perceived as a threat to fair and just treatment,
resulting in favouritism, nepotism and patronage. Moreover, the concept of
informality often seems to be treated as a very convenient device, used to
explain almost everything that is new or points to new trends or new fashion.

Anita Brookner in her recent novel describes the surprise of her heroine,
old Mrs May, on seeing the 'informality' exposed by her new solicitor:
'Young Mr Zeber was in a canary yellow waistcoat and blue shirt sleeves, at
which she found herself staring rather fixedly. "It's the new informality", he
explained, smiling. "For the weekend, you know. It is Friday" he reminded
her' (1997:226–7). Furthermore, even Mrs May, a middle class, respectable
widow, who is 'bound by certain rules, of observance, of behaviour, of formality', dreams about becoming a 'bare feet, adventurous, informal, different, unkempt, ill-natured' woman (Brookner 1997:23, 227). Here
informality is presented by way of contrast with formality.

This contrast becomes splendidly visible if we compare the Dutch family
portraits from the sixteenth and earlier seventeenth century with the same
type of paintings from the later seventeenth and eighteenth century. The
earlier studies present serious couples seated, with 'the formal gestures' and
'the stiff decorousness', and who wear 'that grave and statuesque formality.
Such self-images present the ceremonious aspect of marriage rather than its
intimacy' (Schama 1988:425). The later portraits, instead of an expression of
'sacramental gravity', display dynamically posed and lively interacting couples in more 'informal settings', show 'the affectionate pleasure of married
companionship' and illustrate how 'informality necessarily equalized the
role of two partners' (Schama 1988:426–7). While informality is connected
here with spontaneity and 'more companionable manners', formality is seen
as 'solemnity' and an absence of 'warmth'.

A literary example further illustrates this contrast by describing a writer's
uneasiness with his host's 'habit of formality' and uncertainty as to when and
how strong feelings should be expressed: 'The alarming formality of that eve-
ning [...] suggested that in such a house something had intervened to
replace not only the ordinary small talk but even those casual yet important
expressions of affection, the brief bursts of quarrelling, the random endless
chat about acquaintances, that I was myself more accustomed to' (Kermode
1997:75). Here informality is seen as constituted in small talk, gossip, unrestricted expressions of emotions and the indeterminacy of exchange.

It is also difficult to find a clear and uniform definition of informality in
sociological texts, where this concept does not enjoy an independent standing but rather has the status of an ephemeral or residual concept. It is normally used to describe either more intimate, face-to-face social relationships
or more personal modes of social control or types of social organizations and
pressures, while formality is thought to enable the preservation of social distance and structures of power. Informality is identified with co-presence,
which 'utilises the duality of perception and communication' (Fuchs

1988:123) and is seen as a feature of interpersonal, less routine, less rigid and less ceremonial relationships, which rely more on tacit knowledge than on prescribed norms. Informal behaviour is also often seen as not following any precise procedures and as not being subject to organized sanctions. In contrast, formality is identified with the impersonal, transparent and explicit aspects of interactions, which rely on a formal universalism of procedural, official and legal rules, being results of the increasing expansion of institutions, which through challenging human activity into prestructured patterns, reduce the opportunity for informality. The impact of many one-dimensional studies of informal or formal structures, which conceptualized these two phenomena in contrast or opposition to each other, is still visible in today's split in sociology between those who place individual actors at the centre of their analysis and those who relegate actors to the periphery and view society primarily in terms of institutions.

Until recently informality has been seen as alien to modernity and capitalism, which are perceived as connected with the dynamic of modernization, rationalization and with the processes of centralization and concentration. The traditional use of the concept of informality in the social sciences tends to connect it with the backward looking process, which fits to the unlinear models of development, being functional or Marxist. At the same time, however, the sociological vision of the great transformation, which is described as the movement from informal, face-to-face, homogeneous, communal and spontaneous types of relations to the formal, heterogeneous, rational, contract-based, calculative types of relations, has always looked nostalgically at informality. The concept of informality in this perspective is commonly viewed as a more intimate and dialogical type of face-to-face encounter in which our sense of responsibility and reciprocal obligations is cultivated. A system of informal social control developed in the course of interaction is seen as ensuring that participants' responses construct and sustain shared norms and expectations. The integration of pre-modern society is presented as guarded by conformity to tradition and customs, and by informal control exercised by the community, while the integration of a modern society is perceived as the result of differentiation, individualization, rationalization, expansion of formalistic, depersonalized rules and the move towards impersonality in the exercise of power. The idea of informality, as the condition of an ethical universe, points to the socially beneficial outcomes of cooperative behaviour, while the process of formalization 'leads to a reduced concern for particulars of situations and to an increasing rigidity of action' (Wagner 1994:29).

In this type of approach, informal and formal are taken for granted as respective characteristics of communal and contractual relationships. This distinction is, furthermore, identified with the micro–macro dualism. However, talking about informality does not necessarily imply an exclusive focus on the micro level of social analysis or, in other words, concentrating on what is going on in the local episode of face-to-face interaction. To understand the role and meaning of the concept of informality, we need to realize that since face-to-face interaction can involve different processes (informal as well as formal) and can have various impacts (local as well as not limited by space and/or time), they do not necessarily entail micro-levels (Mouzelis 1991: 31–4). Hence, informality denotes informal processes of face-to-face interaction, which can be either of local space and/or time importance or unlimited space and/or time importance (see Chapter 5). On the other hand, since co-presence is not the only form of communication that involves actors facing complex contingencies of social coordination and relying largely upon tacit assumptions and mutual adjustment, informality cannot be restricted only to face-to-face interaction. Furthermore, seeing informality as limited to face-to-face interaction and a local context is called into question by innovations in information technology which permit us to overcome 'the distance', facilitates mediated communication and enable horizontal flows of conversation (see Chapter 7). Thus informality, instead of being seen as an obvious element of every face-to-face communication, should be conceptualized as existing in any communicational network with a space for interactive indeterminacy or uncertainty.

Modernist assumptions about the homogenization of economic and social life in rationalized forms also found expression in the popularity of the 'formal–informal' distinction in organizational studies. It has been conventional knowledge in this field, following Mayo's discovery that informal groups underlie the formal structure of the Hawthorne plant, that official and formal rules are often not those found to be operating in practice. This type of study has also stressed that formally instituted and informally emerging patterns are practically interwoven and mutually dependent upon one another. 'In every formal organization there arises informal organization [...]. The roots of these informal systems are embedded in the formal organization itself and nurtured by the very formality of its arrangements' (Burns and Flam 1987:223). Many empirical investigations, which assume that it is impossible to understand the nature of formal organizations without investigating the networks of informal relations and unofficial norms, describe how informal, unofficial rules govern the daily operation of organizations or institutions and explain this by defining them as 'local subcultures'. Corridor conversations, chats before and after meetings, exchanges during lunch breaks – these are seen as means by which not only official versions of organizational life can be challenged and reinterpreted, but also as the basis of 'a diverse network of bonds and obligations, friendships and animosities, that humanize and socialize work experience' (Roberts 1996:49).

The argument, starting with the early researchers of the Hawthorne plant, was that people's 'informal social relations tied them into cohesive sub-groupings which had their own norms, values, orientation and subcultures, and which may run counter to the "official" or formal social structure' (Scott 1991:103). Contrasting formal and informal, by pointing to the disparity between official rules and values and concrete behaviour, was supplemented by observations that: 'Behind every formal network and often giving it the breath of life are usually one or more informal networks' (Freeman 1991:503). In this perspective, formal and informal rules and conducts, while seen as being the mutual frames of reference for each other, are also presented as performing different functions, with informal relations being a source of group solidarity and emotional well-being for its members and contributing to their identity and feeling of belonging. Informality here, as in the earlier approach, is seen as the type of everpresent bond, which – by facilitating 'group feeling' or common expectations – produces social integration. Such informal relationships are between individuals of equal status or with no direct functional relationships, thus they are unmediated by hierarchy and therefore power cannot be used to impose a point of view or to hierarchize individual differences. Formal relations, that is, neutral, legally circumscribed or depersonalized and structured types of behaviour, are seen as a means to sustain power relationships and as methods of exercising formal control, and therefore being more instrumental and excluding mutual understanding.

However, while informal relations contribute to cooperative relations, they also function to protect employees' interests (for example, the informal imposition of lower productivity by work teams). Similarly, the experience of formal relations and rules can expand beyond instrumental concerns as 'the narrative mode of cognition is inherent in both the formal and informal organization' (Boland and Schultze 1996:65). Furthermore, face-to-face interaction routinely brings together subordinates and superordinates and informality often equalizes their status; therefore, our search for conditions that enable an enhancement of social capital should be expanded to include broader institutionalized structures and the hierarchical organization of modern societies. Hence, the main difference between formal and informal organizations cannot be reduced to seeing informal groups as a source of emotional and moral ties, whereas more formal relations are viewed as reproducing distinctions and power structures; rather, both realms should be seen as defining themselves concomitantly and in mutual recognition. Moreover, it should be noticed, following Giddens (1984), that organizations not only constrain us, but they also enable us to undertake new tasks and to adopt more reflexive questioning and re-thinking of the adequacy and desirability of formal structures.

The 'formal–informal' distinction can also be uncovered in debates of the public and private realms. In classical theory the private realm was, according to Arendt, 'a sphere of intimacy', while the public realm was the sphere where one could excel: 'for excellence by definition, the presence of others is always required, and this presence needs the formality of the public, constituted by one's peers, it cannot be the casual familiar presence of one's equals or inferiors' (1958:48–9). The development of privacy as a product of concrete historical actions, which in the mid-eighteenth century led to the identification of the idea of privacy with the morally autonomous individual, established new distinctions 'essentially between formal relations regulated by public law and the search for new basis of individual trust and a matrix of interpersonal relations beyond contract and law' (Seligman 1998:34). Since the eighteenth century, with the development of bourgeois culture, the gap between the private and public domains has been expanded. As Elias (1978) notes, in the course of the civilizing process the privatization, intimacy and distinctive emotional culture of aristocratic society were replaced by privacy of the world of the bourgeois. In modern societies, the particularistic, hidden intimacies of individuals' 'private' life and the extreme impersonality, universalism and instrumentalism of open collectivities of the public realm, epitomized by the market and bureaucratically administrated formal organizations, summarized the fundamental distinction between the two spheres (Weintraub 1997:5–8).

This demarcation between private and public, between the personal domain of family, friendship, and the primary group and the impersonal instrumental domain of the market and formal institutions, although still sharply experienced by many people, has been eroded and 'the two realms indeed constantly flow into each other' (Arendt 1958:33). Modern political theory's new interests in the politics of identity and in civil society, seen as constituted by the tensions between public and private or universal and particular (Seligman 1998:29), suggest that this new relationship between private and public does not neatly correspond to the division between formal and informal. The overlapping of these realms results in the increasing role of social networks, which encompass 'the general structure of informal relationships as well as those operating within defined associational structures' (Boswell 1969:255) and which become platforms for discussion of social problems and exchange of opinions.

The above review of the main empirically oriented approaches illustrates the lack of coherent approach to the issue of informality. The search for similarities across the different uses of the concept of informality testifies that the formal–informal distinction tends to be taken for granted and identified with other dichotomous visions, such as the micro–macro dualism, the non-instrumental–instrumental division and the public and private distinction. In order to discover a more theoretical potential of the concept of informality, we now need to look at sociological theories, which – although not directly discussing the issue of informality – may contribute to the description of informal style of interaction.

EXTRACTING THE CONCEPT OF INFORMALITY FROM SOCIAL THEORY

Although there are not many sociological theories explicitly dealing with the issue of informality, the works of Simmel, Mead, Goffman and Schutz seem to have some implications for our debate on informality as those writers enriched our understanding of the basis of social interaction. The examination of these theoretical writings will be essentially a preparatory exercise intended to lay the groundwork for explaining and defining the concept of informality.

The founding fathers of sociology did not scrutinize ephemeral phenomena such as informality. Their attention was directed towards social structures and social processes as such. For these theorists, the most important problem of the social sciences was the construction of a general theory of institutions and institutional change. Following the sociologism of the original founders, the main European social thinkers' writing about modernity and its characteristics at the turn of the century did not pay much attention to the more personal and immediate aspects of face-to-face encounters either. Instead, they searched for mechanisms that might provide for an orderly and cohesive development of society and focused on what they perceived as the uniqueness of the modern era. Nonetheless, in some sociological writings, particularly those of Simmel and Weber, the main vision is supplemented by a sense of the ambivalence or duality of modernity and by a focus on the micro level of social life.

Although Max Weber is 'by no stretch of the imagination an interactionist social theorist' (Barnes 1995:142), his description of status groups concentrates on their constitution as interacting networks and the importance of non-instrumental interaction defined as 'intercourse which is not subservient to economic or any other purposes' (Weber 1968:932). Weber's insistence on the significance of non-instrumentally oriented types of interaction, seen as responsible for the existence and operation of status groups, is connected with his assumption about the role of lifestyles and social relationships in enacting the collective good. Since Weber implies that it is interaction patterns and not interest that explain collective action, his analysis provides a general scheme for the description of informality as a pattern or style of interaction. Furthermore, his theory of the development of Western rationalism, which casts the future in terms of 'iron cage' with little place for individual freedom, warns against progressive bureaucratization, a process aiming at increasing formal control of human action.

Simmel, like Weber, also defended the spontaneity of life against rational bureaucratic regulations. His notion of ceaseless, interrelated interactions, his perception of individuals as not limited only to their roles and his treatment of sociability as making for at least a pretence of equality, implies the openness of social reality. Despite the impersonality, fragmentation and instrumentality of modern society, a human agent – argues Simmel – is still able to enjoy individual liberty and autonomy, mainly thanks to shifting involvements among various fragmented spheres of life and among various groups. Simmel's definition of society 'as interaction among individuals' formulates the task of sociology as the study of the forms of interaction and the rules of sociation between individuals (1950:21–2). He argues that interaction seldom takes the shape of rule-governed behaviour, although he recognizes that interaction can be institutionalized. This viewing of social life in terms of a multiplicity of interactions between individuals and Simmel's insistence of the avoidance of 'fallacy of separateness', which considers actors without reference to the interactions in which they are engaged, grants social interaction the status of 'the most elementary unit of sociological analysis' (Turner 1988:13). Simmel distinguishes between 'forms', seen as the central organizing characteristics of social life (for example, subordination, conflict and leadership) and 'contents' of diverse situations in social life such as war, education or politics. The content of interaction refers to the motives or purposes of interactions, while forms are the ways in which those interactions are organized. The social reality is represented by the foundational notion of forms of interaction, hence, the main task of sociology is to identify and analyze the constitutive forms of interaction. Thus, following Simmel, researching informality means studying ways in which this specific form of interaction is organized.

Another contribution to our understanding of the concept of informality comes from American pragmatist thinkers, interactionists and social phenomenologists, who insist that action should not be 'perceived as the pursuit of preestablished ends, abstracted from concrete situations, but rather that ends and means develop coterminously within contexts' (Emirbayer and Mische 1998:967). Their emphasis on the indeterminacy of interaction and fluid nature of social reality allow them to see the role of spontaneity and creativity in shaping social encounters. However, despite the original American interactionist theorists' ambition to move beyond the dualism of micro and macro and beyond the division between instrumental and normative action, the truth was that they 'had no taste for macro theory' (Barnes 1995: 86). Consequently, a cultural clash between micro and macro sociologists in the USA resulted in several decades of separation of their spheres of operation (Rock 1978). Nonetheless, some basic premises permit the pragmatist thinkers to lay foundations for developing an account of variability and creativity of actors' responses.

The representatives of American social pragmatism focused on the links between society and the self and argued, as Cooley did, that 'self and society are twin-born' and that society consists of a network of communication between people and groups. This ensures the exchange and clash of ideas, resulting in the emergence of mature public opinion, seen as the main integrating factor. Cooley's idea of communicative action, supplemented by the concept of understanding as the source of knowledge about human conduct, as well as his emphasis on the role of primary groups in integrating and linking individuals with society, are important contributions to the development of an understanding of the conditions of modern life. An observation of the realities of American society led Cooley to declare that in modern social life a significant role is assumed by formal, impersonal forms and phenomena, such as institutions, money and public opinion, while the role of primary groups is in decline. Cooley warned against the effect of formalism upon personality by pointing out that the formalization of social contacts will 'starve its higher life and leave it the prey of apathy and self-complacency' (Cooley 1962:343). Depersonalization is described by Cooley as the condition in which the individual does not participate in most groups as a full person but enters into them 'with a trained and specialized part of himself' (Cooley 1962:319). This change in human relations is accompanied, however, by an expansion and multiplication of contacts due to the emergence of new means of communication. Pointing in a Simmel-like way to the multiplicity and overlapping of social groups, Cooley defines the individual as 'the point of intersection of an indefinite number of circles representing social groups' (1902:148). Cooley's famous distinction between primary and secondary groups as well as the importance he attached to the role of the primary group was later adopted by Homans in his description of informal, face-to-face, spontaneous and non-institutionalized forms of behaviour, so called 'elementary social behaviour', as the simplest, most fundamental and universal form of human behaviour.

Homans, like Simmel, identifies exchange as the basic structure and dynamic of social action. He portrays social behaviour as essentially a negotiation with others who have their own interests and who are motivated by the attempt to satisfy them. Furthermore, he argues that informal face-to-face interactions are basic to direct exchange and that more complex societal processes are growing out of these primary elements. Rules of spontaneous interactions are independent of the context; therefore, informal interaction can be seen as the primary or basic source of more complex social systems. 'The ultimate explanatory principles in sociology were neither structural nor functional but psychological; they were propositions about the people's behaviour' (Homans 1962:29). The primary goal of studies of small groups or 'elementary' social behaviour is to analyse variables entering into the process of exchange, while their secondary aim is to study 'the effect of the informal exchange on the institution' (Homans 1962:296). Homans, for example, shows that increased interaction, under the condition that 'a man is free to break off interaction with another whose behaviour he finds punishing', would contribute to partners' more positive attitudes towards each other (1961:187). Informal groups grow alongside institutionalization, not only just in 'the gaps between institutions', but they can do both: support the institutional aims and work against them (Homans 1961:391). According to Homans, any conflict between formal and informal spheres can only be solved by the adjustment of institutional structures to the requirements of informal exchange (1961:392–4). Homans' awareness of the dynamics of the exchange processes and his emphasis on the significance and the durability of informal elements in social life shed new light on the role of informality.

Although George Herbert Mead, like Homans, asserted that a comprehensive explanation of human behaviour should proceed on the psychological level, his approach does not share Homans' reductionism or assumptions about the nature of human beings and the conditions of their interaction.

Mead looked at society as a structure emerging through an ongoing process of communicative social acts. He applied the term society to all situations in which there is interaction among individuals and argued that, since human interaction is mainly symbolic, the limits of society are marked by the limits of communication. All social actions, being cooperative or conflictual, involve a mutual orientation of actors to one another based on 'an object of common interest to all individuals involved' (Mead 1934: 178). In Mead's analysis, human communicative processes consist of definitions and redefinitions through which self-conscious actors try to adjust their conduct to others' actions. He held that it is 'the ability of the person to put himself in other people's place that gives him cues as to what he is to do under a specific situation' (1934:270). This importance attached to taking the role of the other, however, does not mean that a self is a mere reflection of the attitudes of others. Although Mead argues that the subjective self and its capacities are a consequence of the individual's objective sociability, where first we get an objective sense of our own self, he also stresses that this subjective attitude has both a moral and a cultural aspect, as well as a personal and innovative sense.

In Mead's intersubjectivist conception of the self, 'I' is the pre-conscious source of innovation due to its impulses that 'are geared towards distinguishing from all other partners in interaction in order to gain a consciousness of one's individual uniqueness' (Honneth 1995: 86). This involvement in a 'struggle for recognition', a struggle which challenges the existing institutionalized order, leads to the expansion in personal autonomy and to the increased space allowed for individual liberty and uniqueness. 'The great characters have been those who, by being what they were in the community, made that community a different one. They have enlarged and enriched the community' (Mead 1934 :216).

Mead's theory points out two complementary aspects of agency: creativity, which is reflected by the 'I', and control, which is reflected by the 'me'. Mead believes that the essence of the self is its reflexivity, whereby people are able to reinterpret and form a new self. An individual's responsible decisions are seen as a result of 'organic and creative processes of reflective intelligence; and in these processes, the social values and control functions of the "me" are counterbalanced by the innovative function of the "I"' (Baldwin 1988:157). Such a creative and conscious self reflects the structure of the more generalized attitudes of 'significant others' and it comprises what Cooley termed a 'looking glass self'. People visualize others in terms of an abstract relation. This abstractness, however, can be overcome through an 'increase of content in the relation' (Mead 1934:178). Thus, through an accident of encounter or face-to-face interaction (often therefore through informal conversation) some people, out of a mass of others, may become for us vivid, singular and special. Mead's insight into the internal structuring and developing of actors' deliberative capacities as they confront emergent situations provides a step towards a conception of informality as an interactional resource. Because Mead implies 'that individuals, even when in a clear "social context", are able to act out of inner imperatives which override any social pressures they might experience' (Campbell 1996:109), he helps to account for the fact of indeterminacy of interaction and for the possibility of spontaneous and informal actions. The emphasis on the indeterminacy of action and the recognition of the possibility for spontaneous actions, which can be traced to the achievement of 'I', are Mead's main contributions to the advancement of sociological analysis, and, indeed, to our appreciation of informality and spontaneity as driving forces of change and innovation.

For social pragmatism, social life consists of social interactions in which people adjust to each other thanks to their ability to interpret symbols and reflect upon them. Interaction or communicative exchange takes place between individuals as independent selves or personalities, not between their roles or aspects of roles. What is interesting to note here is that this position does not assume that structural or normative conditions are sufficient to explain human action. The emphasis on interactional rules, communicative exchange and on the understanding that others' responses to one's actions, which are always problematic and unpredictable, allows for the distinction or differentiation between the individual and his/her role and for studying individualized responses to the social environment. The American social pragmatists' contribution is essential in terms of formulating one of the most important problems in the social sciences, that is, how to combine analyses of face-to-face interaction and institutional action. However, they did not construct a general theory of institutions and institutional change, consequently, '[t]he problems of social personality and the idea of finding the golden mean between sociologism and psychologism have largely become the common property of all present-day sociology' (Szacki 1979:434).

The theoretical heritage of social pragmatism has been taken over by symbolic interactionism, which emphasizes the relationship between the meanings of social action and the behaviour of the persons involved. This perspective, having its origins not only in the writings of Cooley or Mead but also in Simmel's perception of society as 'a network of interacting individuals' (Rose 1962:13), elevates interaction to a universal principle. It hoped to overcome the past discrepancies of sociological theories by using observation from 'everyday life', by seeing social life as being 'in process' and by assuming that all social behaviours and actions are interpreted by the individual and that the meaning associated with action is important for forming interaction. These tendencies were supposed to tie 'these things together in such a way that sociology cannot be divorced from social psychology' (Blumer 1962:179). However, this approach's rejection of structures, norms and roles as strictly determining behaviour resulted in its inability to fulfil this promise.

Blumer, who coined the term 'symbolic interactionism', stresses that 'meaning' is determined by individual negotiation, thus it is constructed and reconstructed in the process of social interaction. He criticizes previous sociological views for being too deterministic because they assumed human beings 'to be merely organisms with some kind of organization, responding to forces which play upon them' (Blumer 1962:185). Describing practically all sociological perspectives as being unable to 'regard the social actions of individuals in human society as being constructed by them through a process of interpretation' (*ibid*), leads Blumer to stress the spontaneity, indeterminacy and creativity of interaction. He insists that although actors usually bring some previously acquired common understandings or definitions of how to act into interaction, they nonetheless need to be seen as always engaged in 'fluid interpretative, evolutional, and definitional processes so that only strictly inductive procedures can help elucidate their behaviour' (Coser 1977:574). It is immediate situational relevance, not internalization, that defines attitudes. Consequently, human actions are seen as being in a continuous process of change and social reality as being unstable. Blumer's development of Mead's ideas resulted in an extreme situational model, one in which social reality is not only constructed but is also in the process of change. Particularly in modern society, due to its instability and the increased number of 'underdefined' situations, the influence of social organization declines. 'In modern society, with its increasing cris-crossing of lines of action, it is common for situations to arise in which the actions of participants are not previously regularized and standardised' (Blumer 1962:190). Mutual susceptibility of interacting individuals gives a special and distinctive character to interactional encounters. This distinctiveness manifests itself in interactions' improvisatory qualities and their role in the constitution and reconstitution of the meaning and the individual (Barnes 1995:68–72). Social interactionists directed efforts to overcome the shortcomings of their predecessors by postulating a view of social organization as temporary and constantly changing and by calling for an incorporation of the interpretative process seen as a means by which human beings act in society. However, despite Blumer's awareness of the discrepancy between structural and interpretative perspectives, his theory has not been able to 'link conceptually the processes of symbolic interaction to the formation of different patterns of social organizations' (Turner 1982:339). Blumer's search for a more extensive perspective resulted mainly in analyses of the micro processes among individuals within small group contexts.

An emphasis on micro social patterns is also present in two other streams within North American sociology, both of which refer back to the tradition begun by Mead. The two most prominent figures here are Goffman and Garfinkel. Like the symbolic interactionists, Goffman's major concern was with face-to-face relationships and interaction, but in many respects he was critical of them and tried to extend their analyses in the direction of a more formal sociology. His effort towards 'the abstraction from everyday life of the very definite and limited number of forms or modes in which this life occurs' (Gonos 1977:856) suggests some similarities with Simmel's concentration on the form of interaction itself rather than its content or on the structure it creates. While interactionists defined situations as not constituted of imposed formal rules but of informal ones, which are negotiated through the duration of interaction, for Goffman the nature of social encounters is less precarious and based on stable rules or interactional rituals. Unlike Homans, who perceives the elementary, spontaneous and informal type of behaviour as the foundation or the basic unit of formal organizations, Goffman discovers this spontaneous, informal, face-to-face type of interaction within the organized public space and sees it as being constrained by routinized roles. Like Mead, Goffman sees the individual as having a multiplicity of selves, each attuned to a new situation, and this dynamic capability is essential for the development of performance on stage. 'As human beings we are presumably creatures of variable impulse with moods and energies that change from one moment to the next. As characters put on for an audience, however, we must not be subject to ups and downs ... . A certain bureaucratization of the spirit is expected so that we can be relied upon to give a perfectly homogeneous performance at every appointed time' (Goffman 1959:56).

For Goffman, the problem of interaction is the problem of situational control over the 'giving' and 'giving off' impressions in manufacturing normal appearances. However, despite his attempts to combine face-to-face interaction with the production and reproduction of social structures and the fact that he 'was usually careful to avoid the connotation that the micro level is somehow more fundamental than the macro' (Giddens 1987:111), Goffman was unable to overcome the dualism of micro and macro. At the same time, although Goffman himself was conscious of the fact that his approach is illustrative of microsociology, his affinity with the Durkheimian perspective, as visible in his recognition of the importance of collective orientation and rituals (Collins 1988, 1994), placed him at odds with most microtheorists.

Goffman's conviction that most transactions of social life occur at the face-to-face level led him to argue that the interaction order is 'a substantive domain in its own right' (1983:2) and that it possesses its own inner workings and mechanisms, which are derived from and give shape to this sphere itself. Yet, although the interaction order is a separate domain, there is the mutual interchange of effects between the structural and interactional order, or 'loose coupling between the interaction order and social structure', which allows one to find 'a proper place for the apparent power of fads and fashions to effect change in ritual practices' (Goffman 1983:12). Manners of interactional practices are shaped by wider social trends and developments; for instance, the 1960s social movements have contributed to the emergence of more informal ways of interaction. But at the same time, through 'social discipline, then a mask of manner can be held in place from within' (Goffman 1959:57). Thus, creativity and constraints in social life are filtered upwards and downwards between the interaction and structural orders.

A preoccupation with face-to-face interaction also made Goffman aware of the importance of time, space and the orderliness of interactional activities.

Orderliness of interactional activity is predicated 'on a large base of shared cognitive presuppositions, if not normative ones, and self-sustained restraints' (Goffman 1983:5). The workings of the interaction order are seen as 'the consequences of systems of enabling conventions, in the sense of the ground rules for a game, the provisions of the traffic code or the rule of syntax of a language' (*ibid*). For Goffman, all meaningful relationships are based on a tacit commitment or involvement in the face of others which is 'immediate and spontaneous' (1972:6). People produce order by making their intention readable to others and by continuously reading others' intentions. Through their capacities to provide others with 'a window to their intents' people display their moral commitment to the 'working consensus', subsequently renewing and affirming their relationship to one another (Goffman 1969:126). Seeing collaboration as a natural consequence of face-to-face interaction results in Goffman's conceptualization of morality as 'born out of an understanding of the general need to bring off, or successfully manage, the great majority of encounters in order that social business is able to proceed' (Layder 1994:174).

For Goffman, the world of interaction was a moral realm able to generate in people a sense of effectiveness. Yet, it is difficult to assess how profound, according to Goffman, this moral integration is. On one hand, Goffman's claim that people have a tendency to expect and maintain a reciprocity of perspectives stresses too strongly that people routinely preserve distinctions between clearly marked spheres of life, between their 'backstage' and 'frontstage' spheres, which determine whether the dominant type of relationships is more personalized and equal or whether the dominant type of behaviour is formal and framed in a fixed and general fashion. On the other hand, Goffman demonstrates that people do not blindly follow rules and rituals but that they rather use them to score points and that they skilfully manipulate them. The difficulty of evaluating how serious Goffman himself was regarding the assumption about moral integration is, moreover, increased by his empirical case studies, which do not support the picture of the orderly encounter sustained by the common internalization of social norms. Rather they demonstrate the manipulability of norms and their strategic use, thereby implying distancing from norms. This distancing from norms is a constitutive element of Goffman's metaphor of dramatic performance and his concept of framing, seen as a practical agreement on the definition of the situation. Goffman's differentiation between various settings of interaction and his concern with the contingency of everyday situations will provide a useful starting point for defining informality, which will be undertaken in the final part of this chapter.

Goffman's way of thinking about people as able to use and skilfully manipulate rules is taken and followed systematically by an ethnomethodological approach. There is a clear affinity between Goffman's later works, indicating his increasing interest in phenomenology, and those of Garfinkel, who continues Goffman's attempts to combine the classical sociological assumption that rules are skills governing interaction with the realization that rules are also resources used in interaction. For ethnomethodologists social behaviour is always situated and the setting in which the action occurs determines its meaning. They, like symbolic interactionists, stress the importance of commonsense knowledge for understanding social behaviour; however, they also acknowledge that people must learn how to produce social actions. Emphasizing action as a situated accomplishment led them, however, to rely upon a one-sided conception of agency. Their examination of how individuals manage to make their action intelligible focuses on human agency as habitual, repetitive and taken-for-granted.

Garfinkel defines actors as approaching situations with a presumption that they share in the common world. Reality is always contextually constructed through mutual account-making and account-taking of individuals in concrete settings. From the ethnomethodological perspective, interest, norms and rules are merely interpretive schemes which actors use to justify their own actions *post factum*. In short, '[w]ith respect to the production of normatively appropriate conduct, all that is required is that the actors have, and attribute to one another, a reflexive awareness of the normative accountability of their actions' (Heritage 1984:117). The actors themselves explain the meaning of their own actions (reflexivity) and therefore establish what is relevant in everyday life. Although reflexivity is a necessary part of members' 'rational accounting' for their activities, its importance is reduced by the predominance of regular and meaningful behaviour, or rule-following action. Thus, reflexivity is not seen as a common characteristic of action in normal daily life.

Garfinkel's studies were carried out primarily in social settings in which activities were highly organized and routinized, thus the modes in which actors go about showing each other the 'rational accountability' of their organized activities were presented as deeply taken-for-granted ways. In such routinized situations meanings are taken for granted by actors and therefore habit gains an important role in generating social order. Garfinkel also stresses the routine nature of the implementation of common procedures for maintaining normal courses of action. According to ethnomethodology, the human reliance on a taken-for-granted sense of order demonstrates a preference for normalcy; people are usually interested in following ordinary routine since they routinely find that this is the best way of securing the realization of their tasks. Garfinkel's demonstration of how rules, as taken-for-granted assumptions that make up attitudes of daily life, produce actions that confirm the individuals' expectations, points to this approach having affinity with Schutz's perspective.

This main connection of ethnomethodological theory with Schutz's perspective manifests itself in Garfinkel's adoption of Schutz's 'thesis of reciprocity'. According to Schutz, our knowledge of others is always fragmentary and imperfect; it takes the form of typification, that is, the mode of socially standardized and shared knowledge of the everyday world that ensures that actors are able to maintain the 'reciprocity of perspective' and, by the same token, sustain cooperative actions. When entering any social relation, people generally take for granted a 'reciprocity of perspectives' and their 'stock of knowledge', which is defined as a cognitive structure that orders interactions in terms of past experiences, secures a sense of continuity, time, space and meaning of exchange. Although typification, by necessity, entails a narrowing, deformation and standardization of knowledge, nonetheless, some types of interaction with others permit an alteration of typologies. In the continuing process of face-to-face interaction, typifications of the other are tested, revised, reenacted and modified, while in less immediate types of interaction our knowledge of others will be incompletely formulated, unclear and indeterminate (Schutz 1967).

In face-to-face relations, which Schutz calls 'the pure-we relation', we share with the other time, space, environment and a homogeneous system of relevances: 'face-to-face interaction involves mutual engagement in which the partners can witness the literal coming-to-birth of each other's experiences' (Schutz 1967:179). Schutz tries to establish a continuum between taken-for-granted and accomplished intersubjectivity, which is accompanied by a parallel continuum of relations, stretching on the scale of 'we-relations' from concrete individuality on one end, to anonymous types on the 'they-relations' end. A step away from the immediacy of face-to-face relationships, which are seen as the most central dimension of the social world, there is the world of the potential reach, that is, the 'world of contemporaries' whose subjects co-exist with me in time, thus, there is mutual influence without being in actual reach. If the pure 'we-relation' refers to social relationships based on a community of space and time, the 'world of contemporaries' merely involves the expectation on the part of each partner that the other will respond in a relevant way. 'But this expectation is always a shot in the dark compared to the knowledge one has of one's consociate in the face-to-face interaction. Actions between contemporaries are only mutually *related*, whereas actions between consociates are mutually *interlocked*' (Schutz 1967:181). The contemporary is only indirectly accessible and her or his subjective experiences can only be known in the form of general types of subjective experiences, which is determined by the interpreter's point of view (Schutz 1967:189–90). The world of contemporaries consists of a world of 'restorable we-relations' and a world of 'attainable we-relations', which correspond respectively to the worlds of restorable reach and attainable reach.

In sharp contrast to the 'we-relations', which involve an immediate interchange of meanings and where there is less typification as people relate to each other in more personalized ways, there is the 'they-relation'. Whereas in face-to-face situations we are 'sensitively aware of the nuances of each other's subjective experiences' and we are constantly revising and enlarging our knowledge of each other, in the 'they relationship' we only 'share the interpretative scheme' (Schutz 1967:202–3). In indirect social experience, the more anonymous my partner is, the more 'objective' signs must be used and the greater the need for questioning about meanings. Schutz's idea of the integrity of the situation, which implies the contextual determination of social events, can be an interesting framework for discussing changes in interactional styles brought by new means of communication which are discussed in Chapter 7.

Garfinkel's interpretation of Schutz's approach, by stressing the contextual determination of meaning, which maintains that individual actions are only meaningful within the contexts which produce them and that meaning is always fragile and ambiguous, has introduced the investigation of the indexicality of everyday practices as the main task of enthnomethodology. Unlike Goffman, who does not postulate the construction of a common reason for which people accept the way things are ordered, Garfinkel argues that it is the actors themselves who constitute what is relevant in everyday life. For Garfinkel, action coincides with performance and 'the actor appears to be disinterested in anything apart from delineating himself in a coherent fashion during his most obvious routines' (Bovone 1989:48). The orderliness of interaction, seen as 'an ongoing practical accomplishment' (Garfinkel and Sacks 1970:341) created by people from within a given situation, has been best illustrated by studies of ordinary conversations that expose the indexical nature of meaning. Conversation analysis, as a study of the socially accomplished and organized resources used for the production and understanding of indexical expressions, provides very interesting evidence about people's perception and evaluation of various situations as 'formal' or 'informal'. In what follows we look at these empirical research attempts at the conceptualization of the term 'informality'.

INFORMALITY AS AN INTERACTIONAL RESOURCE

In searching for differences between various styles of interaction conversation, analysts try to uncover the social competence underlying social interaction. Such attempts to describe the procedures and expectations through which interaction develops start from the assumption that contributions to interaction are 'both context-shaped and context-renewing, in that each current action will propose a current here-and-now definition of the situation to which subsequent talk will be oriented' (Heritage 1987:258). Thus, conversation is joint action not just in the sense that it is negotiated locally but also in the sense that 'talk and task are mutually elaborative in a turn manner' (Boden 1990:255). The norms or rules that regulate behaviour in circumstances of co-presence therefore have a special form. Locally placed conversation becomes mutually cooperative action through its specific characteristics, such as the richness of information in every co-present situation, turn-taking and turn-making, sequentiality and an ability on the part of participants to deal with 'circumstantial contingencies'. For example, sequential and temporal order plays a crucial role in the constitution of everyday experience. In informal interaction people can cooperatively change the course and speed of conversational flow, thereby maximizing the amount of information and exploration of the topic. Sequence turns action into narrative or collective effects because actors align 'local agendas with larger goals and do so in such a way as to significantly create or subvert those distant and abstract issues' (Boden 1994:128). Routine preferences for 'face-saving' behaviour in interaction under conditions of co-presence dictate, for example, delaying a negative response, increasing cooperative attitudes and the display of solidarity. In effect, this is a message of trust, 'a trust that derives from the observable timing and placement of talk and gesture [...]. For actors to use time to achieve solidarity and trust, there must be a mini-mum amount of space between them' (Boden and Molotch 1994:267). It should be borne in mind, however, as ethnomethodologists remind us, that socially established rules regarding turn-taking and reciprocal monitoring vary between contexts, cultures and among different groups, and so the pro-cedures that align and coordinate face-to-face interaction do not necessarily determine them (Heritage 1984). The work of interaction is to communi-cate rational and sense-making versions of reality. In order to accomplish it, actors employ various practices that sustain their trust in the tacit acceptance of a taken-for-granted reality. Ethnomethodological and conversation analy-sis studies typically demonstrate that actors – in order to complete their tasks and in their general dealings with others – employ unofficial and informal practices, which are not intended to violate existing rules but are meaning-creating and meaning-endowing procedures that make activity possible. Consequently, styles of interaction and their characteristics are seen as essen-tial in the practical accomplishment of common understanding among people. Understanding is seen as resulting not only from verbally transmit-ted meanings but also from the tacit knowledge and the invariant and uni-versal properties of communication (Mitchell 1978: 150–5).

Studies conducted within the framework of ethnomethodology and con-versation analysis focus on spoken mundane conversation, because for con-versation analysts it has 'the authenticity of presence' (Atkinson 1985: 53). Assuming that we cannot understand actions and meanings outside their particular context, conversation analysis focuses on the sequential organiza-tion of activity, such as patterns of turn-taking, adjacency of utterances and methods used by speakers to generate orderly talk. This type of investigation demonstrates that the distinction between formal and informal interaction is readily and commonly used in everyday life and that people in their everyday conversations evaluate 'informal' in a more positive way than 'formal'.

Atkinson (1982) points out that we all use a taken-for-granted model of conversational interaction as a comparative reference point against which certain actions are defined as 'formal'. Therefore it could be said that the method used to identify some interactions as 'formal' or 'informal' relies on the taken-for-granted model of everyday conversational interaction. We arrive at a definition of interaction as 'formal' or 'informal' by relying on 'nothing more than our taken for granted competences as speakers of English, and the ability to analyse sequences of talk that is an essential feature of such competences' (Atkinson 1982:91). Atkinson suggests that in 'the course of monitoring some sequence of utterances, we identify particular features of them as standing out as "noticeable" because of the ways in which they differ from details of talk in other settings with which we are familiar' (1982:91–2). The identification of sequences of interaction as 'formal' or 'informal' is therefore the result of ongoing conversational partners' analysis, sensitive to the extent to which details in the construction and sequential placement of activities are noticeably different from, or similar to, those found in conversational interaction. A list of these details allowing us to define the informality of an interactional situation includes features that tend to be referred to as 'normal ', 'familiar', 'more usual' as well as many others terms that are indicative of small-scale conversations (the frequency and length of pauses within turns, gaps between turns, relative freedom of allocation procedure and so on). Everyday talk is remarkable for its looseness in terms of topics, speakers' participation, allocation of turns and forms of speech. In an ordinary conversation, turn size, turn content and type and turn order are locally and interactionally determined, thus free to vary (Boden and Zimmerman 1991).

To sum up, people generally do not experience any difficulties in evaluating situations as either formal or informal. For them 'formality' implies 'intimidating', 'unfamiliar' or even 'oppressive character of action', while 'informality' is equated with a 'relaxed atmosphere' and is described as a more desirable practice. Yet not all sorts of interactional tasks can be accomplished by relying on the unmodified use of informal practices that work more or less effectively in the production of informal conversational interaction. Therefore, instead of seeing informality and formality as two differently evaluated interactional practices, formality and informality should be seen, argues Atkinson, as two procedures that provide practical solutions to situated interactional problems and, therefore, facilitate the local production of social order. Consequently, it can be said that informal conversational practices are avoided in the situation where they are found to be ineffective in providing for the practical accomplishment of certain interactional tasks. Atkinson's discussion focuses particularly on one type of problem that is more readily solved by using various 'non-conversational' formal procedures, that is, the problem of achieving and sustaining the shared attentiveness of co-present parties in multi-party settings to a single sequence of actions.

The increase in group size tends to erode the effectiveness of the distribution of turns of participation to all co-present parties; therefore large groups have to solve the problem of orderliness of conversational interactions. As the number of co-present participants increases, special procedures are required for making the identities of different parties publicly available. Furthermore, in contrast with informal conversation in small groups, multi-party settings provide less scope for all those present to display their under-standing of an utterance. And since the majority of them do not have the chance to speak in turn, they do not have any incentive to remain continually attentive. Therefore orderliness in multi-party settings (such as court hear-ings) is crucially dependent upon practical solutions being found to the issue of allocation procedure, speaker identification and visibility, utterance design and production and the scope for non-speakers and so on. Unlike courtroom proceedings, in casual conversation turns are not preallocated in any specific way, people are not expected to use complete sentences and they can cooperatively change the course and speed of conversational flow (Atkinson 1982:101–13).

Apart from large gatherings, encounters between professionals and lay people are also faced with interactional problems which are more readily solved through the use of various 'non-conversational' procedures than by relying on 'informality'. Reliance on a rather formal script of conversation practice can be found in different types of professional–lay interactions, as these interactions are still mono-topical in focus and frequently conducted within a framework of alternative turns that can be identified as 'questions' and 'answers', with the professional doing most of the former. This system-atic difference between informal conversational interaction and the type of conversation occurring between professionals and their clients protects the competence or expertise of professionals. Their professionalism might seri-ously be put in doubt if the interaction became so 'informal' as to be more or less indistinguishable from any other conversational encounter.

Borrowing the lay evaluative distinction can lead to a 'call for the abolition of a whole range of evidential and procedural rules' and in the case of court hearings, for example, it can result in the inclusion of the public so 'the par-ticipants could talk "more conversationally"' (Atkinson 1982:113). But the elimination of 'formal' practices could result in very impractical and not nec-essarily better developments. Therefore, understanding the practical and ideological limits of the achievement of 'informality' should be the basis for developing a more comprehensive framework for studying this procedure, for providing practical solutions to situated interactional problems and hence for facilitating the local production of social order.

Other ethnomethodological studies, which also contribute to the develop-ment of the notion of informality, demonstrate the inadequacy of formal rules and official procedures in performing certain kinds of work. Unlike conversational analysis, this type of research does not concentrate on the methods people rely upon for locating noticeable divergences from taken-for-granted models of everyday conversational interaction. Instead this research focuses on the various ways in which people depart from formal procedures and rules. These studies show that in face-to-face interactions people retreat from tested ideas and conventions and that codified rules and procedures cannot exhaust the range of situations to which these conven-tions apply, so that more informal judgemental work is required.

One example of such analysis is the work of Ego Bittner (1967) in which he focuses on the peace-keeping activities of the police on skid row, that is, in those districts with high levels of risk and low levels of predictability and orderliness of the streets. Keeping the peace is an activity developed as 'a craft in response to a variety of demand conditions' and which depends upon 'an aggressive personalized approach' (Bittner 1967:699). Procedures used in this activity are not determined by legal mandates but are instead informal rules constituted on the job, developed out of the practical experience of officers and which practitioners themselves view as proper and efficient.

Indicative of police officers' subordination of strict enforcement of the law to such broader concerns as 'keeping the peace' is the particularization and personalization of knowledge. Patrolmen 'know the people'; they possess an immensely detailed factual knowledge of their district gained through informal small talk. 'The conversational style that characterizes these exchanges is casual to an extent that by non-skid row standards might suggest intimacy' (Bittner 1967:708). Patrolmen enjoy the privilege of expressive freedom and they grant the same to people if they recognize patrolmen's access to their private lives. 'While patrolmen accept and seemingly even cultivate the rough *quid pro quo* of informality, and while they do not expect sincerity, candor or obedience in their dealings with the inhabitants, they do not allow the rejection of their approach' (*ibid*).

The fact that patrolmen tend to proceed against inhabitants mainly on the basis of perceived risk rather than on the basis of culpability suggests 'that patrolmen do not really enforce the law, even when they do invoke it, but merely use it as a resource to solve pressing practical problems in keeping the peace' (Bittner 1967:710). The basic routine of keeping the peace on skid row involves a process of matching the resources of control with situational exigencies and aims at producing relative order on the streets. Since patrolmen know that due to the sheer amount of crime they would be unable to take all necessary legal actions, they perceived informality as the most efficient way of achieving their goal of maintaining operational control. Because in attempts to reduce risk practical considerations are more important than legal ones, the patrolmen rely on 'means of individualized access to persons', which ensure the reduction of ambiguity, extension of trust and favours, but not immunity. 'The informality of interaction on skid row always contains some indications of the hierarchical superiority of the patrolman and the reality of the potential power lurks in the background of every encounter' (Bittner 1967:714).

Thus, informality is a tacit device to reduce ambiguity and increase control over the situation. Since such action can overlook the individual's rights to privacy, informality is often negatively evaluated by outsiders. In contrast to Atkinson's claim that in the commonsense understanding all positive connotations are placed at the 'informal' end of the distinction, here informality is perceived as a threat to cultivated values. However, Bittner, like Atkinson, goes beyond the surface of commonsense comprehension and suggests that in ambiguous and complex situations the effectiveness of performance depends upon the actors' judgement and more dialogical involvement. Officers are aware that the directness and informality of their approach is not always in accordance with civil rights legislation or more professional standards, but they believe that 'the imposition to personalized and far-reaching control is in tune with standard expectancies' (Bittner 1967:714). The fact that policemen exercise discretionary freedom in invoking the law is commonly perceived solely in a negative light, yet Bittner points out that we need to accept that some situations cannot be organizationally constrained and that in such an environment, people, in order to perform their organizational task, must be granted autonomy. We need to realize that these kinds of work cannot avoid relying on rather informal ways of making decisions because such decisions should be attuned to the realities of complex situations and should be based on immensely detailed knowledge. In order to avoid malpractice or abuse of discretionary freedom, people in these types of jobs must be assisted with acquiring knowledge and some particular personal dispositions in order to become 'successful craftsmen'.

To paraphrase Garfinkel, informality can be seen as a familiar aspect of everyday activity, treated by members as the 'natural fact of life'. From this perspective, informality is an unproblematic characteristic of commonsense activities, interpreted with the use of background expectancies, allowing partners to interpret the reality as 'recognizable and intelligible as the appearances-of-familiar-events' (Garfinkel 1967:36). However, we also need to recall Bittner's claim that informal 'expectations' grow up in and around even the most routine and seemingly rule-bound activities, such as those involved in work and occupational tasks. Employing Schutz's classification of the different realms of social reality, it can be said that informality refers to situations characterized by a high degree of immediacy, that is, the degree to which situations are within reach of the actor, and that the practice of informality is used in order to increase the determinability of the situation, that is, the degree to which it can be controlled by the actor. Here informality is seen as a practical solution to situated interactional problems and hence functional in facilitating the local production of social order.

Atkinson's research shows that the accomplishment of the interactional task, that is, the local production of order, can sometimes be achieved by relying on 'informal' practices, while on other occasions there is a need for more 'formal' procedures. This raises an important question: in what kind of settings can the informal conversational practices facilitate the production of order? Since informality, as a pre-existing set of social arrangements that people enter into while interacting, is a culturally prescribed model of conversational interaction, and since actions of individuals are guided by a local logic, it can be assumed that the scope and applicability of informal practices of various local orders differ not only within different historical periods but also from one setting to another.

This difference in the importance of informality for the production of order in various settings is well illustrated by the contrary evidence provided by Atkinson's and Bittner's studies. While in the first case informality is perceived as a 'familiar' practice which is contrasted with 'intimidating' formality, in the second case 'informality' tends to be evaluated less favourably than formal options of actions. Furthermore, while in the first case informality constitutes the basis for a comparison with formality, hence promoting formality's negative evaluation, in the second case, formal rules and actions are considered to be the frame of reference for informality. In both cases, however, the interactional task expresses itself in the continuous practical attempts towards the constitution of the orderliness of social life through the trusted use of shared expectations along with rules and conventions. Consequently, both informality and formality can be seen as significant interactional resources contributing to the stabilization and routinization of various spheres of daily encounters. People follow formal rules and enact social routines but they are also capable of a more reflexive and innovative approach to social arguments. They relate to institutionalized rules in a strategic-monitoring manner, as well as in a taken-for-granted way, and they are capable of using various mixtures of these interactional resources in different situations.

The dynamics of the relationship between the formal and informal can be partially explained, on the one hand, by Schutz's claim that the continuing process of interaction necessarily modifies and changes our typical knowledge of others. On the other hand, it can be explained by the ethnomethodologists' claim that 'people do what they do, right there and then, to be reasonable and effective and they do so for pervasively practical reasons and under unavoidable local conditions of knowledge, action and material resources' (Boden 1990:189). Such an understanding of informality, as the practice of managing social relations that are not bound to instrumental considerations, assumes that people have a relative freedom in interpreting the requirements of their formal roles. In this perspective, characteristics of the interaction are not seen as having a direct impact on social structure but rather as selecting 'how various externally relevant social distinctions will be managed within the interaction' (Goffman 1983:11). Following Goffman's assumption about the loose coupling between social structures and the interaction order, the main task of which is not the endorsement of *status quo* but the display of orderliness, it can be said that an accepted form of interaction is a result of 'a set of transformation rules or a membrane'. Such a definition of interaction as having 'a preinstitutional and therefore a pre-*status quo* order' (Rawls 1984:240) and as relying on various culturally established resources or procedures, allows us to see informality as 'constituted out of interactional materials' and to define the various social circles that draw on these resources as 'merely sharing some affinities' (Goffman 1983:11). Therefore, in order to provide a full explanation of informality, one must analyse interactional practices as the primary point of connection between people and social structures.

INFORMALITY AND THE OPPORTUNITY TO SHIFT FRAMES

In order to meet our responsibilities and commitments, even in institutionalized settings, we need to rely on more than merely our trained skills and official roles. In situations of team work, people's cooperation depends upon their capacity for interpersonal concordance, which is a capacity 'which comes directly not so much from a propensity to identify with others as from an ability and readiness to assume their point of view and interpret their intentions' (Burns 1992:74). Goffman's example of a chief surgeon's informal behaviour well illustrates how people, in order to achieve integration and ensure a successful team performance, make use of various styles of informal behaviour. A chief surgeon, who wants to assure that the members of his team sustain the rigour and pressure of the operation, employs functionally useful informalities, such as uttering supportive remarks, telling jokes or playing the 'good guy' (Goffman 1961:124). The informality 'displayed' in an interaction order by an individual in a position of power is a functional strategy permitting to do a 'morale maintaining job', and therefore it profits all participants. This example, by pointing out that besides the trained skills and the formal prescription of the role, cooperation relies on a more basic 'human capacity' for communication and understanding, suggests several important problems connected with the issue of informality.

In order to cooperate with others, we need to make sense of what we are doing. It means that in order to secure collaboration, we need to share a tacit understanding of the situation with other members of a group. However, the impression of reality, as granted in common meaning and 'fostered by a performance, is a delicate, fragile thing that can be shattered by very minor mishaps' (Goffman 1959:56). Therefore, we can understand our social world only in terms of a practical agreement on the 'frame' of the moment. Interaction proceeds smoothly through the use of frames and it is stabilized by frames, which are accepted by all the parties to the interaction. 'Frames organise involvement as well as meaning; any frame imparts not only a sense of what is going on but also expectations of a normative kind as to how deeply and fully the individual is to be carried into the activity organised by the frame' (Burns 1992:248). Frames, as elements out of which definitions of situations are built up, specify the meaning of social situations and help us organize our experiences (Goffman 1974:10). Their primary reference is not so much to social structures but to the organization of individual experience; therefore Goffman's perspective on frame analysis cannot be thought to be merely a theory of situation. Instead, social structures are seen as involving meanings systems and treated as 'merely forms that multiple actors produce' (Secord 1997:75). Framing is, therefore, a complex and subtle process in which individuals use implicit understanding and their common knowledge to make actions intelligible.

Since social interaction is made meaningful by the conventional frames we put around our social worlds, our interpretative skills and our ability to manipulate social situations are essential for achieving our goals. People use many tactics to maintain trust in the reality of everyday frames. These strategies depend upon the degree to which the participants identify with the roles they play. 'In situations where participants take their role very seriously there is likely to be little doubt of the frame's meaning; in situations where the participants are easily visible behind their roles, there is likely to be some confusion about what is going on' (Manning 1992:128). While 'one can never expect complete freedom between individual and role and never complete constraint' (Goffman 1974:269), differences in the scope of role distance result in various styles of interaction. Consequently, Goffman equates the notion of informality with role distance by arguing that when a performer shows his/her distanciation to the role, s/he puts brackets around the central task activity and enjoys more freedom in selecting the style or form of interaction (1961:123–5). With the expansion of role negotiability and self-reflexivity, the relationship between the self and the role changes, and by the same token, the adherence to the formalities of a role declines and informality increases.

Since normally we perform many roles in different settings, the calls of our other roles and the fact that we need to protect ourselves from the embarrassing feeling that with each role we are taking on a different identity, increase our distance to our roles. The distance to the role caused by these two factors, or the 'out-of-role rights', as Goffman calls them, can result in a multiplicity of different ways of playing the part such as, for example, parodying or simply overplaying the role.

Informality, therefore, needs to be seen as referring to situations with a wider scope of choices of behaviour where, in order to make the most of the possibilities in given circumstances, to reach 'a working understanding' (Goffman1983:9), people employ various forms of action that are not premade. However, it does not mean that informality necessarily means the total freedom to reject social roles. It involves more freedom to choose roles and more freedom to control the types of audiences for our performances. The space for informality or the opportunity to shift frames is indicative of actors' social sophistication, which consists largely 'in how easily one can move among frames and either fit them together smoothly with other people's frames or else deliberately manipulate frames to mislead other people about what we are doing' (Collins 1994:283). In this model of multiple frames, 'the first issue is not interaction but frame' (Goffman 1974:127) and the underlying message is that the fewer opportunities there are in interactional processes for shifting frames, the less informality.

The amount of freedom one has to break one's own frame (for instance, the frame prescribed by the organizational role) and to shift to another one, differs from one setting to another. It is smaller in highly organized than in more loosely coupled environments; it is also smaller in organized settings of the 'frontstage' than in the 'backstage' arenas of co-presence relationships. 'The more formal the situation, the more the performer tries to hide any notion of the performance process itself, so that attention will be concentrated only on what is on the stage' (Collins 1988:56). Staging the front region role is not, however, a synonym for dishonest behaviour. The main difference between honest and dishonest performers, according to Goffman, is not 'the need for performance, but rather the attitude of the performers toward their roles. In one sense, honest people are those who are at least partially taken in by their own performances and come to think of them as the characters they portray' (Meyrowitz 1985:30).

Acting informally, which ensures more personalized relationships with those with whom one shares this activity, is not only determined by the type of setting or stage, but also by social ranking. The chief surgeon from Goffman's example can assert a role distance, which is perceived as his willingness to relax the *status quo*, while subordinates' attempt to exercise role distance will be met with suspicion and seen as a refusal to keep their place (Goffman 1961:128–32). According to Goffman, 'we can expect that the more is demanded from a subordinate in the way of delicacy, skill, and pure concentration, the more informal and friendly the superordinate is likely to become' (1961b:124). In his discussion of the special responsibilities of the chief surgeon and his frequent need to draw on informality in order to meet these responsibilities, Goffman implies that the superordinate may have a special right to exhibit role distance, whilst a subordinate has to meet formal exceptions of her or his role in order to be treated as a fully fledged person. However, if in the 1960s a nurse could be penalized for showing too much distance to her role, today her joking behaviour will not attract any negative reactions. The modern advancement of the process of informalization, seen as 'demise of organized institutions and the emergence of new modes of action and control' (Wagner 1994:191), does not mean that all differences in the opportunity to shift frames has totally disappeared, yet it points to the fact that the amount of freedom one has to shift frames is historically determined.

THE PROCESS OF INFORMALIZATION

The process of informalization of Western societies has been captured in Elias' notion of the civilizing process, which describes changes in the relation between external social constraints and individual self-constraints. In order to clearly understand this aspect of the civilizing process we must work out sociologically 'the formality-informality span of society' (Elias 1996:28). This span concerns the synchronic gradient between formality and informality and is different from 'the successive informalization gradients observed in the course of social development, the *diachronic gradient of informalization*' (*ibid*:29). Informalization, as an aspect of the civilizing process (see Chapter 3), means the relaxation of previously formal behaviour. Each society strives to find its own mixture of rule-bound formality and rule-independent informality. In each society informality of conduct and formality of rules are joined together in their opposition and tensions. Their relation is never fixed for all time and their dynamism results in the evolution of styles of interaction. In order to avoid reducing this complex process to a static and simple phenomenon, the relation between informality and formality ought to be seen and investigated as changing and as reflecting changes in the nature of society.

The role of the formality–informality gradient as a criterion of the social distance between different strata has been continuously eroded because of the increasing material security of the West. Greater economic security and equality reduce the importance of the display of formal codes. Modern society puts less pressure on people to conform to the formalities of roles and protects individual rights, also as a result of such changes as the growing division of labour, the effects of new media of communication and the increasing complexity and pluralization of social life (Elias 1996). As the weight of the dominant role declines, society allows us to be more multi-role performers and cultivate our various obligations. 'While some degree of role distance and instrumental attitudes towards role-taking no doubt existed in all social formations, it would certainly seem that the greater degree of differentiation and complexity which characterizes postmodernity brings with it much greater role distance and looser fit between any particular social role and the social actor' (Seligman 1997:166). Trends in the direction towards the differentiation of roles, the increasing division of labour, the emergence of individualism, loosening of formal hierarchies and de-conventionalization of organized practices as well as the dynamic, complex and rapidly changing environment, demand that individuals' ability to monitor their situation is not reduced by too formalistic restrictions on interaction. In the course of the changes that mark the end of the organized form of modernity (Wagner 1994:191), most of the restrictions have become more flexible and differentiated and this process implies further democratization of informality.

In our society, where the gradient between formality and informality is no longer so steep, informalization means emancipation from external constraints. However, informalization, at the same time, brings also a higher level of structural insecurity as today we are left without models to follow, and consequently one has to 'work out for oneself a dating strategy as well as a strategy for living together through a variety of ongoing experiments' (Elias 1996:37). For example, looking at letter writing styles or rituals of addressing women in the last hundred years, we will notice the disappearance of many of the previously customary polite phrases and manners, which, when translated into behaviour, can give rise to confusion, as when the rules of etiquette of gender precedence through doorways are no longer shared. The process of democratization of informality further lowers the synchronic gradient between formality and informality; thus, in modern societies the formality–informality span is relatively small. However, people are not fully aware of the fact 'that at the same time the scope of informality in the key areas of informal behaviour has decreased. The tendency – partly unintended, partly intended – is towards the same behaviour in all situations' (Elias 1996:29).

In the past the strict formalization of behaviour characterized contacts between people of socially higher and lower standing, while informality dominated behaviour within one's own group. Now, with people being formally equal and with the formal code no longer corresponding to the actual relationships, informality emerges as the main code of behaviour, especially among the younger generations. Here we can point to the growing fashion for informality, 'in which the conventional attributes of a role are shed in favour of those of personal identity or "character"' (Burns 1992:275). In this example 'informality' is prescribed by the fashion standard way of playing the role and as such it can lead to 'the tyranny of informality' where 'being informal' is the order of the day.

This new significance of informality can be illustrated by a recent trend in some American companies, which in the process of adjusting to new global conditions and new means of communication, are moving towards becoming downsized and less hierarchically structured organizations. Employees of these firms are expected to be casual, down-dressed, unofficial and more relaxed, and to develop a more personalized and intimate style of relations with others (Weiser 1996). This interesting example of democratization of informality, while showing that in our culture being informal has a relatively well-defined content (e.g., coming informally dressed means coming in jeans), only describes the situation in which some previously unacceptable forms of behaviour have been incorporated into the official role. Such a situation does not really allow for a more independent choice of behaviour and can easily end up in the hyper-rationality trap of formally demanding informality or 'willing what cannot be willed' (Elster 1989).

According to Elias (1996), the breakdown of customary formalization in modern societies demands the search for a code of behaviour that corresponds to the actual relationships between members of various groups. This slow and gradual process cannot be stopped because only gradually and through many experiments a new balance between external social constraints and individual self-constraints can emerge. The problem posed by the breakdown of customary formalization can be formulated only when the extent and character of the informalizing process is seen in relation to the extent and character of formalization. 'An answer to the question of what are reasons for and what is the structure of the contemporary informalizing spurt depends, in short, on examining the formalizing spurt of the previous phase' (Elias 1996:75).

Although Elias realizes that one of the effects of the stronger demands on the apparatus of self-constraint can be the emergence of 'the permissive society', he does not despair because he recognizes that the process of informalization is not an unlinear development. Only from a broarder historical perspective is it possible to evaluate the nature of contemporary informality since our experiments with informality – in the context of a change in power relations of many groups and a widespread feeling of status uncertainty – 'perhaps obscure the difficulty which stands in the way of efforts to achieve total absence of formality and norms' (Elias 1996:29). With the main burden of shaping life together lying now on the shoulders of the individual, we are facing a less predictable, but not necessarily bleak, world. We still 'live in a world of strangers', therefore the need 'for emotional and behavioural restraint remains', although now there is 'no longer such a need for a "class act", and in consequence there is a lessening of a desire for the formality that went with this act' (Newton 1998:74).

Because the nature of the distinction between person and role is itself socially framed, socially better situated or economically better off groups are also better situated in terms of interactional resources and opportunities for individualization of their patterns of interaction. Following Collins' (1994) extrapolation of Goffman's theory, it can be argued that society could be seen as divided by invisible barriers resulting from differences in the framing techniques of different stratified groups, where patterned social behaviour reaffirms the definition of how society is organized.

In this vision, the differences in kinds of interactional material used by various groups can result in distinctive styles of interaction, whereby informality plays a dual role. On one hand, informality ensures the preservation of distinctions between groups, the phenomenon of 'old boy networks' or informal talks in the corridor are often quoted, for example, by many professional women in academia, as the principal factor restricting their access to important resources such as information, grants or teamwork projects. On the other hand, informality also reinforces the emotional and moral ties within the respective groups.

Seeing informality as 'constituted out of interactional materials' used by various social circles to establish their claims to uniqueness (Goffman 1983:11) redirects our attention away from Elias' focus on the relation between emotions and social figuration towards an examination of informality's capacity to mark and maintain social boundaries. This approach, by the same token, allows us to avoid the ambiguity of Elias' stand on the issue of connections between the process of informalization and both the internalization of restraint and the conformity to external rules. Within Elias' perspective it can be argued either that more lenient patterns of self-control go hand in hand with lower levels of emotional control, or that as self-constraints become more flexible, they are, at the same time, more deeply internalized. Wouters, for instance, asserts that 'the different patterns of self-restraints that came into being demanded not only greater sensitivity to varieties and greater flexibility in social conduct, but also a higher level of self control' (1986:1). The argument that a new informal standard of conduct implied lesser use of constraints by others and a stronger use of exercise by oneself does not, however, address a possibility that this new informality may not represent 'a radical change in the internalization of restraint, but instead heralded the need to "exhibit" publicly the fitness of one's skills in restraint' (Newton 1998:76). Such arguments point to the advantage of adopting Goffman's perspective as its focus on role distance allows us to avoid the difficulty of Elias' approach in determining whether informalization is about changes 'in tacit rules of emotional display' or about 'some suddenly learnt self-regulation' (Newton 1998:76).

To sum up, following Goffman, informality is defined as a form of interaction among partners enjoying relative freedom in interpretation of their roles' requirements. Our capacities for interpersonal concordance and our socially, culturally and economically determined opportunities to distance ourself from the role allow us to shift frames, and – by the same token – permit some space for informality. Following Elias, we assume that the expanding scope for informality is challenged by the increase in the number of formal rules and by the expansion of the formalization of rights in the public sphere, so we look at the process of informalization as occurring in the context of the continuous tendency to formalization. While the occurring structural and cultural changes are expanding the scope and the practical importance of various non-hierarchical, voluntary negotiated forms of self-coordination, at the same time the growing reliance on legal and administrative ways of solving problems accelerates the process of formalization. In order to improve the quality of social life we should search for a more balanced shape of the 'informality–formality span'. To construct such a balanced relationship requires us to learn more about styles of interaction.

Therefore our main aim is not only to point to the continuous relevance of informality but also to shed some light on a dynamic balance between formal and informal interactional practices. Since a full explanation of how actors strike the optimal balance between informal and formal styles of interaction requires a more careful examination of the social contexts in which interaction takes place, the next chapter will look at the structural changes that demand a rethinking of the relationship between formality and informality. An examination of the processes of the de-conventionalization, the blurring of the boundaries between public and private regulations and between the frontstage and backstage regions, will show how these changes have been contributing to the creation of new opportunities to escape role obligation, to flee restrictions on relations and conduct and to unfold one's emotions.

2 The growing formlessness and unpredictability of social life

> This society is characterized by hybrid forms, contradictions, ambivalences (Beck and Beck-Gernsheim 1996:31).

BECOMING UNCONVENTIONAL

Despite the fact that social interactions are increasing between people in their formal roles, many previously assumed trends towards the formalization and standardization of interaction now look less obvious because of broader, more fluid and flexible definitions of roles as well as because of the growing plurality of roles and more frequent changes of roles (Thompson 1995; Seligman 1997). For example, an American college graduate can expect to change job at least eleven times and to change his or her skills at least three times, while job categories are becoming more amorphous (Sennett 1998:22; Castells 1996:219–20). Furthermore, cultural changes have undermined the value of unreflective, role-bound and role-obedient conduct. They have contributed to new differences in the constructing of identities, as illustrated by the case of Dana International, a Israeli transsexual singer who does not conform with and thus does not reproduce the 'natural-moral' institutional order. Both the opaque surfaces of work and 'the growing attractiveness of more personal, informal and spontaneous ways of dealing with oneself and others' (Wouters 1986:4) have eroded the importance of the formal role as a source of meaning, enjoyment and social status and led to the present articulation of group differences and demands to abandon the concept of unifying standard of 'normal' (as 'normal sexuality', 'normal division of household duties'). So, whereas we were once all citizens and then producers, 'now our identity is increasingly detached from what we do and more and more dependent upon what we are, on our needs as expressed through economic consumption' (Touraine 1998:168).

This weakening of institutionalized social order means that roles cannot be 'solely defined by statutes, forms of authority, norms and values' and that all our roles, connected with both production and consumption, are part of 'formulating life projects' (Touraine 1998:178). The growing separation between economic and technological activity, on one hand, and self-identity, on the other, is seen as accelerated by the process of globalization, which by removing economic exchange from political and social control, creates perception that 'things are getting out of hand', that 'no one seems to be now in control' (Bauman 1998:57–9).

These trends, together with the rise of new forms of interaction in which information and symbolic content could be exchanged between individuals who did not share the same spatio-temporal setting, have been increasing the diversity of cultural scripts, strategies and expectations upon which people draw as they devise their performances. Consequently, one of the most 'personally burdensome characteristics of a sharply differentiated society is the absence of socially approved models for how to combine a plurality of roles into coherent life stories' (Luhmann 1982:xxi). This lack of common coherent stories or cultural codes, fixed forms or agreed upon styles of conduct contributes to today's commonly reported feeling of chaos, fragmentation, shapelessness and disintegration. Such feelings are a result of the fact that 'individual persons can no longer be firmly located in one single subsystem of society, but must be regarded *a propri* as socially displaced' (Luhmann 1986:15). Due to this process of functional differentiation, the contemporary individual 'inhibits simultaneously several divergent social worlds' (Bauman 1991:95), while the process of globalization brings 'the growing experience of weakness, indeed impotence, of habitual, taken for granted ordering agencies' (Bauman 1998:60).

Fears of the uncertainty, unpredictability and provisionality of all arrangements can easily lead to anomie. The loss of integrity in people's lives, the lack of a stable frame of reference for identity and the absence of a commonly accepted framework for interaction can undermine the capacity for cooperation and creativity. In their efforts to improve the quality of life, people try to cope with the 'normal chaos' (to use Beck and Beck-Gernsheim's phrase) of modern life, which, I argue, is a result of shifts in the boundaries between roles and identities, between private and public regulations and between frontstage and backstage regions. In what follows we look at problems resulting from the 'formlessness' of daily life in order to evaluate the complexity and difficulties of the tasks faced by people in their attempts to create coherence and orderliness across widely divergent worlds.

The shifts in the boundaries between roles and identities and between private and public regulations, together with the impact of the process of globalization and the spread of new electronic means of communication, have been changing our lives in a way that we are still unable fully to understand. It seems that the dominant sentiment is that today's life is characterized by ambivalence and contingency. It is argued that in the absence of any centralizing or 'totalizing' force, the expanding choice, uncertainty, pluralism, decentralization and the growing complexity of contemporary life increase social ambivalence. Thus, since modern culture 'does not effectively resolve ambivalence but increasingly generates it', we are 'condemned not so much to be free, as to be ambivalent' (Weigert 1991:159 and 21). Consequently, ambivalence, as a form of modern life generated by 'the rapidity, complexity, precariousness, and intensity of today's world', needs to adopted as an interpretative aid for making sense out of contemporary interpersonal relationships (*ibid*:58). Bauman, like Weigert, considers ambivalence to be at the heart of a world of globalization and new information technologies, the world that promotes dislocations and fragmentation. This 'endemic' and 'irreparable and irredeemable ambivalence', which seems to 'be immune to all efforts to trim it down' (Bauman 1995:43,66), reflects the end of modernist dreams of rational ordering, legalized ethical codes and planned control and, thus, leaves us with new questions to which there are no clear-cut answers any more. The main issue here is that change 'does not consistently conform either to human expectation or to human control', consequently uncertainty and contingency are bound up with the main characteristic of 'high modernity' (Giddens 1991:28). The decline in the boundaries of groups, the impact of the mass media and the transgression of boundaries (between private and public, frontstage and backstage regions) have been resulting in the decentring of identities (Lash and Urry 1987:295–9). Hence, in the 'age of contingency', characterized by the disintegration of previously existing social forms, both tradition and identity are missing since 'it is now all too easy to choose identity, but no longer possible to hold it' (Bauman 1996:50).

Modern untying and dis-embedding of situated identities mean that we are released from traditional roles and that traditional norms are fading and losing their power to determine behaviour, while the significance attached to authenticity is growing. However, with the further growth of individuality, personal responsibility and internal norms have been delegitimated as constraints on personal autonomy, thus – in turn – power of social sanctions over personal behaviour have again increased (Seligman 1997). Furthermore, as traditional social roles became less constraining, and with the further advancement of the process of individualization, instability, formlessness and ambivalence have become to be seen as a normal part of life. Consequences of the absence of a way of life that can claim universal authority and the lack of fixed moral norms are complex and differently evaluated by various writers, with some of them praising the process of individualization as the expansion of individual choices, while others stress new dependencies brought about by this trend.

In general terms, the process of individualization, being a complex and ambiguous phenomenon, does not make the task of constructing identity easier but only less determined and more accidental. The 'freer the choice, the less it feels like a choice' (Bauman 1996:51) since certainty, determination and what used to be carried out as a matter of course now has to be discussed, justified, negotiated and agreed, and for that very reason it can always be revoked or cancelled; therefore, our free choice lacks weight and binding power. Furthermore, as the Becks (1995:7) note, the very conditions that encourage individualism also produce new, unfamiliar dependencies as 'you are obliged to standardize your own existence'. Arguing that our autonomy cannot be seen as 'unfettered', they point to the importance of institutional constraints and considerations marking out our actions. Not only are we under pressure simultaneously to become individuals and adopt standardized strategies, but also, moreover, the requirements to be uniquely yourself and the requirements of the outside world are contradictory, and of unequal weight. Consequently, the outside world becomes an internal part of individual scripts. As our private decisions become heavily dependent on outside influences and by circumstances 'outside our reach', we are increasingly 'confronted by risks, friction and difficulties which we cannot possibly deal with' (Beck and Beck-Gernsheim 1995:40). Therefore, while from one perspective individualization means the freedom to choose, the expansion of choices and the reduction of the pressure to follow old norms and traditions, from a different angle, it also means 'being dependent on conditions which completely elude your grasp' (Beck and Beck-Gernsheim 1995:7).

Looking at the process of individualization, understood as the expansion of individual choices, pluralization of world views and liberalization of lifestyles, focuses our attention on this trend's capacity to create the opportunity for less rule-bound behaviour. Individualization, seen from this perspective, allows for less conventional conduct, which frequently makes use of less hierarchical and orthodox institutions or relies on more personalized, less bureaucratic structures and cultures. 'We acquire a new freedom of choice, we may realize our private ends by going along with the demands of the world, or we may choose a cross-grained existence, exhibiting our freedom precisely by not living up to expectations' (Ryan 1983:150). The modern emphasis on individuality and the growing freedom of choice manifest themselves in the increasing number of people living and acting in unconventional ways. As people's behaviour deviates from traditional, institutionalized value systems, they increasingly strive for the realization of personal desires and aspirations. Unconventional choices are directing people's conduct in many areas of social and political life in Western societies. For example, studies of political involvement of citizens in Western societies between 1981 and 1990 are showing that the increase in political participation in general can be attributed to unconventional participation (Ester *et al* 1993:87–96). In the last several decades, 'unconventional political action transformed from a movement of broad political protests of short duration and small numbers into a great variety of contestations and civic interventions with often greater continuity and more limited, often local objectives' (Wagner 1994:134).

The growth in popularity of alternative forms of political behaviour, such as signing petitions, taking part in demonstrations, political boycotts, strikes, sit-ins and involvement in various social movements, suggests that people 'prefer the more informal grassroots activities to the formal, more structured and more binding activities of the political parties' (Gundelach 1992:317).

Their political participation, oriented towards challenging the legitimacy of political systems, is organized by non-party-like institutions, which are submerged in the social networks of everyday life. These various networks are composed of a multiplicity of groups that are dispersed, fragmented and mobilized only periodically (Melucci 1989). This increase in unconventional political participation results in the growing support of a variety of 'third party' forces, protest voting, the growing fragmentation of the political system, penetration of the political system by symbolic politics, single-issue mobilizations, localism and personalization of politics (Allum 1995; Meny 1996).

Such developments in unconventional political participation are in sharp contrast to the decline in public trust in, and satisfaction with, the functioning of democracy. Individualism, therefore, is also blamed for the growing scepticism towards mainstream parties and politics and the decline in traditional public political involvement (Castells 1997:343–6). By subverting and questioning the conventions of traditional institutions, extra-institutional, unconventional involvement has undermined the boundaries of organized democracy and weakened the linkage between individuals and the polity (Wagner 1994). The overall consequence is the unpredictability of the political system and the singularization of politics (Castells 1997:349). Furthermore, the expansion of individualization not only leads to both the expansion of unconventional personal choice and an increasing reliance on less rigid and less hierarchical institutions than traditional organizations, but it can likewise mean a push towards repression and social control because the process of individualization also brings new dependencies.

From this perspective, individualization does not only free us from various economic, social and organizational conditions that constrain our choices, it also manifests itself in the growing search for identity and authenticity. The expansion of the process of individualization introduces new dependencies as for many people this search for 'their true selves' results in a voluntary acceptance of new types of subordination and rules. A number of people participating in various sects, new religious groups, practising astrology, searching for fortune tellers' or sorcerers' advice and so on, is on the increase in modern societies. New types of associations, characterized by very fluid and non-hierarchical, flexible structures and offering a more 'informal' form of individual gratification are increasingly popular. This type of gathering addresses people's emotions, anxieties and fears. 'We're building on exactly that kind of association .... We aim to bring religion down to an informal level, make it correspond to natural impulses, make it fun. When people realise it can be fun they let God into their lives on a daily basis' explains a young religious teacher in Brookner's (1997:100) recent novel.

This type of involvement, as shown in Stacey's (1993) ethnographic survey of American families experiencing the unsettling economic and social conditions of the last decade, provides for many people an answer to their 'cravings for security and spirituality' and the retreat from rationalism and secularism (which resulted in a 'resurgence of fundamentalist religious reviv-alism'). Stacey's case studies illustrate how women are grappling with the contradictory character of their postmodern family options. While freed from the restrictions and protections of the modern family, they often expe-rience difficult choices. One such woman, Pamela, sympathetic to feminist and union movements, after family emotional and economic crises, decided to resume her unsatisfactory marriage by having a fundamentalist wedding. Pamela's conversion to 'patriarchal Christianity', seen by her friends as a vio-lation of her emotional and political integrity, was her attempt to find a shel-ter which would help her to stay in the marriage and which could protect her from her overly high expectations for total honesty and openness that she realized could not be met. The main attraction of the Christian marriage rested on the fact that although it did not change her husband's inability to be open and to communicate (which was Pamela's main disappointment), it did, however, provide her with the security of the 'absolute commitment' which was comparable with the value of emotional intimacy.

This example illustrates that complex modern societies offer individuals increasing opportunities to define themselves as individuals by the choices they make; it also shows that at the same time, pressures develop that push actors towards dependence. Pamela's creative use of patriarchal ideology to serve her family's purposes is also indicative of another characteristic mark of today's intimate relationship, that is, its self-reflexivity. The growing aware-ness of the need to construct and negotiate decent trust, which could pro-vide a good ground for emotionally gratifying relations, also necessarily incorporates an element of self-discipline. The process of individualization, which once helped women to express their own aspirations and flee their marriages, now often demands from them to discipline these impulses in order to overcome rupture and family crisis. 'Whereas once it helped them to reform or leave unsatisfactory relationships, now it can intensify the pain and difficulty of the compromises many feel they must make to sustain inti-macy and to cope with family crisis under postindustrial circumstances' (Stacey 1993:263). While the underdetermination of identity in modern society increases the level of insecurity, various local cultures, for example, a local church or work place culture, try to set the social boundaries between the right and wrong way to feel in a range of contexts.

To sum up, our main problem today is how to combine the plurality of unconventional scripts in a coherent story in such a way that the process of the fragmentation and the growing unpredictability of social life can be arrested, without, however, impacting negatively on our freedom and cre-ativity. With the transformation of the modern relationship between individ-uality and role and with the growing multiplicity of roles 'the potential for mediating and blurring the boundaries between roles in a singular manner has been increased' (Seligman 1998:31). Connected to this process is the expansion of self-reflexivity 'as each role can become the archemedian point from which others can be judged' (*ibid*). With role differentiation and its complexity growing, a much greater role distance and looser 'fit' between the actor and her or his role is facilitated. Role distance and the instrumental attitudes towards role-taking, as manifest in the process of individualization, expand unconventional personal choices and the increasing reliance on unorthodox institutions, which are generally less hierarchical and more flexible than traditional organizations. On the other hand, the process of individualization also means the existence of pressures for standardization, social control and dependence on influences and decisions outside our reach. Hence, the assessment of the consequences of the process of individualization also varies, with some writers perceiving the trend towards individualization as only expanding hedonism, passivity and consumerism, whereas others adopt a more optimistic view, which assumes that a higher level of individualization can offer opportunities for free creativity, fulfilment, personal development and self-expression. While it is true that the process of individualization creates a threat to social bonds and makes the foundations of solidarity more fragile, it is also true that it does not necessarily make all our relationships instrumental, strategic and calculable or free of any personal responsibility. The acceptance of both facts can be a good starting point for the conceptualization of the basis for a new solidarity. When human relations are governed by choice, the foundation of solidarity depends upon people's chances and ability to communicate about, negotiate and agree on their goals and their criteria of choice. Since, as Durkheim notes, for society to exist there must be a limit to negotiations, a chance of reaching agreements, and therefore solidarity, depends upon finding such a form of communication, which would allow us to strike a proper balance between forging new bonds and embracing the risk of choice, between fostering change and preserving 'an aspiration to a human life endowed with sense' (Melucci 1996:131). Thus, finding new bases for solidarity requires the discovery of an optimal balance between the informality and formality of interactional practices.

With the development of the process of individualization, the most important dynamic of modernity is connected with the inevitable tension and complementarity between rationalization and subjectivation or universalism and particularism (Touraine 1995; Melucci 1996). As the emphasis on individual choice and cultural identities is growing, there is a need to recognize the value of universality because, as Touraine (1995) argues, a cultural identity shorn of its ties to rationality becomes reactionary. Moreover, since the creation of the public sphere requires the fostering of more universalistic arguments, there is also a need for the opening of possibilities for a more universalistic subjectivity. At the same time, however, growing pluralism means a stronger importance of individual differences, which cannot now be overlooked. In order to accommodate all these tensions, we need to come to terms with complex actualities of contemporary pluralist societies by means of combining inclusion and exclusion or democratic incorporation and pluralistic particularism (Wolfe 1992). This can be realized when civil society, as a progressive force for deepening democracy in a substantive sense, becomes 'a sphere of solidarity in which abstract universalism and particularistic versions of community are tensely intertwined' (Alexander 1998:97). In order to know conditions for the existence of civil society, we need to apprehend how inclusive citizenship rights actually are and how widespread is social acceptance of a normative framework of shared purposes and consensus, within which diversity can be both cultivated and contained. Understanding of civil society as 'informal, non-state, and non-economic realm of public and personal life' (Alexander 1995:34) allows us to examine the relation between universal individual rights and particularistic restrictions on these rights and to look at how in the shared space of interaction interpersonal trust is formed.

Civil society, that is, the arena of social solidarity, which provides 'a thread of identity uniting people dispersed by religion, class or race' (Alexander 1997:118), is defined in universalistic terms and is 'rooted simultaneously in a radical individualisation and a thoroughgoing collectivism' (*ibid*:125). It is argued that the tension between the individual and collective dimensions of civil society can be moderated by the creation of conducive conditions for the concretization of universalistic attitudes and codes. It means fostering civility as an appropriate style of interactional practices. Civility, which is further discussed in Chapter 3, implies respect for others and control of oneself and also adherence to a social code of behaviour, therefore it expresses the optimal balance between universal and particularistic and between formal and informal. The argument that vital civil society would manifest itself by high levels of civility asserts that 'democracy depends on the self-control and individual initiates' (Alexander 1998:99), while at the same time stressing the role of the macrostructural factors in ensuring people's opportunities for autonomy and participation. So, a revitalization of civil society can be assisted by the process of individualization if the inclusion and the acceptance of individual differences do not prevent the development of more universalistic identities of communicative rationality.

TOWARDS MORE LOOSELY COUPLED SYSTEMS

The movement towards the de-conventionalization of organized practices provides opportunities for less formalized, less strictly defined relations between various actors in an interaction chain, as well as for transgressing boundaries between the spheres of public and private regulation. The trend toward less hierarchically and more loosely coupled systems of interaction also has a clear institutional basis since, at least to some degree, it can be attributed to the result of technological innovations in the domains of communication and information as well as changes in the sphere of production. Among many modern institutional changes, the transformation to an information society and the evolution towards post-industrial society are of crucial importance. For instance, the development of new methods of communication and more flexible, less hierarchical and less standardized ways of organizing economic production, together with the process of globalization, result in important changes in the way in which the political and economic subsystems are integrated and in changes to their interaction patterns.

As a result of all these new developments and structural processes of the last two decades, several important macrostructural changes in the economy and in the functioning of Western states have been taking place. In the 1980s and in the 1990s we have witnessed the emergence of many new markets, the deregulation of national economies, their radical and universal transformation brought about by liberalization and privatization, as well as the movement towards more flexible modes of production. In the same period Western states have been losing their power to supranational levels (e.g. through the process of European integration), to the lower levels of governance (e.g. to regional governments) and to the global market, all of which undermine the steering capacities of national governments. Since the early 1970s the concept of democracy, on one hand, has become more encompassing in its cultural and social implications and issues such as cultural lifestyles, family structures and minority entailments have been included. On the other hand, the concept of democracy has grown more restrictive as the basis for economic policy has become dominated by Thatcherism, globalism and the control of money (Maier 1992:125–8). At the same time, states' fiscal problems, the decline of the welfare state, the proliferation of interest groups and states' reduced ability to control their fate – these have created a new situation where the political system is less transparent and less trusted. Consequently, 'the all pervasive interventionist state has disappeared and has given way to a new diffuseness of the boundaries between the spheres of public and private regulation' (Wagner 1994:134). What we are witnessing is not merely the reversal of the historical trend towards increasing public regulation, but rather it is the entirely new openness of the relationship between the public and private sectors that is in motion. Consequently, within 'this fluid structure, new possibilities for manoeuvre between the public and private sector came to light' (Meny 1996 :116).

This blurring of boundaries also raises questions about the links between the state and citizens and the state and the various elites. Changes in relations between economic and political actors, for instance, the state, employers and trade unions, have been driven to a large extent by the external context, for example, by the constraints of the European Union integration criteria, the globalization of markets and the intensification of international competition. The crisis of institutions responsible for consensus building helps contribute to the fragility of these new relations and arrangements. At the same time, in order to compensate for the decline of committed support and to meet the growing cost of electoral campaigns, political parties' increased need for money has transformed them from being 'organizations devoted to the mobilization of the electorate and the expression of the ideological and political preferences, to being machines for mobilising, distributing and exchanging resources' (Bull and Rhodes 1997:4). In the context of this continued privatization of the public sphere, opportunism of the dominant strategies, unable to generate trust, has resulted in a growth of inter-personal alliances based on shared interests, various trade-offs and informal instrumental exchanges (Meny 1996:116).

The new possibilities for manoeuvre between the public and the private sector have led to informal and usually decentralized modes of exercising influence. Since the cooptation of the powerful is informal (Oommen 1995:251–68), the evolution, which has been undermining the separation of politics and economics and has been fusing business and politics, further strengthens the bonds of allegiance between various elites and interest groups and further facilitates the personalization of relations in these realms (Meny 1996:116). Corruption, cronyism and clientelism are among the negative consequences of this trend. The fact that power now often manifests itself in terms of personalized and informal interactions does not mean, of course, that structural features, such as inequality or ethnic divisions, are not essential factors in shaping society. Forms of power that reside in the structural features of society are highly influential, and, moreover, the decline of formal rational domination of the hierarchical type has – by removing many checks and balances – made the power of private interests, and thus also the power of money, less restricted.

With the crisis of political parties and the decline of corporatist arrangements, politicians have increasingly become entrepreneurs, while businessmen 'have been ousted by a new species of economic agents characterised by their "bargaining" capacity, their ability as intermediaries and "brokers"' (Meny 1996:116). In this way, the economy enriches politics and vice versa and this process, consequently, results in the accumulation of wealth and in the increase of inequalities, which both erode democracy. Because democracy depends 'on social structures that allow egoism to be pursued but make the aggregation of egoism impossible' (Alexander 1991:160), the fusion of politics and business, by reducing the distinction between the public and the private and increasing the accumulation of chances, increases societal inequality and, by the same token, presents a threat to democracy.

The fusion of the state and the economy was the principal characteristic of the former communist countries, where it was, as the main structural feature of these societies, responsible for their disintegration. The unforeseen consequences of the institutionalized amalgamation of the state and the economy in the centrally controlled monoparty system resulted in the 'informalization' of the system, which slowly led to the system losing its structural coherence, therefore becoming ripe for change (see Chapter 8). The situation in Western countries, however, differs significantly from that of state socialism because the blending of business and politics is not the structural feature of the liberal democratic system, so it should not be understood as structural crisis but only as a potential threat. Although the evolution towards the diffuseness of the boundaries between the spheres of public and private regulation and the growth of personal alliances between political and economic players taking place in Western liberal countries are not a functional equivalent of the informalization in state socialism, these processes may, nonetheless, lead to remaking the economic and social institutions of these societies.

The blurring of boundaries has brought about the trends that run against Weber's account of the role of impersonality in both the state and the market. According to Weber, impersonality, calculability, formalism, rationality and the separation of the market and the state are all hallmarks of modern society. Weber's presentation of the push for calculability and impersonality in state administration as a consequence of the requirements of bourgeois capitalism, connects the rationalization of bureaucracy with democratization. His description of the instrumental rationality of the market and bureaucratic organization, as the most favourable conditions for formal rationality, and his stressing of the increasing impersonality and instrumentality have been challenged by the movement towards the loosening of formal hierarchies, personalization of social relations and de-conventionalization of organized practices. So maybe we escape the threat of the 'iron cage' of overall bureaucratization and rationalization, while, however, confronting another danger. This time the threat is not symbolized by the cage where everyone is involved in the impersonal regulation and control of everyone, but results from the decline in importance of impersonal, rational regulations and hierarchical structures. However, this does not mean that bureaucracy is not present in the public realm, but rather that in a dialectical turn of the modern tendency towards the depersonalization of social relations, we can now expect, as discussed further in this chapter, the bureaucratization of informality, feelings and emotions.

The structural changes, which have resulted in the transformation of the rules of economic and political games, have upset the *status quo* between the political and economic subsystems, have created new possibilities for movements between public and private spheres and have undermined the significance of the rules and principles which previously controlled the intersystem flow. The withdrawal of formal controls and the expansion of new market opportunities create the threat of the penetration of monetary transactions into activities formerly governed by rules or traditional customs as well as to personal forms of exchange. Money, as Simmel (1978) argues, more than other forms of value, makes secrecy possible and ensures invisibility and silence of exchange. Furthermore, following Simmel's point that money is a source of legitimacy for polity capable of maintaining stability of currency, it can be said that now, with the depreciation of the state as an economic player and the denationalization of money, new opportunities for a less fair and transparent system emerge. As money manages to 'seep across boundaries' and to buy things that should not be for sale (Walzer 1983), various types of more or less corrupt behaviour take place more easily.

The danger of the contemporary situation is that this process of the increased penetration of money to other than economic spheres takes place in the context of the transgression of so many boundaries and the general crisis of legitimacy. Consequently, all these factors, together with the lack of a political centre and the lack of a political vision of the future, seem to be contributing to uplifting money to the role of the main motivational force in contemporary societies. The observed great change in public sentiment, from thinking money is evil to thinking it a worthy desire, has even resulted in some writers seeing this inversion in the moral sentiments of the West as signifying the arrival of 'the age of money' (Buchan 1997). Furthermore, money is not only thought to be the only good or praised for increasing our power as consumers but also only money is now to be trusted. The Gallup pollsters show that growing trust in Wall Street has been accompanied by a falling trust in government, media, Congress and the White House. Looking at figures from the USA, which point out that 70% of Americans believe that Wall Street benefits America and that Americans' trust in government is declining, testifies that 'Americans have lost faith in people who claim to promote the public interest, believing that their words are empty. Meanwhile they have warmed to people who are efficient, but make no claims to lofty motives' (*The Economist*, 1 November, 1996:37).

This illustrates the crisis of power, the decline of credibility and legitimacy of the political system. If we remember that Americans likewise worry about their personal dependence, it also portrays the other aspect of money, that is, its impersonality, which makes for freedom and independence (Simmel 1978). Money, apart from leading to the commodification of social relations, can free the individual of personal obligation and can increase individual sense of value since in exchange 'each is mutually and equally enriched by the others' and since exchange presupposes 'an objective appraisal, consideration, mutual acknowledgment' (Simmel 1978:289–90). Simmel, in contrast to Marx who saw money as the symbol of alienation and enslavement, values individual freedom and liberation secured by the existence of the monetary economy, where people's interdependence is greater in scope but looser and more depersonalized. Money's abilities to dissolve people's dependence on things, together with the growing complexity and multiplicity of groups in modern society creates 'the most favorable situation for bringing about inner independence, the feeling of individual self-sufficiency' (Simmel 1978:298). Hence, at the same time, while the penetration of money can 'breed egoism' and reduce 'all quality and individuality to a purely quantitative level' (Simmel 1978:437, 325), money also contributes to the loosening of personal dependence, and the expansion of freedom and is an essential factor in sustaining our ability to defend spontaneity of life against rational bureaucratic regulations. So, freedom, which thrives in the monetary economy and signals a breakdown of chains of personal dependency and surveillance, can be seen as an important part of our protection against too much administrative control and formalization of social life. The issue is how to strike a proper balance between these two functions of money.

The failure to achieve this balance means that in our 'age of money' (Buchan 1997), monetary freedom has caused alienation. 'In the mature money economy, money's empowering features have compromised that very freedom which money itself promises to embrace' (Dodd 1994:49). From the point of view of the quality of human relations the cost of instrumental rationality of the market and impersonality in the exercise of power seems to be very high. The tensions between freedom offered by money and its alienating nature, the opposition between rational domination within the state and the instrumental rationality of money as on the open market, show the difficulties of the reconciliation of autonomy and the relations of association between human beings. Since the role and significance attached to money as an end depends on the cultural tendencies of the epoch (Simmel 1978:232), our problem today is how to stop or limit the progressive expansion of money to all other spheres of life without, however, undermining the increase of freedom secured by the monetary economy.

With the growing challenges to the previous model of reconciliation of autonomy and rational domination, we now witness the creation of communities on other substantive grounds, and this can be seen as 'approaching real individual autonomy as the right and ability to choose the others one wants to associate with as well as the substantive and procedural terms of association' (Wagner 1994:186). However, this process of the creation of a certain overlap between social identities, community boundaries and social practices is not easy and not without dangers. It can be successful, if a strong sense of a weak community, as manifest in the concept of long, more loosely and openly related interaction chains, can be created (Wagner 1994; Walzer 1983). The best strategy to secure this strong sense of weak community, which will be described in the following chapter as sociability, is parallel to a search for a new and more adequate balance between informality and formality for the present conditions. The reconciliation of freedom and dependence and instrumental and non-instrumental motivation is best served by accepting some conventionalized practices which set limits to the instrumental orientations of action, while at the same time opening communication in the public sphere in order to ensure the inclusion, dialogue and self-realization of all.

TRANSGRESSING BOUNDARIES: THE BACKSTAGE AND THE FRONTSTAGE

Despite many recent structural changes undermining rigid hierarchical systems, bureaucracies still exist and are of great importance in the modern world. Ritzer (1993), for example, maintains that four elements of Weber's formal rationality, that is, efficiency, predictability, calculability and control over people, are also constitutive of McDonaldization, which he sees as the essence of modern social life. However, Ritzer's criticism of McDonaldization notices only some aspects of what is happening in the interactive service industry. In addition to rationalization processes, McDonaldization should be noticed for its attempts to produce a 'climate of authenticity' through the application of bureaucratic rules. McDonald's' persistent efforts to create a new 'aura of sincerity' can be illustrated by the latest development resulting in McDonald's dropping its 'Have a nice day' trademark in favour of greater staff 'spontaneity' (Bewes 1997:51). McDonaldization with its attempts to standardize 'informality', understood as pseudo-friendliness, spontaneity and being personal, is an example of commercially driven efforts to transgress the boundaries between the backstage and the frontstage regions. Evidence of the growing popularity of the organizational culture incorporating 'informality in the line of duty' and of the employment of backstage intimacy as a frontstage strategy to lift sales or to market goods raises several questions. What are the reasons for such an appreciation of 'informality', understood here as showing emotions, a personal touch, and being yourself? Why is the reality of the backstage region assumed to be so important? In what follows, I try to answer these questions, but first we will take a quick look at the nature of frontstage and backstage conduct.

The differentiation between the frontstage and backstage regions is a part of Goffman's vision of society as being a very complex drama, in which participants present claims for deference based upon a definition of themselves and the situation. When people perform at the frontstage, writes Goffman, the performance must be appropriate, that is 'molded and modified to fit into the understanding and expectations of the society in which it is presented' (1959:35), it must be well executed and actors should be in control of their expressions since even 'a single note off key can disrupt the tone of the entire presentation' (*ibid*:52). As scripts are never fully written, actors are required to 'learn enough pieces of expression to be able to "fill in" and manage more or less, any part that he is likely to be given' (Goffman 1959:73). The process of negotiations over the definition of roles, and therefore over the social order, is a carefully crafted ritual, which collectively reaffirms status differences. 'On the surface, then we all grant due deference to each other [....]. Underneath the surface, or backstage, so to speak, a vigorous process is at work seeking to ensure that the apparently spontaneous mutual celebration taking place on the surface comes off' (Schwartz 1993:209).

While in the frontstage region actors ought to perform according to the script of their roles, in the backstage region they can relax and abandon their roles. For Goffman, therefore, the reality of the backstage plays an important social function because it allows people truly to be themselves and to deflate tensions. 'The backstage language consists of reciprocal first-naming, co-operative decision making, profanity, open sexual remarks, elaborate griping, smoking, rough informal dress' and of many other activities characteristic of a performance which is not fully public (Goffman 1959:128). The backstage intimacies and relaxation, together with its world of informal groups, are seen as sources of emotional and moral ties, whereas the more formal rituals of the 'frontstage' arena ensure the preservation of distinctions and different symbolic cultures of various social groups (Goffman 1959:200–4).

By using Mayo's discovery that informal groups underlie the formal structure of the Hawthorne plant, Goffman was able to see the frontstage as the ritual performance which sustains power relations between workers and managers, and the backstage as less formal behaviour within their respective informal groups, the performance that contributes to cooperative relations within both groups. The investigations of informal relations in large-scale systems, such as factories, emphasize the importance of informality and interpersonal relations in all social systems and view informal social relations as tying people into cohesive sub-groupings which have their own norms, values, orientation and subcultures, and which may run counter to the formal organization structure. The backstage or informal sphere of interpersonal relations is seen as an important part of people's everyday existence, contributing to their identity and feeling of belonging. The backstage informality is the type of everpresent bond, which – by facilitating 'group feeling' or common expectations – produces social integration. The main difference between frontstage and backstage can be summarized in terms of the amount of freedom or secrecy one has when performing. In highly organized and ritual settings of co-presence, in which the timing and spacing of appropriate responses is much more formalized (the frontstage), performers define in a general and fixed fashion the situation for those who observe the performance. Therefore, at the frontstage performance there is no mixing with the audience, whose attention is concentrated only on what is on the stage, due to actors hiding any notion of the performance process itself. At the other extreme from the formal frontstage is the informality of the backstage, for instance, everyday conversation, which 'consists of mixing together the performer and audience so thoroughly that neither has many secrets from the other – that is, secrets in the problems of performing' (Collins 1988:56).

Among many factors contributing to the increasing incidence of the commercialization of informality, understood here as backstage intimacy, is the growing significance of the service sector in post-industrial society. In *The Coming of Post-industrial Society* Daniel Bell argues that the growth of the service sector means that 'communication' and 'encounter' or the response of 'ego to alter ego and back' is central to today's work relationships: 'the fact that individuals now talk to other individuals, rather than interact with a machine, is the fundamental fact about work in the post-industrial society' (1973:6). Also the increasing importance of knowledge in post-industrial society is presented as contributing to changes in the nature of work. While some post-industrial society theorists exaggerate the extension of freedom and creativity in these new types of jobs, others, like Ritzer, deny that there are any advantages in this new development. Although there is reason to believe that the dominant characteristics of work have changed and that those changes in some way have affected our lives, the overall picture is more complicated due to the fact that different sections of industries and different types of industries and services, because of their different sensitivity to process, quality of goods or their own traditions, have reacted differently to the new developments. It seems that elements of both the old work requirements and the new job characteristics can be found in contemporary work settings.

In all work situations people draw upon wider cultural resources; however, this is especially crucial in the mass service sectors where a common understanding seems to prevail 'that all candidates for service will be treated "the same" or "equal", none being favoured or disfavored over the other' (Goffman 1983:14). This principle of equality is accompanied by the expectation that anyone seeking service will be treated with 'courtesy' (*ibid*). It can be said that routinized face-to-face service jobs require 'emotional labour', that is the commercial exploitation of people's feelings. Employees are paid to smile, to be polite and 'caring'. Therefore, an essential feature of those types of job is 'to maintain the organizationally prescribed demeanour or mask' (Fineman 1993:3). The institutionalization of emotional labour, together with the growing trend towards the de-differentiation of roles, is a deliberate attempt to create an impression of sincerity and spontaneity aimed at serving an organization's commercial and strategic ends. As 'forms of face-to-face life are worn smooth by constant repetition on the part of participants who are heterogeneous in many ways and yet must quickly reach a working understanding' (Goffman 1983:9), so informality of interactions becomes routinized.

The bureaucratization of informality and the compliance to organizational emotional rules can be coercive and alienating, as Hochschild's (1979) study shows. She examines the work of airline flight attendants whose duty is to display enthusiasm, friendliness and caring. Now it is not simply 'individuals who manage their feelings to do a job; whole organizations have entered the game' (Hochschild 1979:185). Spontaneity and cheerfulness in the line of duty become something other than a private act since their standards are now set by companies. The final result of this subordination of 'a private emotional system' to commercial logic is 'the managed heart' (Hochschild 1979:186). As various companies compete to raise ticket sales by ensuring more 'informality' and friendliness, Deutsche BA has recently proposed an innovative new approach relying on the use of humour to attract customers. As part of the ongoing battle to lure passengers, Deutsche BA decided to 'have a more personal and friendly service, so they trained their flight attendants 'to loosen up and be themselves more'. Although the company does not yet tell its staff that they have to tell jokes (even though testing their ability to be spontaneously funny is a part of the recruitment procedure) because 'not everyone can be spontaneously funny', it asks them 'to project their personalities and have fun with passengers'. According to these new guidelines for employees, they should try, for instance, to make people laugh by juggling or announcing on the landing in Munich 'Welcome to New York'. This desire of the company to encourage their employees to 'sparkle' (*The European*, 27 November 1997:62), can be seen as a further step in pushing to the frontstage the type of conduct more characteristic of the backstage region.

This emotional labour, where people are paid to smile, to laugh and to be polite, becomes an essential feature not only of jobs in the face-to-face service industry, where the bureaucratization of feelings rules at its most obvious. Now the 'tyranny of informality' is also a recurrent element of a new corporate culture. These new managerial strategies can be attributed to all factors pressuring for more consensual relations in the workplace. Apart from the fact that employers now are often faced with employees who resent being treated as subordinates, who are critical, who expect to be consulted and to exert influence, there are many structural changes, which – by making competition harder – push for adopting more integrative approaches in the workplace. For example, the movement towards less formalized organizational structures, new means of communication, knowledge-based industries and the smaller size of companies generally increases the importance of horizontal links with more direct contacts and replaces the old vertical forms of communication. With the structural changes in the technology of production and in the information revolution altering organizational structures, the opportunity for success and the importance of innovative input, companies are forced to abandon the zero-sum vision of conflict and adopt a more consensual approach. And as organizations try to discover new ways to increase innovative ideas, in order to enhance quality and productivity, they are forced to pay more attention to cooperation with employees.

The introduction of more consensual and consultational types of management techniques, attempts to democratize work practices, changing forms of communications, encouraging team feelings, creativity and individuality and casual dressing – are all strategies to enhance cooperation. Employees are encouraged to enjoy and conform to a less formal work environment during their Casual Fridays, Business Casual or Dress Down Day, when they are encouraged or ordered to come dressed casually. These type of initiatives originated on the east coast of the United States and became very popular with almost three-quarters of the largest US companies. In 1992 sixty-three per cent of American office workers could wear casual dress occasionally to work; in 1996 this percentage jumped to ninety (Epaminondas 1996:1). 'By creating a culture that enables employees to believe that they have a little more autonomy and security, employees are enjoined to become more committed to corporate objectives' (Willmott 1994:110).

However, the business casual conduct and look are neither quite as egalitarian nor as empowering as they appear. These new strategies often merely replace one form of conformity with another. The tactic of the institutionalization of the presentation of the 'right' emotions, used by the corporate sector where workers are encouraged to get underdressed and be more informal, often results in nothing less than in the creation of a new form of subjection. Organization – by imposing emotions on its members – sometimes helps them to avoid the 'truth of our own powerlessness'. Often, however, the compliance to organizational emotion rules is simply stressful and seen as an additional burden, which consequently results in people feeling that existing institutions are too demanding and inexperienced to cope with the complexity of people's emotion (Fineman 1993:24). Taking this into consideration and noticing that at the same time the gap between the earnings of those at the top and those at the bottom continues to expand and that employees are increasingly on short time contracts, allow us to say that these attempts to increase 'informality' and to manage emotions have not much changed the general picture as the formal structure of power and the role of impersonal bureaucracy have not been undermined.

Looking at the cost and demands of emotional labour from a wider perspective, it is easy to argue that this type of work is no worse than putting windshields on cars on the assembly line. Moreover, having experienced the hostility of the communist service sector, I know that dealing with a salesperson who smiles is more rewarding. Nonetheless, experimenting with 'informality in the line of duty' still does not seem to be the best way of expanding human potential. However, these attempts will not be stopped because where competitive pressures on business have increased significantly, even small improvements are seen as being of critical importance and therefore worth implementing. Because of it and because of today's economic and political environment there is now more than ever the need to remove social constraints that limit the development of alternative strategies for negotiating – the relationships between the backstage and the frontstage regions should be re-thought in such a way as to increase the chances for innovative solutions to our problems. The importance of this search for new alternative processes of bargaining is well illustrated by Friedman's (1994) very interesting study of various traditional and nontraditional negotiating processes between labour and management.

Friedman's use of Goffman's dramaturgical framework allows him to show how actors (negotiators from management and labour in their roles of representatives, opponents and lead bargainers), audience (teammates, constituents and opposing bargainers) perform on the frontstage (where actors are visible to the audience) and on the backstage (where informal discussion and signalling take place). The traditional system of labour negotiations, where 'conflict is expressed in public, understanding is built up in private' (Friedman 1994:111) does not suit the present situation because of today's complex and ambiguous issues, solutions to which require extensive discussions and overcoming the rigidity of the existing roles and divisions. As labour negotiators have less room to manoeuvre in these new circumstances, many of them feel that the old strategies are too confining and ineffective and that the old process could not produce innovative solutions to complex problems. This brings increasing reliance on the backstage for the development of mutual understanding. Hence, the importance of a more integrative style of bargaining, which allows negotiators to spend less time presenting the typical drama of conflict and more time engaging in the backstage meeting and discussion.

The introduction of integrative bargaining means both that the negotiators spent a great deal of time interacting informally and also that an 'informal' type of communication enters the frontstage. Friedman stresses that these informal interactions, now operating at the frontstage, helped to build trust between the two sides and provided a place for negotiators to express their views more openly. As a result the traditional role structure was overshadowed by an understanding that the actions of both teams were shaped by shared expectations. 'The kind of behaviours that had been kept backstage were now formalized and made into a new script for the front stage' (Friedman 1994:206).

However, although a more integrative style of negotiation allows negotiators to escape some of the expectations that are placed on them, it does not change those expectations. Providing an alternative model of negotiations is not enough to actually change the process of bargaining. As long as negotiators are pressured by the unchanged legal, political and social characteristics of their respective positions, integrative negotiations will be flawed or abandoned. Therefore, although there were good reasons for overcoming the weaknesses of the traditional model, the effort to expand the backstage and drop public displays of conflict proved to be very difficult. 'Any far-reaching effort to change the traditional process in a way that eliminates either the frontstage drama or backstage contacts risks destroying this balance' (Friedman 1994:230–31). For change to occur requires not just a new process of bargaining but a shift in the social structure of negotiations able to alter the influence of role pressures and audience expectations. Nonetheless, if we want to increase 'the chance that very innovative ideas are created' (Friedman 1994:234), we need to continue experimenting with integrative bargaining.

With the increasing complexity and ambiguity of economic and political contexts and the growing formlessness and unpredictability of social life, the transgressing boundaries between the frontstage and backstage regions is often seen as a source of diversity and innovation and as an essential element of social change aimed at improving the quality of life. However, the same ambiguity, complexity and unpredictability of our lives, which encourages us to rely on more personalized, less rigid, more informal means of solving our problems, also facilitates our search for more formalized protection of our rights and norms of inter-personal behaviour. This trend, enhanced by declining of the practice of ascribing responsibility for their action to individuals, expresses itself in the expansion of the legal regulation of the private realm and in the growth of individual rights. As more realms of interaction are defined solely by formal regulations and constraints, it becomes less possible to assume a shared understanding with others and to trust others. Our increasing reliance on formal rules and regulation, which has replaced 'the open-ended negotiation of trust', erodes our shared sense of familiarity and the resulting 'contingencies of alter's activity can thus no longer be framed internally but only externally, as dangerous threats' (Seligman 1997:173).

In the context of the disappearance of preconditions for commitment, the sense of danger dominates. The awareness of many dangers, from street crimes, through AIDS, to nuclear disasters, holds us back and puts restraints on our conduct and action. 'The culture of fear' (Furedi 1997) can be seen as imposing limits to our freedom, introducing or conserving the rules and constraints on conduct and closing us in collective identities, often of an ascribed or primordial nature. Fear restricts the importance of experimenting and limits more flexible and open interaction. Seeing interactions with others as full of potential danger, together with the development of various formalized instructions or codes of conduct and speech, restrains freedom and spontaneity of action.

When our conduct in the more ambiguous and complex world is constrained by imposed strict legal codes and regulations, our behaviour is expected to be a function of legal scripts. The implications of following such guidelines could sometimes be funny, if they there were not so tragic. An example is the case of a code of conduct introduced by Antioch College and described by Etzioni as 'a menace to spontaneity' (1996:xiii). The College produced a very lengthy list of instructions to students and staff in order to provide them with detailed prescriptions of how to ask for exact permission from a partner at every stage and move of courtship. If members of the community violate the code by not asking permission at each step ('if you want to take off her blouse ... you need to ask' ... and so the list continues), they can even be expelled from the College.

And finally, the most common way of dealing with the growing complexity and difficulties of life is simply by escaping from those difficult, unpredictable and too demanding regions of our lives. Now, paradoxically, very often it is the backstage, namely home, the family or problems in dealing with intimacy, from which we are escaping. The frontstage, that is, our official roles and workplace, are seen as providing us with a new comfort of coherence, predictability and orderliness. According to Hochschild (1997), in the new model of family and work life, tired parents, both mothers and fathers, flee a world of unresolved quarrels, domestic problems and troublesome children for the reliable orderliness, harmony and managed world of work. In a similar way, a recent study of Australians driving more than one hour to work discovered that the driving time for a large majority is the best part of their day, the period where they are free from both the emotional tangles of home and the stressful duties of work (*The Australian*, 12 November, 1996:2).

All these examples show that life becomes more complicated and less predictable. On one hand, home is not necessarily any more a haven because domestic ties are increasingly tenuous, while, on the other, work demands a more innovative input and more 'emotional labour', without, however, necessarily securing stability, clear marked career prospects or protection. The situation of the increased de-conventionalization, the blurring of the boundaries between public and private realms and between the frontstage and backstage regions creates new opportunities to escape role obligation, to flee restrictions on relations and conduct and to unfold one's emotions. It seems that in order fully to enjoy the quality of life, it is necessary to adopt effective strategies that can, without undermining our freedom and choice, help us to cope with the ambivalence and contingency of a pluralistic world. To develop such strategies means to formulate an optimal equilibrium between a relatively greater individuality of people and their understanding of mutual dependence. This new balance can be achieved by strengthening individual agency through the internalization of norms and values, or through what Elias calls individual self-constraints, and by the existence of a clear set of social constraints 'which people exercise over each other because of their interdependence' (Elias 1996:32).

With the main features of modern institutions driven by the force of a pluralistic, uncertain and ambivalence-inducing culture, the expansion of scope allowing for civility, sociability and intimacy – defined as three ways of balancing the informality and formality of interactional practices – seems to be the best response to the complexity of contemporary life. The value of these balanced interactional practices as strategies for alleviating contingency and ambiguity lies in their ability to enhance our knowledge and creativity. Secondly, they are also effective ways of coping with uncertain and changing environments because they permit flexibility, which is absent from formalized and rigid structures. Thirdly, today, when universal principles are being tested by the realities of a pluralist society, the balanced approach, such as manifest in civility's joint universalistic and particularistic standards, ensures respect for all without undermining individual uniqueness. The next chapter's closer look at civility, sociability and intimacy will put more light on their roles and their potential functions for enriching our lives.

3 Informality and styles of interaction

ENCOUNTERS, EXCHANGE AND PURE RELATIONSHIPS

> Whatever it is that generates human want for social contact and for companionship, the effect seems to take two forms: a need for audience before which to try out one's vaunted selves, and a need for team-mates with whom to enter into collusive intimacies and backstage relaxation (Goffman 1959:201).

Modernity has not only encouraged contrasting trends towards formalization and informalization, it has also complicated the relations between the sphere of intimate and closed human relationships and the public world of large scale organizations. The initial growth of polarization between private and public, which resulted in the shrinking of the intermediate sphere of networks of social activities and social institutions, has stopped at the boundaries of the nuclear family. Now the split between the formal world of organization and the informal sphere of personal relationships is taken so much for granted that informal, private, personalized relationships are still presented as being under threat from the abstract and impersonal structures of modern society.

However, the relation between rule-bound formality of the public sphere and rule-independent informality of the private realm is never fixed for all time and, even more importantly, in the contemporary context boundaries between private and public are more than ever vulnerable to shift. So, despite the fact that the contrast between the informal, private, intimate domain of family, friendship and the primary group and the impersonal, instrumental public domain of formal institutions is widely experienced, this dichotomized vision is rather unsatisfactory. Hence, as the search for a solution to tensions between informality of the private sphere and formality of the public realm has become an integral part of modern society, there is a need to conceptualize these relations in such a way as to overcome this dichotomous vision.

Following Walzer (1983), who treats the issue of the quality of social life as a problem of such boundaries and argues that 'good fences' make not only 'good neighbours' but also that they 'make just societies', it can be said that the moment boundaries collapse and one dimension is made superior, both freedom and justice become threatened. Thus, today, when boundaries between private and public are more precarious and unprotected, our main dilemma is where to put demarcation lines, or, in other words, what style of interaction should we adopt in order to achieve a better quality of individual and social life?

This line of investigation, by assuming that the nature of relations between private and public influences the quality of all social interaction, opens a promising way of a new reconciliation between informality and formality. To grasp crucial factors influencing how people behave towards each other requires us to examine particularities of a given kind of interaction. So, it can be argued that treating others as a matter of 'having the right touch', or tact, depends upon the specific characteristics of three realms of interaction, namely encounters, exchange and pure relationships. It means that a different tactful behaviour, manifesting itself by 'a particular sensitivity and sensitiveness to situations, and how to behave in them' (Gadamer 1975:16), is essential for each of these types of interaction. Encounters, exchange and pure relationships are inclusive in their character, with encounters being the most general, the broadest and the most elementary one, while pure relationships denote the smallest but the more inclusive domain of the two others. Since interaction dictates 'how one must display one's self with respect to others' (Collins 1988:54), the issue of the equilibrium between self-revelation and self-restraint is of essential importance for understanding human conduct. Consequently, different ways of balancing self-revelation, or three different styles of interaction, can be distinguished.

While compliance with rules of conduct in all three types of interaction 'has to be tacit' (Burns 1992:76), tact required in each of them reflects, however, a different balance between informal and formal elements of conduct. These three realms of interaction differ in terms of the nature of interaction between partners, in terms of the framework of the interaction and in terms of actors' mutual influence. Hence, they can be described according to their respective levels of impersonality, emotional commitment, disclosure of private emotions, voluntary sharing of private knowledge, warmth in dealing with others, their degree of institutionalization and according to the strategies of their respective actors.

Consequently, encounters can be described as characterized by the lowest level of close association and voluntary sharing of personal information and private emotions, occurring mainly in non-institutional settings, where people do not exhibit their identities, their roles, expectations or interests. 'Persons' in this type of interaction are bound by general social norms and conventions. Their encounters are accidental and momentary, although based on some kind of mutual awareness and rules of politeness that sustain the orderliness of interaction. These rules of conduct apply not to the ends sought by participant individuals nor to any consequent patterns of relationships but to 'the ways in which those ends may be pursued. In this, they are rather like traffic rules, which are concerned with how you go, not with where you are going' (Burns 1992:36). Encounters can be seen as a kind of rudimentary form of social behaviour in the sense that they normally take place in circumstances of co-presence, because they lack institutional control and also because these rules of conduct are fundamental for all other types of interaction. Consequently, the proposed understanding of encounters breaks from Goffman's view of encounters as always lodged in a more macro structural unit of rules.

The second type of interaction is exchange, which is, according to Simmel, the dominant social relation because it teaches us not only the relative value of things but also reciprocity, which is a constitutive factor in all social relationships. Exchange or 'sacrifice in return for gain' (Simmel 1978:175) is about transactions between people who occupy certain social positions. Their conduct is not merely a function of their individual character and personality, it also reflects the social roles that they are enacting (such as role co-workers, neighbours or fellow researchers). Others, that is, people in their roles, are seen here as important to achieving various goals, therefore mutual relations can be both instrumental and non-instrumental. Furthermore, although in this type of interaction social conduct is regulated by social conventions and more or less formal rules concerning specific roles, people performing their roles are motivated by individual goals and aspirations, and therefore they employ an immense repertoire of behaviour.

The third type of interaction, the highest on our scale of sharing emotions and personal information and voluntary engagement in dealing with others, refers to social situations where others are close and familiar individuals (e.g. friends) with whom spontaneous, individualized and emotionally responsive communication is established. Here individualized norms and rules dictate the selves' mutual actions. Co-identification and sharing values are the main source of motivation, while intimacy is based on authenticity and self-disclosure (Giddens 1992). The pure relationship is described as a situation where 'a social relation is entered into for its own sake, for what can be derived by each person from a sustained association with another, and which is continued only in so far as it is thought by both parties to deliver enough satisfactions for each individual to stay within it' (Giddens 1992:58). A constitutive element of this kind of interaction is the voluntary and spontaneous sharing of personal information between partners, friends or lovers.

Since a particular tact or a balance between formality and informality is required in every one of these three kinds of interaction, these three styles of interaction – namely civility, sociability and intimacy – are respectively characteristics of encounters, exchange and pure relationships. These styles of interaction are of an inclusive nature, with intimacy, while being different from civility and sociability, also relying on both practices. Likewise, sociability is a feature of more intimate contacts as well as characteristic of less primordial groups, but not social encounters, where civility is the sufficient

Table 3.1   Three realms of social interaction

	Encounters	*Exchange*	*Pure relationships*
Partners' identity	persons	roles	individuals
Motivation	self-presentation	particular goals and aspirations	co-identification
Normative regulation	non-codified general rules	rules and norms, sometimes codified	individualized rules of conduct
Style of interaction	civility	sociability	intimacy
Content of relation	respect	reciprocity	responsibility

practice. Sociability should be seen as a web of social networks that is distinct from the intimacy of private interaction, ruled by particularistic obligations, and civility, often ordered by more universal norms. Civility, sociability and intimacy, as kinds of context-specific tact, help to preserve distance, to avoid offensive, intrusive violations of the private sphere of the person and to suppress socially unacceptable levels of spontaneity and particularism within their respective realms. On the other hand, they mitigate the unnecessary formalism and abstractness of universalism and help to train receptivity and sensitivity towards others.

Assuming that scrutinizing the concepts of civility, sociability and intimacy can tell us something about changing relationships between formality and informality in the modern world, we will start our discussion with an examination of civility, which is seen as a manifestation of these relationships in the first type of interaction, that is, encounters.

CIVILITY AND RESPECT

> I would like to follow these laws, but not so timidly that my life would remain constrained (Montaigne, quoted in Revel 1989:201.

Writing in the 1970s, Sennett noticed that it is rather difficult to talk about the issue of civility 'without appearing to be a snob or a reactionary' (1974:264). His fear to address the matter was an effect of, at least to some degree, the 1960s critique of the 'formal politeness' of mass society, its routinization, standardization and the dominance of technical rationality and bureaucratization. The new generation's craving for new forms of social practices, for an authentic democratic culture and a new style of social relations gave a bad press to civility, which was seen as a formalized and impersonal form of social oppression, while its conceptions of appropriate social roles and the balance between public and private behaviour had eroded respect for rigid forms of conventional upbringing and conduct. The new spirit encouraged 'the public display of formerly back region features', such as informal dress, intimate self-disclosures, emotions, consequently it blurred 'onstage and backstage regions' (Meyrowitz 1985:139).

A highly idealized image of the social transformations of the 1960s, often presented as a period of the highest advancement of informalization (Wouters 1986), has introduced a view of civility as an example of the empty and unhappy old universalism. This portrayal of civility, together with today's mood of anti-politics or anti-institutionalism, is responsible for recent diffi-culties with the concept of civility. The domination of rhetoric of authentic-ity, personal commitment and integrity in our contemporary culture sharpens people's contempt for rule-bound and more formal styles of public behaviour, which are therefore perceived as superficial. However, the impor-tance of the sixties' rebellion as well as subsequent waves of cultural protest cannot be grasped without stressing the importance and persistence of institutionalism. Since the publication of Weber's article on the routinization of charisma, sociologists have known that the process of institutionalization of social life continues because people always return to institutions to provide an ordered reality, normality and predictability. At the end of the day, people will continue to accept that regulations are preferable to chaos and they will always agree that a degree of impersonally adminis-trated constraint is 'a price worth paying for security' (Barnes 1995:221). It seems that while calling for more freedom from rule-bound conduct, we also need to realize that there will never be a total escape from rules and routines, that even the most rebellious movement can be 'fairly pedantic', to use the Australian poet Les Murray's (1997) description of 'the tyranny of the 1960s swinging era of self-proclaimed freedom'. Therefore, while confronting and rebelling against formalized routines and manners are important and neces-sary experiences, they have – in order not be disruptive or empty practices – to rely on, and define themselves within, the existing system of meanings and authorities. Furthermore, formal and informal should be seen as the frame of reference for each other or as the basis for comparison of each other.

The evolution of the concept of civility is not, however, limited to the last several decades, which witnessed successive processes of formalization and informalization of ways of interaction and conduct. Until the late eighteenth century the terms civility and civilization were used interchangeably. The concept of civility, which is the older of the two, had practically the same function as the concept of civilization. They both expressed the self-image of the west and the sense of superiority and 'the self-image of the European upper class in relation to others whom its members considered simpler or more primitive, and at the same time to characterize the specific kind of behaviour through which this upper class felt itself different to all simpler and more primitive people' (Elias 1978:39).

The notion of civility, understood as the civil treatment of others and respect for their sensibilities, also tended to be included into the conception of civil society, understood as the relations between urban people of different interests and as being different from the personalized relations of the close-knit community of the past. For representatives of the Scottish Enlightenment, who distinguished between civil society and the state, civility had to do with manners, education and cultivation. These Scottish moralists spoke often of civilized societies of polished manners, of taste, of the softening of social relationships in modernity, of the 'gentle mores' of commercial societies, as distinct from less amiable habits of earlier societies (Keane 1988: 42–46). They understood commercial society as offering new possibilities of personal relations, creating non-instrumental friendships and bonds of real sociability (Silver 1997:43–67). However, with societies becoming larger and more anonymous, civility, understood as good manners in the public realm, started to be seen as making 'a difference in the quality of the daily life of the members of society' but being 'not directly important in politics' (Shils 1992:5).

Since the sixteenth century the concept of civility has also been connected with courtesy. With the growing efforts to control social interactions through the rules or techniques for disciplining behaviour, civility became a central element in the scholastic curriculum. The most famous book of manners at that time, Erasmus' treatise *On Civility In Children* (published in 1530), instructed people on the civil way to behave in public and emphasized manners and appearances for two reasons: self-presentation implied self-control and it created the condition necessary for social interaction (Revel 1989:169–73). Furthermore, the willingness to 'do service' for others was one of the principle marks of civil men, whose main duty, as one of the main eighteenth-century courtesy books says, was politeness, which gentlemen 'owe reciprocally to one another' (quoted in Goldgar 1995:20). In 1615 Eustache du Refuge wrote that civility consists principally in two points: 'One is certain Decency, Goodwill, or good grace, to which one must conform oneself as much as one can: the other is an agreeable Affability which not only makes us accessible to all who want to approach us, but also makes our ... conversation desirable' (quoted in Goldgar 1995:20).

In the second half of the seventeenth century manners ceased to be a private matter and became signs of perfection, with courtesy and etiquette governed by the rules of rank (Revel 1989:191–5). By the end of that century, the literature on manners did not at all include emphasis on virtue but rather emphasized the significance of appearance, grace and style of conducts. 'The stress was on form alone, and that form was one which could not be learned, but rather ... something which could be grasped only by those already in the know' (Goldgar 1995:236). In the eighteenth century the rules of civility enjoyed their widest social acceptance and were extended to diversified and wider segments of Western European societies. However, by the end of the eighteenth century the old civility was seen as outmoded or 'old-fashioned' ways of conduct and the old manners ceased to be regarded as natural, thereby ceasing to be valued as marks of social standing. 'The status of the civility concept was even more radically jeopardised by its very success

... there was conflict over whether to define civility in terms of rules applicable to all or in terms of conformity with a model established by a small elite' (Revel 1989:200). The French Revolution, as Arendt says, teared 'the masks of hypocrisy off the face of French society' and introduced the preoccupation with sincerity (1963:101). Rousseau's description of manners as falsifying the relations between men seemed to express the growing uneasiness towards civility, which came to be seen as an artificial strategy that destroys the intimacy and warmth of human relations. Consequently, the expanded appreciation of individualism, intimacy and spontaneity undermined the importance of formal manners in public life.

Finally, the concept of civility shares ground with city life. City and civility have a common root etymologically. Civility, defined as 'treating others as though they were strangers and forging a social bond upon that social distance' (Sennett 1974:264), is the essential element of city life, which consists of continuous encounters with strangers. To protect themselves from unknown others, while preserving some illusion of fraternity and communal experience, people need a mask of civility. The same argument is put forward by Simmel who argues that 'the metropolitan type of man develops an organ protecting him against the threatening currents and discrepancies of his external environment' (1950:410). In the metropolis, because of the necessity of self-preservation in the face of what Simmel calls the 'objectification of culture', its dwellers, instead of reacting emotionally as is common in rural settings, react primarily in a rational manner, thus creating a mental distance between themselves and others: 'He reacts with his head instead of his heart ... Metropolitan life, thus underlines a heightened awareness and a predominance of intelligence in metropolitan man' (Simmel 1950:410). Since this mental strategy has its root in the pervasiveness of a money culture, city dwellers are characterized by calculability, exactness, precision, a lack of warmth and the impersonality of their conduct.

The importance of the division of labour and money for the evolution of civility has also been the main topic of Elias' (1978 and 1982) work on 'the civilizing process', which shows how changes in manners are part of the social process of transformation, which emerged from the changing balance of power in society and involved the transformation of the structure of human personality as a whole. The civilizing process is seen as resulting from changes in the network of interdependencies, which are a direct outcome of changes in the balance of power.

In Elias' view, civility is a new mode of social control or medium by which hierarchies are maintained. The standards of courtly behaviour were used to keep subordinates in their place and to keep questions of social legitimacy off the public agenda. Civility's central role was to serve the courtly aristocratic upper class as a justification of their rule. The process of changes in manners went hand in hand with corresponding changes in people's personality structure. The making of the civilized individual meant especially a 'particularly strong shift in individual self-control, above all, in self-control acting independently of external agents as a self activating automatism' (Elias 1978:257), while socially the civilizing process brought the growing distance between people as the result of stratification. With the conversion of external social constraints into self-restraints and self-regulation, people learnt to conceal their passion, act against their feelings, 'disavow' their hearts, therefore, the core of personality, as an encapsulated 'inside himself' is though as 'hidden from all others, and often as the true self' (Elias 1982:258, 244). Due to these developments as well as to the process of democratization of civility, 'life becomes in a sense less dangerous, but also less emotional or pleasurable' (Elias 1982:242).

The suppression of spontaneous impulses and the development of formal manners with the purpose of exclusion had also created a social space and the borders within which the private individual is located. This expansion of the concept of privacy formed the basis of the modern notion of social respect. Since one's ability to sustain boundaries between the private and the public is so essential for maintaining one's identity and autonomy, some scope of privacy is necessary for one's well being and, more generally, for the quality of social life. So respect, as based on the principle that protects privacy, constitutes the fundamental condition for an individual autonomy and civil life.

Privacy, defined as 'the right to control what information people possess about certain areas of our lives' (Ryan 1983:151), provides a protection of persons' ability to develop and realize their projects in their own ways (Benn 1988; Reiman 1988; Schoeman 1988). The right to privacy plays an important role in 'protecting the capacities of individuals to form, maintain and present to others a coherent, authentic, and distinct self-conception' (Cohen 1997:152). Privacy, seen as providing a precondition for having an identity of one's own, ensures respect and protection for individual differences. Moreover, it can be argued that through recognizing others' need for privacy, we are also expressing our respect for people as trustworthy and reasonable individuals, securing, subsequently, others' recognition of our privacy and their respect for us. Thereby, people's perception of themselves as 'mutually recognizing each other' (Walzer 1983:278) upholds social collaboration and nourishes self-respect. As many writers (for instance, Walzer, Rawls, Margalit) argue, self-respect, seen as depending on the attitude of others towards the individual, is the primary good because without self-respect one lacks the self-confidence to make full use of freedom. Furthermore, in order to enjoy self-respect we need to be part of the larger community or group, which rightly distributes rewards, that is, we need to live in civil society. So, in today's multicultural societies, civility and respect, as its essential elements, are crucial, because they strengthen tolerance and good relationships among individuals and their groups (Glazer 1997).

During the twentieth century the power balance between established and formerly weak outsider groups (e.g. between men and women or between rulers and ruled) has changed and resulted in the transformation of the code of behaviour. The process of democratization of modern societies, by reducing the difference of social conduct, has contributed to the growing equalization of participation in social respect. Emancipation movements, consequently, have brought with them 'the relaxation of previously formal behaviour' (Elias 1996:29). 'The contrasts in conduct between the upper and lower groups are reduced with the spread of civilization; the varieties or nuances of civilized conduct are increased' (Elias 1982:255). These variations in conduct do not point any more to deep social partitions in terms of the claimed respect, they rather only mark differences in social milieus or subcultures. Furthermore, in the course of the civilizing process the self-constraints become stronger, more even and all-embracing than external constraints, thus in modern societies we 'have had to develop a relatively high degree of self-restraint in dealing with all people, including social subordinates' (Elias 1996:34). This informalization process, or the change in the relation between external social constraints and individual self-constraints, seen as the 'hallmark of civilizing process', allows for more egalitarian social relationships, since they are not regulated now by formalized codes of conduct, while at the same time placing stronger demands on our 'apparatuses of self-constraints' (Elias 1996:33).

Elias' description of the reduction of difference in standards of behaviour in modern societies, where codes of conduct are not any more 'markers of distinction and prestige' and where people express a total emotional control over their behaviour, comes close to Simmel's presentation of the style of behaviour in modern urban environments. Elias' argument that forms of conducts of various classes are becoming more similar due to the spread of a modern type of social interdependence resembles Simmel's view of connections between styles of modern life and the predominance of a money economy and the growing division of labour. In the same way as Elias' modern men internalize anxiety and fears of 'personal degradation or merely loss of prestige in his own society', which assures the habitual reproduction of distinctive conduct (Elias 1982:254), Simmel's 'metropolitan type' develops a 'structure of highest impersonality' (1950:413). Furthermore, both Simmel and Elias suggest that with the changes in external conditions and with the conversion of external social constrains into internal self-regulation, people cannot really be truly themselves in public as the core of personality needs to be hidden from all others (Elias 1982:244). When 'life is composed more and more of these impersonal contents and offerings which tend to displace the genuine personal colorations and incomparabilities', the preservation of the personal core often takes the form of mannerisms and extravagancies, which are strategies aimed at being different or at standing out used by people in order to save 'for themselves some modicum of self-esteem' (Simmel 1950:418, 422).

Striking a proper balance between formality and informality, or finding the right style for a specific encounter, is the necessary first step in attempts to revitalized civil society. However, to find such an equilibrium becomes increasingly more difficult because of continuous erosion of conditions able to facilitate the experience of trust. Changes in people's experience of social relations and their increasing inability to engage in the negotiation of trust relationships should be seen as linked to changes in economic and political dimensions of societies. In Elias' approach 'civilised political action presupposes a sense of proportion, tolerance, detachment *vis-à-vis* one's own affects, and the recognition of civil and liberal principles such as the obligation to behave decently in personal interaction with others' (Kuzmics 1988:170). This perspective stresses the links between 'civilized' structures of personality and structural conditions within a society, while seeing the mechanism of self-control as developed in the context of the specific power structure. Following Elias' approach, it can be said that the construction of an appropriate balance between formality and informality or self-restraint and spontaneity should draw not only on the capacity of individuals but also on many structural resources. In similar vein, Sennett, in his new book (*The Corrosion of Character*), argues that the conditions of work in modern capitalism, especially its flexible methods of working, downsizing and re-engineering, have corroded workers' ability to experience commitment, loyalty and trust. Because modern conditions of work do not provide us with a reason to care about one another, they also do not socialize us to practise civility in the realm outside of work. Consequently, people increasingly rely on the formal rules and rights to regulate their interaction. By defining interaction solely by formal constraints, the responsibility for negotiating the boundaries of acceptable behaviour, and subsequently the opportunity to establish trust relations, is taken from its participants.

The increased replacement of the open-ended negotiation of boundaries of interaction with rule-bound behaviour has many shortcomings. For example, as legal categories reduce the variance and the uniqueness of persons and as typification takes the place of personal familiarity, people increasingly show the tendency to give 'meaning of crime' to 'more and more of what is seen as unwanted or at least dubious acts', so consequently 'more and more of these crimes are met with imprisonment' (Christie 1993:86–7). The process of formalization cannot continue for ever. It diminishes our willingness and relative freedom in conducting encounters with others and does not facilitate the expression of respect for people as trustworthy and reasonable individuals; also, it erodes social collaboration and the legitimacy of the system. And, in any case, it would not acquire social approval because today's society – due to such processes as the reduction of differences in the standards of behaviour, the democratization of respect and the increased need for privacy and social distance, all of which cultivate openness and distrust to established hierarchies – strongly values an open mood of interaction based on tact, imagination and understanding of the context of encounters. Furthermore, remembering the very human dislike of rigid rules, so well expressed by Montaigne in the phrase opening this discussion, civility – in order to be an accepted style of interaction – cannot be perceived as a constraint on people's freedom. Thus, civility, as the style of conduct that in essence is the affirmation of others' worth, cannot be anything else than a style of interaction that leaves enough space for individual expression, interpretation and input into an encounter.

This means that attempts to strike a balance between the demand not to violate others' privacy and the demand for the articulation of individual desires and opinions should rely to a high degree on the internalization of norms and self-discipline. This proposed understanding of civility, by rejecting Sennett's (1974) claim that authenticity does not occur in public encounters, offers sufficient freedom to shift frames to avoid the empty routinization of manners, while, at the same time, stresses the necessity of some restraints to avoid 'incivil' society, that is, society suffering from the deficit of respect.

All these various meanings of the concept of civility saw incivility as a lack of effort to extend courtesies or show respect to others. Incivility is subject to social rather than legal sanctions and the evolution of the importance attached to the formalization of rules of civility has been shaping the severity of these sanctions. Showing mutual respect, while at the same time preserving social distance, needs to be supported by the existence of some generalized norms and values; it does not need, however, to be rested in formalized means of control or codifed legal rules. This means that people meet others' need for respect, and consequently preserve a pattern of orderly behaviour in public encounters, as a result of their socialization to general norms.

It seems that civility, as a style of conduct that – by balancing informal and formal interactional practices – provides the affirmation of others' worth, can be undermined in two types of social systems. The expression of mutual respect is, on one hand, based on the common perception of the existing division of labour as legitimate (Elias 1978), and on the other hand, on the principle of the protection of privacy, which can be defined as people's right to control what information others possess about them. Hence, the deficit of respect can threaten societies that violate privacy because the violation of privacy can cause people to lose control over their lives, and this can serve as an extreme form of humiliation. The deficit of respect can also be expected in societies that have delegalized the social division of labour (for example, in former communist countries salaries and wages did not reflect people's real contributions, levels of education or experience, while promotions were not related to reliable and meritocratic assessments; Zaborowski 1998). Such a delegalization of the social division of labour, in turn, results in the societal perception of the existing social differences as not fair, namely, as not justified by rational or technological requirements of the division of labour and this can, subsequently, lead to societal rejection of the norm of generalized respect (Margalit 1996:204–8).

The obvious example of a society characterized by the deficit of respect on account of both factors is a totalitarian system. When the common understanding of deserts or reward is undermined by the political centre, the conception of human autonomy is under threat. This line of argument follows Durkheim's (1984:121–3) remark that external differences endanger industrial societies and their division of labour. According to him, although social inequalities are unavoidable in a mature industrial society, they can be perceived as just and fair to the extent that they are 'natural inequalities', that is, real differences in innate ability, rather than 'external' inequalities, that is, differences secured by rights of inheritance, nepotism or arbitrarily introduced by the political authorities. For instance, one of the main consequences of Stalin's Stakanovite awards for heroes of socialist labour (aimed at conditioning other workers to perform in a similar fashion), was a growing fear, distrust and divisions among workers, since this award was 'not a recognition but an incentive, a gad, one of these offers that turns very easily into a threat' (Walzer 1983:263). Consequently, this type of reward created a social climate of distrust, mutual suspicion and disregard, with many 'Stakanovite heroes of labour' being ostracized by their fellow workers, who felt that political manipulations and unjust criteria were undermining their self-respect and the dignity of their jobs. Thus, the problem of the deficit of respect can only be overcome in the system that treats people's preferences seriously and where these revealed preferences are the limit and the arbiter of political practice. This line of defence of liberty and pluralism as the best guarantee of freedom and decency is stressed by Isaiah Berlin. According to him, liberty, as negative freedom from oppression and positive freedom of rational control of one's life, is 'essential to decent existence' because human self-respect and dignity depend upon the possession of human rights as well as upon people's values and forms of life being embodied in the social and political institutions (Berlin 1992:47).

However, not only power but also money has the tendency, as Simmel (1950) and Walzer (1983) suggest, to cross boundaries and transform every social good, including social respect, into a commodity. Generalizing, it can be said that any society that does not set limits on the dominance of power and the dominance of money, so it does not protect its members' privacy, could suffer from a deficit of respect. In this way, civility is essentially a by-product of a given society's members' general behaviour towards each other, which is determined by the socio-political characteristics of a given society. In a 'civil' society ordinary people tend to respect each other and social differences sustain their neutral character, while in an 'incivil' society, where people's desire for social respect can only be met by participation in informal groups (such as circles of friends or any ethos groups), social divisions tend to lose their neutral character and this can result in social intolerance and fragmentation (see Chapter 8). Therefore it can be argued that civility, understood as a style of interactional practice rested in the universal norm of respect for others and allowing for shifting frames, is a significant factor shaping the quality of life.

SOCIABILITY AND RECIPROCITY

> Causality and utilitarianism alone are insufficient to explain the propensity for association. Despite the various egos and interests involved, there remains a glue which guarantees perdurability (Maffesoli 1996:41).

The second type of interaction, exchange, is about interactions that transcend the boundaries of the household but are not predominantly shaped by the logic of the state or market. It is commonly assumed that there are two types of exchange – social and economic exchange – and that the main difference between them is that social exchange entails unspecified obligation and 'involves the principle that one person does another a favour, and while there is a general expectation of some future return, its exact nature is not definitely stipulated in advance' (Blau 1964:93). Here we will be concerned only with social exchange, that is, exchange where partners have an opportunity to negotiate their particular expectations about what inputs and returns are relevant as well as their timetables and nature. However, since partners' opportunity to negotiate the returns and their nature depends upon the characteristics of the context, we can distinguish three types of social exchange: clientelism, sociability and bureaucratic exchange. While the latter can be considered to be a type of role-based and instrumental exchange, which is rooted in abstract, universal rules of the rational culture of modern organization, clientelism is seen as exchange involving asymmetrical personal relations and obligations. Yet only sociability can be seen as a style of exchange which comes close to balancing informality and formality of relations because, although unregulated by rationalized conventions, it is limited by the norm of reciprocity, one of the universal 'principal components of moral codes' which is 'implicated in the maintenance of stable social systems' (Gouldner 1960:163).

Thus, the main function of exchange is the creation of feelings that can result in an atmosphere of reciprocity and mutual obligation, which ties 'one element of society to another, and thus eventually all of them together in a stable collective life' (Simmel 1950:387). Reciprocity, seen as supplementing formal procedural rules, creates 'an inner bond between people – a society' (Simmel 1978:175). It can be defined as a continuing relationship of exchange that 'involves mutual expectations that a benefit granted now should be repaid in the future' (Putnam 1993:172). The density of networks of exchange is seen as responsible for their participants' ability to cooperate for mutual benefit because the norm of reciprocity, which is built into these relations, typically makes 'every participant better off' (Taylor 1982:29). Sociability is also seen as securing a fine tuning between instrumental and non-instrumental types of motivation because it utilizes the self-interest of individuals, while the norm of reciprocity 'serves to reconcile self-interest and solidarity' (Putnam 1993:172).

Sociability embraces the realm of neighbourhood relations, communal associations and network ties between, for example, fellow researchers or webs of mutuality between colleagues from work. By their nature, these ties belong both to the institutionalized world and to a more personal sphere. They occupy the intermediary sphere between public and private and connect people in their not-so-intimate roles. Therefore, sociability can be seen as being capable of mediating between 'the particularistic intimacies of "private" life and the extreme impersonality and instrumentalism of *gesellschaft*' (Weintraub 1997:22).

Sociability, as public relationships between equals, is a modern phenomenon because its emergence required the constitution of the public realm and the private individual. Both these changes were brought about by 'the newly emergent idea of the individual and of individual agency as coming to exist beyond the normative expectations of what we would term status and role' (Seligman 1997:124). In the eighteenth century universal rules of the public sphere 'secure a space for what is most subjective; because they are abstract, for what is most concrete' (Habermas 1987:54). In the second part of the twentieth century 'the public sector of the nineteenth century collapsed and people thought they could fill the void by extending the private, family, sector' (Aries 1977:234). The current interest in the concepts of public and private is based on the growing awareness that the sharp division between private and public is misleading and that this false dichotomy should be seen as mediated by the concept of sociability. 'This sociability – the means by which people constructed and maintained communities, mobilized social movements, and expressed moral sensibilities – is distinct from purely private interactions, often ruled by intimate emotions and particularistic obligations, and from strictly public affairs, which are ordered by legislation and formal organization' (Hansen 1997:270).

The attraction of this type of network depends on those bonds being able to offer both freedom of personal choice and some feeling of belonging. While the formal nature of sociability, which manifests itself in rituals of impersonality sustaining the predictability of this type of interaction, provides for our need of belonging, its informal nature, which expresses itself in partners' capacity to choose, shape and model the main features of relationships, secures our sense of freedom. In this type of exchange people rely on informal control and on more or less codified norms (e.g. ethical codes, etiquette, occupational rules). Although Simmel argued that 'sociability presents perhaps the only case in which talk is its own legitimate purpose' (1950:53), I think that the appeal of sociability is also connected with sociability's instrumental as well as non-instrumental means of motivating people. Simmel saw the commitment of the individual to the conversation as being non-instrumental and he therefore argued that 'as soon as the discussion becomes objective, as soon as it makes the ascertainment of truth its purpose, it ceases to be sociable' (1950:52). However, it seems that people engage in this type of exchange for non-instrumental reasons, such as the pleasure of conversation or to improve their social standing or social approval rating, as well as for strategic reasons, such as to enhance their particular interests. When the rules of social exchange are rested on the norm of reciprocity, which reflects both a more general concern for others and a more particularistic preoccupation with the specific other, they can foster a poised relationship between 'individual' and 'society'. In order for this to happen, sociability should be the expression of an appropriate, for a given situation, equilibrium between formal and informal interactional practices, such as tact and discretion, on one hand, and more formalized group rituals which play regulatory functions, on the other hand (Simmel 1950:43–9).

Tact is of enormous significance in this type of relationship because it draws 'the limits, which result from claims of others, of the individual's impulses, ego-stresses and intellectual and material desires'; it excludes the most personal elements and generally allows us to 'enter the social work of art called sociability', which permits us to sustain, at least, the illusion of the equality of partners' social standing (Simmel 1950:45–6). The other important condition of sociability, according to Simmel, is discretion, without which sociability ceases to be 'the central and formative principle of sociation' (1950:46). Manners and rituals of sociability, by excluding the most personal elements, made sure the presumption of equality, which Simmel describes as the first rule of sociability, is met. Although equality of partners is only 'the game in which one "does as if" all were equal, and at the same time, as if one honored each of them in particular' (Simmel 1950:49), therefore not really altering the real inequalities, it expands the scope for egalitarian manners. So, groups enjoying such sociability 'were held together formally' (Simmel 1950:46) by formalistic and superficially mediated connections with people hiding behind the impersonality of a mask. However, while maybe during the Victorian period the first duty in life was 'to be as artificial as possible' (Wilde 1970:433), the contemporary transformation of social relations in the public realm has rejected such view of sociability and has questioned the need for hiding behind the impersonality of a mask.

The erosion of a balance between public and private life means these masks 'have ceased to matter in impersonal situations or seem to be the property only of snobs; in closer relationships, they appear to get in the way of knowing someone else' (Sennett 1974:15). For Sennett, unlike Simmel, sociability is not 'mere play' but the achievement of civilization, which allows us to handle public matters and deal with each other in a proper way, that is, on the basis of equality. Sociability, in this view, represents the best of the eighteenth-century public culture: its new civil bonds, its new forms of mediating institutions, its new types of associations and varieties of public places as avenues for vibrant social interactions. Sennett worries that this contempt for masks of sociability has made us more primitive culturally and that without barriers, boundaries and without mutual distance we lose the ability to play and this means that we can lose 'the sense that worldly conditions are plastic' and any motivation to be politically active

(1974:267). Because Sennett assumes 'that we can choose our selves in order to regain a better perspective on social reality' (Kuzmics 1988:172), his explanation of political apathy, understood as a consequence of the decline of sociability or the fall of public man, is a case of reverse causality. So, if we want fully to understand changes in the nature of sociability, we need to avoid Sennett's error of underplaying the role of the social environment in the formation of social characters. This means that we need to be sensitive to the role of social, technological and economic contexts in shaping the nature of people interaction. For example, only by analysing of the spread of electronic media and its consequences for the changes in relationships between the public domain and the private realm, formality and informality of exchange, can we become aware of what it does to the nature of social relations (Chapter 7).

Sociability, as an expression of people's strategic as well as non-instrumental (intrinsic) motives, contributes to the collaboration and integration of society. 'The vibrancy of associational life', seen as one of the consequences of sociability (Putnam 1993:91), can be contrasted with the situation of a total lack of societal cooperation, which is best illustrated by the case of 'amoral familism', as described by Banfield (1958). Banfield's study of a southern Italian village shows the absence of sociability, as exemplified by family egoism and societal distrust, all of which limit solidarity only to the nuclear family, leads to atomization, fatalism and suspicion of others and institutions. When everyone is concerned solely with the interest of her or his family and takes it for granted that everyone else does the same, it becomes impossible to bring about any kind of cooperation to improve living conditions in general.

There are many examples, on the other hand, showing how an expanding sociability gives a greater sense of security and improves the society's condition. For instance, various investigations exemplified how collegial sociability of researchers involved in the informal exchange of information secures the distribution of rewards and prestige, and facilitates innovations and new ideas. It is argued that informal networks among scholars in both the past and present attest to the importance of sociability in constructing the community. An exemplary illustration of the interplay of formal and informal elements in scholarly exchange comes from the functioning of the Republic of Letters, which from the fifteenth century functioned, unlike an academy or literary societies, as informal type of linkages between scholars. The Republic of Letters, which existed 'only in the minds of its members', had 'no formal manifestation' and its rules were unwritten, while its 'regulation and even its membership were nebulous at best' (Goldgar 1995:2). This informal community of scholars, which functioned on the basis of rules 'as well-defined as they were usually unexpressed' (*ibid*), was founded on two principles. The first was provided by an 'ethos of personal obligations', which implies reciprocity of service, mutual aid in scholarly work, the sharing of information and knowledge. The second lay in seeing the world of scholars as identical to 'invisible institutions' that one can only join through recognition by one's peers. Thus, most fundamental to the Republic of Letters were forms of interaction rather than their content, the characteristics of conduct of individuals on the micro, day-to-day level, their personal relationships, communication, interchange and assistance. This informal exchange, moreover, branched 'into an extensive network of connections available to provide information and help of all kinds', which constructed the foundation for 'the invisible institutions of the Republic of Letters' (Goldgar 1995:26).

The Republic of Letters' social structure was fundamentally based on personal contacts, with sociability being a social technique to draw scholars closer together for self-protection and social cohesion. However, with the increase in the volume of exchanged information, this 'invisible institution' faced a new problem of controlling and organizing communication. The formalization of the scholarly community, as its response to the above dilemma, was further accelerated by the expansion of the process of professionalization of social life, the developments in literacy and education, the development of commercial institutions and governmental attempts to control education and cultural life. However, the Republic of Letters, the formalization of which manifested itself in the institutionalization of exchange of scholarly information (for instance, by the establishment of professional journals), found it very difficult to abandon informal, interpersonal and individualized relationships for more institutionalized identifications. Consequently, many of its institutions became personalized, while, at the same time, forced to struggle not to allow personal considerations and favours to enter into their scientific judgements. However, with many journals being identified with a single author, it became increasingly difficult for those journals to maintain the status of institutions serving the entire community. This contradiction and confusion of the personal and the institutional undermined the journals' neutrality. 'The journal could not and did not escape from the fact that the world of scholarship revolved around services and favours, politenesses done to serve one's friends and colleagues. Its operations, even when hidden behind an authorless title page, could not be depersonalized' (Goldgar 1995:104).

The move towards a greater liberty of judgement and the attempts to make the journals into more communal institutions, was thus full of internal tensions and conflicts. The problem faced by the journals was how not to offend, how to be sociable, without being dry, boring and cold. 'The conflict was, again, one of form versus content. If the relations of individual scholars with each other was the ultimate goal, the community was well served by its obligation-based social system. But if a higher aim – objective truth, for example – was instead of primary interest, favors and personal obligations were out of place' (Goldgar 1995:242). Moreover, the trend to make the journals into more communal institutions was in contradiction to other types of institutionalization in the Republic of Letters. This institutionalization, manifesting itself in the process of bureaucratization of communal links, increased the impersonality of learned relations and contributed to the formalization of some of the exchange among scholars, hence 'this new system may have cancelled opportunities to create direct bonds between scholars' (Goldgar 1995:227).

This historical example illustrates the tensions characteristic to sociability as a style of exchange. It also suggests that due to these contradictory pressures, accelerated by changes in the social context, sociability can evolve either into clientelism or bureaucratic type of exchange. So, before returning to our main topic of sociability, let us first look at two other types of exchange, namely, clientelist exchange, that is, interaction based on extrinsic or instrumental benefits and guaranteed by personal obligation and gratitude, and bureaucratic exchange, that is, interaction formalized and controlled by impersonal rules.

To start with the former, we can point to clientelism and patron–client relationships as examples of the personalized exchange. They can be described as relationships dominated by vertical networks which link 'unequal agents in asymmetric relations of hierarchy and dependence' (Putnam 1993:173). Patronage and clientelism, although often perceived as the characteristic aspects of developing countries, where they are 'a form of interaction and control over economic and political markets, shaped both by structural factors such as centre–periphery relations and class and elite structures and by cultural factors, primarily the structure of trust and distrust' (Roniger 1990:xiv), are not absent from Western liberal democracies. Despite the formal logic of modern constitutional democracies, many personalized relations of clientelism still play an important role in their everyday pragmatic functioning. This type of personalized relationship can refer to several things; it can mean alegitimate, alegal or even illegal contacts based on particularistic, rather than universal, standards and procedures. However, generally, all personalized ties are asymmetrical and vertical, and create a personal dependency type of exchange. Illustrating how modern forms coexist with clientelism and patronage, Gunes-Ayata (1994:24) argues that clientelism, which 'arises as a blacklash to the centrally imposed, cold, impersonal, even alien political system', undermines the democratic mechanism advocating universalistic rules.

Some researchers expose 'the covered, informal and extralegal character' of clientelism bonds which encompass 'mutual, relatively long-term compromises based on commitments and some kind of solidarity' together with power and instrumentality (Roniger 1994:4–5). From clientelism's contradictory nature, illustrated by its being hierarchical but mutually beneficial, combining inequality and promised reciprocity, voluntarism and coercion, symbolic and instrumental resources, stems the ambiguity and unpredictability of this type of relation (Roniger 1994). The contradictory nature of clientelism and patronage influences the competition for power and within such a context clientelism, as an informal personalized bond, remains in dialectical confrontation with the official networks. Interpersonal relationships, where the exchange is vertical and asymmetrical, are seen as not helping to solve dilemmas of collective action because they do not develop norms of reciprocity between clients and solidarity between patrons and clients. 'In the vertical patron–client relationship, characterized by dependence instead of mutuality, opportunism is more likely on the part of both patron (exploitation) and client (shrinking)' (Putnam 1993:175). Therefore, according to Putnam, only those informal relationships which consist of networks of interpersonal communication and which bring agents of equivalent status together are free of dependence and formal control.

In the long term the existence of patronage, due to a lack of clients' incentives to mobilize for change and an absence of motivation for change on the part of patrons, reproduces the existing order. In the short term, however, not all groups bonded by authority and dependence are unwelcome. In some circumstances patron-client relationships can be a rather unique source of innovation. For example, according to Unger (1987), patronage is one of the ways that society can depart from the extreme condition of closure. This type of bondage can overcome existing rigid, formal structures, it can secure new allocations of scarce resources or allow substitute mechanisms to take over. In peasant communities the institution of patronage, as many empirical studies of Italian villages show, 'is seen as a way for the peasant to cope with the impersonal, unfair and often hostile demands emanating from national and regional centres to the rural hinterlands' (Galt 1974:182). It has been further noticed that peasants' skilfulness in and willingness to deal with patrons is the result of 'believing that impersonal, formal channels are virtually useless, their responses to a wide range of difficulties and opportunities is to think of someone who knows someone in a position to pull a string' (Rogers 1991:110). Furthermore, clientelistic networks may not be egalitarian 'but at least they recognize the individual as an individual in *quid pro quo* relationships. They may not distribute many tangible resources, but at least they offer hope for the future' (Gunes-Ayata 1994:26). Moreover, clientelism, by privatizing public relations, provides the political system with meaning and people with familiar supportive systems. A certain type of clientelistic system 'induced the local political actors to foster development by allowing and even encouraging the formation of networks of cooperation among economic actors' (Piattoni 1995:165). Thus it could be said that sometimes patronage may give people at the bottom of the hierarchy some power and a decision-making role and it does not necessarily hinder modernization. Finally, some writers simply object to 'the whole tone of the debates on clientelism, arguing that all human life is based on networks and calling in of favours' (Delamont 1995:136), thereby supporting a more neutral approach to this unavoidable social phenomenon.

To sum up, although groups bonded together by horizontal relations of reciprocity and cooperation are more beneficial to the whole society than groups consisting of unequal partners, in some circumstances and in some type of societies patronage can also foster welcome redistribution and change. Since cultural norms, which inform patterns of social relationships, differ from country to country, in order to evaluate the role of personalized exchange in a given context, one needs to explore the repertoire of culturally formed styles of interaction. It is commonly assumed that Mediterranean societies are characterized by traditions of paternalism, clientelism and nepotism. And since this type of tradition is perceived as linked to widespread corruption, it is, consequently, assumed that there is a lot of corruption in 'southern or developing societies while democracies, with sturdy bureaucratic traditions, experience no more than the odd scandal to which no society can be altogether immune' (della Porta and Meny 1997:2). However, the 1980s and the 1990s changed this picture and in many Western countries corruption no longer appeared to be a marginal and exceptional problem.

Both clientelism and corruption are types of exchange relationships in which extrinsic or instrumental benefits or motivation dominate. These two types of instrumental personalized relationships are empirically linked to the same aspects of political culture; however, from an analytical point of view they can be seen as two separate phenomena. Firstly, while corruption, which implies a privatization of politics by public administrators, entails the trading of public decisions for economic rewards, clientelism involves the exchange of protection for consensus. Following this difference in the medium of barter, it can be said that only in the case of clientelism 'it is possible to determine a vertical distinction with the subordination of clients to a patron' (della Porta and Meny 1997:173). Moreover, while repayment in the case of corruption is always of a financial type, in the case of clientelism repayment is guaranteed by personal gratitude and obligations. 'Also linked to the medium – money versus consensus – is another difference between the two phenomena: the different degree of perceived illegality' (*ibid* 1997:174). The fact that corruption constitutes not only a violation of ethical but also of legal norms, connects a corrupt exchange, as a separate case of political and administrative malpractice, with our third type of exchange, namely, the bureaucratic type of exchange, where impersonal control is the most significant factor.

While the main difference between sociability and clientelistic exchange is that in the latter partners are equal and have both rights and duties, whereas the complementary exchange of clientelism defines the situation in which one partner's rights are another's obligations, the rational bureaucratic model of social relations is role based. Bureaucratic exchange can be considered to be a style of conduct based on abstract, universal rules of the rational culture of modern organization. Exchange is not a matter of personal relations but depends upon the observation of abstract impersonal rules and routines. Bureaucratic organization is supposed to be the embodiment of rationality and efficiency in the modern world. Weber, who connects the rationalization of bureaucracy with democratization, argues that increasing formality and impersonality, standardization and regulation are justified as a

means of expanding general welfare. 'Bureaucracy develops the more perfectly, the more it is "dehumanised", the more completely it succeeds in elim-
inating from official business love, hatred, and all purely personal, irrational
and emotional elements which escape calculation' (Weber 1968:975).
Bureaucratic administration means domination through knowledge, and
this – in turn – makes it specifically rational and removes any regard for personal considerations. 'The "spirit" of rational formalism, which bureaucracy
(embraces) is promoted by all the interests [...]. Otherwise the door would
be open to arbitrariness' (Weber 1968:985). Such bureaucracy is 'the most
rational known means of exercising authority over human beings' (Weber
1968:223). It stresses the depersonalization of relationships, impersonal
power and the detailed rigidity of some prescribed behaviour, all of which
make the initiation of change very difficult. 'A main rationale of bureaucratic development is the elimination of power relationships and personal
dependencies – to administrate things instead of governing men. The ideal
of bureaucracy is a world where people are bound by impersonal rules and
not by personal influence and arbitrary command' (Crozier 1967:107). All
members of organizations are dependent and controlled by formal rules and
this lowers personal dependency and alleviates the tensions created by subordination. Human behaviour is made predictable, conformist, disciplined,
rigid and oriented towards a secondary formal group designed to perform
according to abstract, universal criteria. 'Since the group is oriented toward
secondary norms of impersonality, any failure to conform to these norms will
arouse antagonism from those who have identified themselves with the legitimacy of these rules. Hence, the substitution of personal for impersonal treatment within the structure is met with widespread disapproval and is
characterized by such epithets as graft, favoritism, nepotism, apple-
polishing, etc.' (Merton 1952:370). From this perspective, bureaucratic
exchange can be seen as conduct that is in compliance with the formalized
norms of rationality, specialization and conformity. As such it does not allow
for flexibility and more particularistic adjustment to local conditions.
Because impersonal rules delimit, in great detail, all the functions of every
individual within the organization, this type of exchange is in sharp contrast
to more informal types of exchange, namely, sociability, that allow for shifting and adjustment to the peculiarities of individual cases.

Of course, the bureaucratic system can never be so tight as in its theoretical models and in real life the ideal type has many dysfunctions and unintended consequences. Much research shows the routine and oppressive
aspects of bureaucracy as well as its 'vicious circle' and role of human relations (Crozier 1967:177). 'Informalization' of formal organization is seen as
a normal response to bureaucratization, which testifies to the 'limits of rationalization' of this type of institution' (Stark 1989:644). Not only does the
standardization of behaviour often result in a displacement of goals, but also
bureaucratic universal abstract rules tend to produce conflict because the
peculiarities of individual cases are frequently ignored. Therefore, the

functioning of bureaucracy can never be totally explained by the combination of impersonality, expertness and the hierarchy of the ideal type. Consequently, Crozier (1967:187) defines bureaucracy as an organization that cannot correct its behaviour by learning from its errors. Furthermore, universalism of bureaucratic impersonal rules is often a rhetoric used by bureaucrats when they want to ignore particularistic claims that they do not wish to acknowledge. Hence, it can be argued that for the rules of exchange to be more than only pale reflections of universal values, a society should also foster consideration for particularities of local contexts.

It seems that in contrast to both clientelism and bureaucratic exchange, sociability, as rested in the norm of reciprocity, is able to cultivate a more balanced relationship between universal and particularistic considerations. While the concretization of partners leads to partiality in personalized exchange not rooted in formal-procedural and universal intentions, bureaucratic exchange's perception of people as abstract, faceless and 'formal' organizational members can bring about other dangers, such as being unable to tune into other people's needs and failing to grant any significance to their specific needs. The degree to which understanding is mutual and supportive is connected with the adoption of less universal, formal procedures and criteria of evaluation. In many everyday situations, the pattern variables guiding people's actions, which, according to Parsons (1951), consist of dichotomous alternatives between affectivity and affective neutrality, between universalism and particularism, between diffuseness and specificity, and between achievement and ascription, include inconsistent orientations. The dichotomous principles create tensions, because 'whenever we think about organisational members developing ties to particular others, we then worry about universalistic standards being undermined by nepotism, friendship, old-boy ties, and the like. At the same time, though, we recognize that in some instances ties to particular others are part of the parcel of a person's job' (Heimer 1992:153). If accepting concern for the needs of others means accepting contingency, that is, locating it in the particularities of our form of life, maybe the dichotomy between universal and particularistic values is a false one. Responsible behaviour is necessarily partly particularistic and necessarily about relationships since it: 'entails providing different things under different circumstances, collecting enough information to know what the other party needs and so what one is obliged to supply, and accepting that one's own welfare varies with what one is required to provide or to do for the other party' (Heimer 1992:159). Consequently, universal principles of sociability should also always be particularistic in the sense that they should take account of the details of the context.

Sociability, as a style of interactional practices not favouring universality over contextuality and instrumentality over non-instrumentality, is rested and supported by more codified rules and norms, while also being rooted in partners' tacit adjustments of their reciprocal obligations towards each other as members of the same circle, network or community. Therefore, sociability fosters people's interest in the integrity of their shared life. In this interpretation, the connotation of the concept of sociability comes close to the meaning of the term social capital, which encapsulates 'such diverse entities as trust, norms, and networks' (Woolcock 1998:161) and which enhances collective action for mutual benefit. On one hand, both concepts are used to refer to people's ability to come and work together; for instance, social capital is seen as embodied in basic social groups, associations or networks, while sociability is seen as referring to various types of intermediate communities. On the other hand, sociability is viewed as constituting 'a subset of social capital' or a useful kind of social capital with 'the capacity to form new associations and to cooperate within the terms of reference they establish' (Fukuyama 1995:27). Usually in such an approach social capital is defined as a form of trust based on commonly shared norms; therefore, social cohesion is explained in terms of people's capacity to create networks of reciprocal relationships. Hence both social capital and sociability are seen as linked to and interchangeably used with the concept of social network.

Similarities between these two concepts, sociability and social capital, have led to the indirect incorporation of the notion of sociability into the stream of a more general sociological discussion about the connection between the quality of life and social capital. While there are many differences between various studies addressing this issue, they all seem to adopt *ad hoc* claims about the capacity of informal interaction to bridge the gap between individuals and, thus, to facilitate cooperative behaviour. Sociability, seen as linked in a rather unspecified way to social integration and cooperation, is granted with some emergent properties, which are supposed to explain these beneficiary developments. Such assumptions are visible, for example, in Simmel's concept of 'reciprocity transactions', that is, the norms and obligations that emerge through personalized networks of exchange, in network theorists' viewing social capital as one's non-rational social ties, and in Coleman's (1988:102–18) definition of social capital as the effective norm which ensures that people work together for common purposes in groups and organizations. Approaches seeing social capital as a public good produced by civic associations (Putnam 1993) and as moral resources such as trust (Fukuyama 1995) also argue that the nature of social ties or 'mediating structures' is essential for the quality of life.

Many of these various conceptualizations of the notion of social capital do not separate the functions of social capital from its essence and do not provide a clear answer as to whether 'social capital is the infrastructure or the content of social relations' (Woolcock 1998:156). They also do not see that both benefits and costs can be connected with this notion and that there are different types of social capital. For example, the literature on social capital often suggests that the higher the density of networks of social relations, the higher the sociability or social capital, consequently, the higher the socio-economic development and quality of life (Putnam 1993). However, this approach leaves out some of the most important questions to be asked. Since a good society depends on trust as well on distrust (Misztal 1996), we need always to look beyond trust and check the accountability, transparency and goals of reciprocal networks. Furthermore, the main difference in the amount of social capital may reflect the different levels of centralization of networks, not necessarily a higher level of social integration since the centralization can overcome the free-rider problem due to 'the effect of selectivity, the organizer's ability to concentrate organizing effort on those individuals whose potential contributions are the largest' (Marwell and Oliver 1988:513). Moreover, the type of social capital matters; for example, cohesive groups made of strong ties (in other words, having a high level of social capital) can obstruct innovation, hence they can reduce the opportunity for the improvement of the quality of life. As such cohesive groups become increasingly self-sufficient, thus increasingly isolated and closed to outsiders, the boundary between members and non-members becomes rigid and less exposed to information sources that provide novel information. Since members of strongly tied groups would reject information that disturbs their group's norms and cohesion, these types of group tend to contribute to the preservation of the *status quo*.

A very similar observation is made by Collins, who notes that the pervasiveness and importance of personalized networks could lead to a pessimistic and static view of societies since they breed stratification and reinforce 'ethnic enclaves in the division of labour. In the same way, gender and class and the cultural boundaries, are reproduced by personalistic networks that take local culture as the medium for enforcement of economic trust' (1995:303). Likewise, many studies of migrant communities stress that the solidarity of these types of collectivities leads to the restriction on their members' individual freedom and outside contacts and an increase of control and pressure to keep members in line, all of which often result in a lowering of the opportunities for social mobility through individual achievements (Porters and Sensenbrenner 1993). Studies from Soviet-type societies (see Chapter 8) also show that some types of social capital facilitate social stagnation and resistance to change, especially when 'the peculiar form of social capital constituted by political capital which has the capacity to yield considerable profits and privileges, in a manner similar to economic capital in other fields', by enhancing 'a "patrimonalization" of collective resources' (Bourdieu and Wacquant 1992:119). In a similar vein, Olson's (1982) argument that distributional coalitions undermine competitiveness and innovation of national economies, counters the assumption that social capital is only beneficial for society.

Such an understanding of social capital, which does not clearly differentiate between distinct forms of social capital and does not specify whether they are the sources or the consequences of group membership, fails to provide a successful explanation of social cooperation (see Chapter 4). In order to be able to differentiate between groups, memberships or networks that are not beneficial to society in the long term and those ones that contribute to an overall higher level of the quality of life, there is a need to clarify the confusion involved in using the same term 'social capital' to describe various types of exchange. The assumption that not all forms of social capital are synonymous with sociability is supplemented here with the definition of social capital as 'the sum of the resources, actual or virtual, that accrue to an individual or a group by virtue of possessing a durable network of more or less institutionalized relationships of mutual acquaintance and recognition' (Bourdieu and Wacquant 1992:119). This definition and the proposed distinction between three styles of social exchange, that is, sociability, clientelism and bureaucratic exchange, allows us to see sociability as the constitutive element of this type of social capital, which is desirable from the point of view of the quality of social life and which shows the capacity for the mobilization of social networks based on reciprocity and vertical links.

Seeing sociability as referring to the specific nature of networks of social relations allows us to identify multilevel networks encompassing formal and informal links as sites of sociability and to stress the possibility of social collaboration through those connections. Because the network perspective assumes that social behaviour depends on the actor's location within patterns of social connections, it does allow for the definition of social capital as something more than the property or deep characteristics of an individual. The other advantage of using the network analysis approach to study forms of sociability is that network analysis does not try to impose any presumption about 'the groupiness' of the world (Wellman 1983). Network studies' critical examination of both mass-society perspectives and community-visions of modern life found a wealth of social networks of various type, size and quality (Fischer 1982). By not assuming that social solidarity is the obvious characteristic of modern life, researchers in this perspective avoid treating social bonds as the self-evident 'social glue' but instead they define the social system as 'a network of networks, overlapping and interacting in various ways' (Wellman 1983:168). This approach facilitates the study of a wide variety of ties and diversity of social networks, which are presented as making for a low density of knit network clusters in modern Western society. 'Social solidarity, analyzed from this perspective, may be the outgrowth of the coordination of activities through network processes rather than the sharing of sentiments through common socialization' (Wellman 1979:226). What is interesting for us in these studies is their focus on the characteristics of the linkages in people's relationships to one another as the means of explaining the behaviour of the people involved in them. They point not only to the importance of sociability, but also to the usefulness of this concept for the description of a new overlap between social identities, community boundaries and social practices. This new 'fit', as formulated in the notion of long, more loosely and openly related chains, creates a strong sense of a weak community (Granovetter 1973, 1985; Wagner 1994).

The usefulness of the network analysis perspective to examine forms of sociability is also connected with its promise to study social change. Now, with the demise of the totalizing vision of change, more attention is paid to the role of informal networks in the emergence of social movements (Melucci 1996) and to informal networks' capacities for mobilization, which expresses itself in their ability to bring together people with common interests, values and norms. Collins (1995), while analyzing the mobilization of the informal economy in response to state regulations, notes that 'it is precisely the mobilization of certain networks on a wide scale, against others mobilized on a narrower scale, that brings about the shifting balance among different kinds of embeddedness' (1995:303). At any point in time, the result of a struggle between demands of wider networks (for example, the state) and networks of defence organized on a narrower scale explains the shape of subsequent social institutions. The mobilization of specific networks may thus be seen as determined by a macrostructure, existing outside the control of the local actors. Groups' capacity for mobilization in defence of their interests increases with the centralization of network ties and when the group's resource or interest heterogeneity increases (Marwell and Oliver 1988).

Until recently sociologists insisted that modern society has been marked by an increasingly sharp polarization between the domain of informal, personal life and the larger world of impersonal, formal and instrumental relations. This habitual way of thinking about the split between private and public has meant that the importance of sociability, as a web of social networks distinct from intimacy and civility, was overlooked in sociological analyses. Now, however, with various attempts to overcome these dichotomized visions of social reality and with the increasing visibility of social networks, sociability is discovered and seen as a useful analytical tool. This realization, that there is a need for a move to a more differentiated and encompassing interpretive framework that can capture more effectively than simple distinction between private–public or formal–informal the complexity of social structure and culture in modern societies, is visible, for example, in Maffesoli's (1996) work, where he argues for the importance of sociality (his term for sociability).

According to Maffesoli, today's significance of sociability is a result of the fact that in postmodern cities people come together in a multiplicity of temporary emotional communities. These tribe-like, fluid forms of being together are oriented towards the local and immediate and are held together by a shared participation in social rituals rather than by an ideology or common programme. 'Consequently, we find that the individual cannot be isolated, but rather he or she is tied, by culture, communication, leisure or fashion, to community which perhaps no longer possesses the same qualities as during the Middle Ages, but has nonetheless the same form' (Maffesoli 1996:81). Describing this form as 'the "thread of reciprocity" that is woven through individuals', Maffesoli defines sociality as 'the pure form of the undirected being-together' (1996:81). These tribe-like forms of being together challenge the existing models of politics and tradition and demonstrate troubling 'barbaric' features. Maffesoli, however, urges us to remember that 'through history it was barbarity that brought many moribund civilizations back to life' (*ibid*:28). He points out how new politics is created by members of new networks or communities in the process of the assertion of sovereignty over their existence with the help of a repertoire of informal strategies that undermine 'the logic of domination' (*ibid*:51).

Unlike Maffesoli, Sennett sees the process of retribalization as 'the mark of an uncivilized society' (1974:340) and stresses that this type of community network only reinforces the forces of domination or inequality since 'a community of power can only be an illusion in a society like that of the industrial West, one in international scale of structures of economic control' (1974:339). However, since the results of more formal attempts to challenge the structural differences are not very impressive, other ways of pursuing interests should not be disregarded. It seems, furthermore, that this new form of networking on the basis of a shared style does not lend itself to the traditional hierarchical order or ranking. In this way, the vitalism of this new form of sociality reflects the same quality as sociability, which can also introduce a new social order and new lifestyles to the existing structures. Sociality is, in the same way as a political and economic society, a social reality, although it functions differently since it 'stylizes the existence and brings its essential characteristic' (Maffesoli 1996:51). The new form of sociability, resulting out of the 'irrepressible and infrangible impulses of sociality' and being the opposite of the politico-economic power, signals the replacement of a rational social by 'an empathetic sociality', which increasingly expands 'an informal underground' (Maffesoli 1996:51 and 5). This assures the continuity of life in society and the creation of 'the conditions necessary for a sort of aura that characterizes a certain period' (Maffesoli 1996:13).

To sum up, the connection between sociability and reciprocity ensures that it is neither wealth nor power that threads ranks and ties a given group network together. For instance, the ranking of members of the Republic of Letters did not rely on the patterns of wealth or power but it was 'generosity to colleagues' that was the most important factor in reaching the higher ranking (Goldgar 1995:28). In this way the norm of reciprocity is both derived from individual self-interest (Blau 1964:90–104) as well as being the 'starting mechanism' of social interaction (Gouldner 1960:176). Consequently, sociability is a style of interaction that can be treated as a blend of instrumentality and non-instrumentality, resulting in the creation of 'a specific ambience' uniting all its elements. It is a style of exchange with reciprocity weaving through it, a style that is capable of creating a feeling of belonging and providing people with social acceptance and position. It can fully exist only under the conditions of a liberal public sphere, while at the same time being its necessary condition since informal communication 'pulls together the scattered critical potentials of a public that was only abstractedly held together through the public media, and it helps this public have a political influence on institutionalized opinion- and will-formation' (Habermas 1996:382). Thus sociability, because of its role in public opinion and identity formation, is essential for collective action.

This argument can be reformulated as Hirschman's (1986) distinction between horizontal and vertical voice, where the latter is more audible socially and includes communication, complaint, petition or protest addressed to authorities and the various organized social and political agents by citizens, the former consisting of informal exchange of opinion: all forms of spontaneous conversation, gossip, criticism, 'murmuring of the people', even jokes, in which people negotiate points of view, similarities and differences of opinion. Horizontal voice is a necessary precondition for the mobilization of vertical voice, while the suppression of horizontal voice is generally the result of the action of undemocratic regimes, converting citizens into isolated, wholly private and narrowly self-centred individuals (Hirschman 1986:81–3). Horizontal voice is 'free, spontaneous activity of women and men ... and extraordinary violence must be deployed to suppress it. Under ordinary circumstances, horizontal voice is continuously generated and has an effect even without becoming vertical' (Hirschman 1986:83). By fostering opinion formation, invention and self-reliance, horizontal voice transcends purely social, spontaneous contacts into public dialogues about rules and standards of fairness, excellence and common sense. This argument resembles Lasch's (1997) idea of the role of common life as capable of nurturing the individual responsibility and courage demanded for democracy, while providing the satisfying life. Seeing modern life as too highly organized and too self-conscious, and thus resulting in a shrinkage of people's imaginative and emotional horizons, Lasch calls our attention to informal groups and gatherings in the so-called 'third place', which is 'a meeting ground midway between the workplace and the family circle', where talks, or 'third place' sociability, encourage 'virtues more properly associated with political life than the "civil society" made up of voluntary associations' (1995:120, 122). Believing that '[d]emocracy depends upon the engagement of individuals, not only with the state, but with each other' (Hansen 1997:289), stresses the importance of links between informal discursive sources of democracy and formal decision-making institutions and, therefore, the crucial role of sociability in democratic societies. The revitalization of the complex world of sociability requires overcoming the inadequacy of the public–private dichotomy as an analytical framework for the understanding of modern societies and the redefinition of the concept of sociability in order to increase its analytical flexibility so its interplay with other forms of life can be systematically explored.

INTIMACY AND RESPONSIBILITY

> Today's society may perhaps be more accommodating as far as motivat-
> ing the construction of a purely personal world is concerned, but one is
> probably only just beginning to discover how improbable this is
> (Luhmann 1986:171).

While the discussion of the concepts of civility and sociability has displayed
the nature of relationships between formality and informality, some doubts
can be expressed about the usefulness of undertaking the same type of examination of the notion of intimacy. It could be argued that there is not much
point, for at least three reasons, to discuss intimacy. Firstly, it could be said
that such a discussion is pointless because informality in pure relationships
can be taken for granted. Secondly, this type of examination could be seen to
be without merit since, due to the fact that 'there is an important solidity and
facticity about everyday life which has been observed by sociologists for many
decades' (Turner 1996:15), not much change has taken place in the nature
of this type of interaction. Finally, it could be argued that, if anything, the
contemporary processes of pluralization and individualization – by introducing complexity, diversity, fragmentation and freedom to individuals' lives –
demand a more active, specific, imaginative and informal type of pure relationship. Nonetheless, there is still some justification for discussing how
informality and formality are balanced in this type of relation. The rationale
for it is connected with the dual consequences of today's main trends. On
one hand, through 'making individual out of social classes' (Beck and Beck-
Gernsheim 1995:24), the contemporary processes of pluralization and individualization expand the opportunity to create a more democratized personal life. On the other hand, these trends increase the possibility for chaos
and, therefore, in order to control it, some movement towards formalization
of rules governing pure relationships can be noticed (for example, as illustrated by the new popularity of prenuptial contracts). Additionally, as Lasch
(1997) argues, the trends towards the privatization of the family and individualization have always been accompanied by the invasion of the family by a
variety of experts and professionals. Therefore, because the private sphere of
intimate relations is a space 'that has been increasingly filled by outside
forces' (Kumar 1997:229), because interaction in private relationships has a
public side and because this type of relationship is affected by large-scale processes, examining relationships between informality and formality in pure
relationships is a valid topic for further discussion.

Although the distinction between the private and intimate, on one hand,
and the public and visible, on the other, has been a central characteristic of
Western thought since the eighteenth century, it still continues to generate
much confusion (Weintraub and Kumar 1997). Privacy and the private
sphere, as products of concrete historical actions, have evolved through the

centuries in a parallel way to changes in the balance between sociability and intimacy (Aries 1973). In the past, home and the family were not cut off from the public realm. For example, the aristocrat's house was a direct symbol of his place within the structure of power (Elias 1978). Its connections to the wider society through webs of sociability bonds, 'through the network of social activities and social institutions', allowed the family to 'preserve some independence and give its members some space for privacy and intimacy' (Kumar 1997:231). Without going any further into the nature of historical relations between the public sphere and private realm, we can observe, while turning to the present, that contemporary conditions are more confusing and that they are characterized by shifting boundaries between the personal, emotionally intense and intimate domain of family, friendship and the primary group, and the impersonal, severely instrumental domain of the market and formal institutions.

Pure relationships, which designate the realm of close and continuing emotional ties with others, include a range of relationships, the most important among them being love, marriage and friendship. All pure relationships are essentially expressions of individuality and freedom. An important feature of this type of relationship is intimacy, which refers to relationships characterized by close association, privileged knowledge, deep knowing and understanding, sharing, commitment and some kind of love (Jamieson 1997). While there are many 'degrees of intimacy' (Klima 1997:385), all these relations are significant sources of psychological satisfaction, identity and personal development. Intimacy should be understood, writes Giddens, as 'a matter of emotional communication, with others and with the self, in the context of interpersonal equality' (1992:131). 'The ultimate degree of intimacy' refers to the 'the capacity to trust utterly' and 'closeness of a loved one' (Klima 1997:385).

The uniqueness of intimate relations is expressed in the importance partners attach to the privacy of their relationships, whose 'whole affective structure is based on what each of the two participants gives or shows only to one other person and to nobody else' (Simmel 1950:126). Intimate information is a kind of secret shared between people that bonds them in trust to each other. Consequently, 'intimacy is not based on the content of the relationships' (Simmel 1950:127), its condition consists in the fact that the participants in a given relationship disclose only to one another, and do not see, at the same time, 'an objective, super-individual structure which they feel exists and operates on its own' (Simmel 1950:127). Intimate relationships, therefore, are characterized by secret, private communication, which must be under the control of the intimate partners themselves.

Intimacy, as the disclosure of very private emotions, is based not only on the development of emotional sympathy with others, but also on being in touch with one's feeling (Giddens 1992). Intimate relations are seen as opening the 'door to the total personality' and as connecting a 'whole person with another person in its entirety' (Simmel 1950:225, 326). Intimate relationships require, therefore, 'a relatively greater individuality of the members' (Simmel 1950:137). In other words, for intimate communication to take place, the persons involved 'must be individualized to such an extent that their behaviour can be read in a specific way; on the basis of a difference' (Luhmann 1986:34). The necessary step in the process of individualization is the privatization of the family, which – in turn – places excessive emotional demands on the relations among family members (Lasch 1997:103–46). This shift toward intimacy, so much honoured in psychotherapy, has resulted in the development of today's culture of autonomy. The spread of therapeutic services can be seen as a response to the emergence of tensions between mutuality and self-fulfilment or responsibility and self-gratification. The therapeutic model of relationships, starting with a search for the true self since only the true self is capable of developing close relations (Bellah *et al* 1985), pushes further the requirement for openness and authenticity. Since only self-actualized persons are assumed to be capable of genuine relationships, the satisfaction from intimate relationships is seen as depending on the development of self-understanding or discovering of one's true self.

While 'disclosing intimacy' has become an important new ideology (Jamieson 1997), its main practical consequence has been the replacement of the significance previously attached to sincerity with the anxious desire for authenticity. While authenticity assumes the direct exposure to intimate partners of one's own attempt to feel, sincerity refers to the societal request that we present ourselves as being sincere and that, consequently, we play the role of being ourselves by the exposure of our private feelings in public (Trilling 1974:10). The present-day addiction to authenticity enlarges the confusion surrounding the dilemmas at the very heart of intimate relations, dilemmas connected with the problems of self-disclosure and privacy. Because the purpose of being true to one's self does not have the public end in view or does not secure social esteem and reputation, it can be said that the replacement of sincerity with authenticity undermines the distinction between public and private and this fact has many consequences for the nature of pure relationships. Some of the consequences of this reduction of the distinction between public and private, such as the tyranny of intimacy, narcissism, boredom, self-reliance, and so on, have one common feature: they all lower the importance attached by partners to their mutual responsibilities and obligations.

The tyranny of intimacy, with its implicit prohibition on maintaining privacy and personal secrets, is closely related to a lack of differentiation of the partners from each other, which reduces, by the same token, the opportunity for autonomy and narrows the assessment of social complexities to a single standard of psychological truth. It can, therefore, lead to the suppression of diversity and avoidance of conflicts and tensions, which all together freezes the development and maturing of personalities. It can also limit our chances for a more satisfying public life since the intensification of intimacy expands ambivalence about the private realm and public arena. With the modern family becoming the 'haven in a heartless world' (to use the title of Lasch's 1977 book, in which he describes the public realm as impersonal, unfulfilling and routinized), people's willingness to participate in public life diminishes as they 'seek out or put pressure on each other to strip away the barriers of custom, manners and gesture which stand in the way of frankness and mutual openness' (Sennett 1974:338).

Since authenticity proposes being true to one's self as an end in itself, it can also result in narcissistic attitudes, which – by facilitating inversion and concentration on feelings rather than on the content of what is felt – reduce a chance of the development of meaningful intimate relationships. The logical consequences of narcissistic attitudes and a lack of discretion is boredom, which – in turn – lowers the attractiveness of intimate relationships. Even in the most intimate relationships, the attractiveness can only be sustained by not compromising the total person since only 'those individuals can give themselves wholly without danger who cannot wholly give themselves, because their wealth consists in a continuous development in which every abandon is at once followed by treasures' (Simmel 1950:328).

Therapeutically liberated individuals are encouraged to show their strength by adopting a strategy of individual self-reliance, which makes partners' interdependence rather problematic. Furthermore, favouring self-reliance undermines the importance of partners' obligations and responsibilities. Because self-reliance is 'a virtue that implies being alone', the therapeutic self-actualized person 'denies all forms of obligation and commitment in relationships, replacing them only with the ideal of full, open, honest communication' (Bellah *et al* 1985:15 and 101). This continuous verbalization of emotions, which is seen as the path to reaching intimacy in the face of the erosion of traditions and binding norms, introduces confusion and ambivalence about obligations by stressing free choice and that no 'binding obligations nor wider social understanding justify a relationship. And should it no longer meet their needs, it must end' (Bellah *et al* 1985:107). This search for one's authentic feeling, combined with the opposition to any outside authority, leads to the rejection of relationships based on socially granted responsibility and agreeing to only one obligation, namely to be honest. And it is probably why the 1990s are labelled as 'the age of honesty' (Bewes 1997:50). Intimate relationships devoted to honesty can easily 'turn totalitarian', inflict deep wounds and bring disappointment to both partners' hopes of 'becoming themselves' (Beck and Beck-Gernsheim 1995:171). To sum up, by teaching people to 'be selfish' as a way of loving and by stressing that 'one has duty to oneself' as a way of personal growth and development, the therapeutic model rejects the grounding of intimate relationships in obligations.

The spread of the therapeutic model of relationships with its search for the true self, seen as the sole source of genuine relationships, has undermined the importance of partners' obligations and responsibilities. This rejection of relationships based on socially granted obligation is additionally reinforced by the declining significance of formal roles and structures as well as supportive frameworks for this type of relationship. The growing individualism within the family and the rejection of socially grounded obligations make family life increasingly subject to complex and difficult negotiations, through which it tries to meet new expectations and build a new type of trust. Personal ties in this new type of intimate relationship are based on voluntary commitments and intensified intimacy. This new partnership involves neither submission nor domination: 'the partners try to listen to each other, while each remains a separate person, conscious that intimacy can be a cause of conflicts, or become too close and stifling, or too defensive' (Zeldin 1994:326). Experimenting with new options and seeking alternatives is an enormously difficult task because couples involved in continuous negotiations of their rights and obligations cannot count on external support and because of the existence of confusion surrounding both the concept of intimacy and the boundaries between the private and public.

Today it is commonly assumed that the formal world not only does not provide external support to intimate relationships (Giddens 1992:138), but also that it is moreover likely to inhibit such intimacy (Bellah *at al* 1985:85). So, in conditions of modernity people must actively search for a sense of security, which would allow them to construct strategies for the preservation of the world of intimate relationships. Spontaneous interpersonal intimacy is aspired to as the ideal, while formal roles, obligations and expectations are increasingly seen in terms of their negative impact on partners' autonomy and identity and, consequently, on intimacy , which is valued as able to provide us with 'a sense of personal validity and worth, and a way of avoiding being quite alone' (Beck and Beck-Gernsheim 1995:191). With modern marriage no longer based on the mutual dependency associated with traditional gender roles, love becomes more important. 'As traditions become diluted, the attractions of a close relationship grow' (Beck and Beck-Gernsheim 1995:32). Consequently, in our individualized society pure relationships are becoming 'a scarce and precious commodity' (Beck and Beck-Gernsheim 1995:190). However, with so many formal rules and moral restrictions gone, the status and the capacity of this type of relationship to shelter and provide solutions to our problems is declining. Bourgeois respectability and taboos demanded strength and risk-taking from unconventional lovers. Now there are no penalties to pay, no barriers to break and the turnover in many relationships leads us to see 'that love did not make us tender, wise or compassionate' (Gornick 1997:31) or that it 'can only concern itself with itself' (Beck and Beck-Gernsheim 1995:190). Today's type of supposedly conflict-free environment does not teach us responsibility, 'that ultimate and indispensable condition of morality of human intercourse', because it cannot be expected to 'grow, let alone thrive, in a hygienically pure space, free of surprises, ambivalence and conflict' (Bauman 1998:46). The failure of intimate relationships to provide insight and self-understanding can be seen as a result of the fact that the external world does not seem to demand that we master the difficult art of acting under conditions of conflict and therefore of the ability to come to grips with those problems and to solve them. This lack of the opportunity for meaning-negotiating can be seen as a result, on one hand, of the process of formalization (for example, the expansion of formal rules about the division of property, custody and divorce or spouses' mutual rights and obligation) and, on the other hand, of the process of removal of the static and formal rules (which were controlling the family life in more traditional societies), with both of these trends contributing to shifts in the boundaries between private and public.

This line of argument, pointing to the specific features of modern society as contributing to the weakening of individual self-understanding and individual character, has been voiced for decades. For example, it can be found in Marcuse's (1969) discussion of the social and political implications of the affluence, permissiveness and pleasure-oriented nature of Western societies. Recently, many scholars note connections between the growing subjective difficulty with identity and the fragmented, unstable and ambiguous nature of social reality (Giddens 1992). It is argued that the contradictory trends and unsettling conditions of the modern world have been transforming intimacy, introducing confusions about obligation and ambivalence, insecurity and distress to the pure relationship. Globalization and uncontrollable risk, which increasingly become a part of our daily life (Beck 1992), are seen as undermining people's sense of security and as, by the same token, facilitating their retreat to privacy and passivism.

The widening scope and increased importance of intimacy might, as argued by Marcuse, Sennett and Lasch, make public life less intelligible. For instance, according to Sennett, a complementary relation exists between the nature of the public realm and the significance attached to private intimacy. The 'tyranny of intimacy' is the main reason why the public space is empty: '[i]ncrease intimate contact and you decrease sociability' (Sennett 1974:15). Other researchers, for example Kuzmics (1988:172), invert the causal relations between intimacy and sociability and argue that it is the nature of the public realm that is responsible for the importance attached to private life. Yet other writers do not worry about the delimitation of individual autonomy into the realms of subjective experience. Giddens, for example, assumes that the concern with intimacy is connected to the very reflexive nature of modernity and represents new forms of social activism, where women become 'charged with managing the transformation of intimacy which modernity set in train' (1992:178). Nevertheless, Giddens does not provide a full answer to the question of how people who are shaped by the comfort and intimacy of pure relationships can 'be strong enough to move in a world founded on injustice' (Sennett 1974:260). On the other side of the spectrum, Sennett exaggerates the threat of intimacy and he fails to recognize that once society has laid down the structural guidelines for public and private relationships in such a way that this demarcation is conducive to political apathy, the problem of tyranny of intimacy is here to stay.

Any discussion of pure relationships should be based on the acknowledgment of two very obvious facts. Firstly, one needs to recognize that there is no going back, that the formalism, impersonality and fatalism of old models of intimate life are things of the past. Secondly, it should be admitted that in our complex and changing society pure relationships are in the process of continuous change and that, because of their role as a shelter for the whole person, they will become more autonomous and more intensified. This process of autonomization creates a new situation, where external supports are dismantled, the internal tensions become more acute and the capacity for stability now depends on purely personal resources. 'A clear-cut attribution of duties and responsibilities is then no longer possible ... Reasons for everything that happens are to be found in the other person or in oneself, and every act of directing attribution to either the ego or the alter in itself constitutes a violation of the code' (Luhmann 1986:57). Shaping intimate relationships in a free, autonomous, flexible way, in accordance to individuals' values and negotiated agreements, and, at the same time, without having the comfort of relying on societal guidance, support or protection, makes many pure relationships very unstable. Some writers see here the core of the problem faced by intimate relations, namely, in the declining ability of society to provide support, control and protection for this type of relationship. Furthermore, since social control has given way to self-imposed consideration, modern society can only provide symbols 'for permissible and protected exclusivity', moreover, it can make the symbols available only 'for quasi-autonomous use' (Luhmann 1986:157). As a consequence, 'a marriage autonomized in this way does not afford adequate protection against the primary danger posed by intimate relationships, namely, their instability' (Luhmann 1986:157).

It seems that in order to reduce the confusions, ambivalence and instability of pure relationships there is a need to redefine the relations between the private and the public in such a way as to connect intimate relations with 'the wider society through the "interstitial space" of sociability, through the network of social activities and social institutions' (Kumar 1997:231). Secondly, because pure relationships in the face of the erosion of traditions and binding norms are the personal responsibility of partners, people's ability to operate within these intimate relations can be enhanced by partners' acceptance of mutual obligations as the foundation of a more intimate style of interaction. The anxiety and problems caused by leaving everything in the hands of lovers, partners and families could be reduced by re-defining pure relationships not as aimed at cutting off all links with the public realm but as attempting to anchor people in a meaningful context and as capable of providing people with the validation of their personality and to teach them to be responsible for others. In this way the world of intimate relations could allow autonomous people to be responsible in a radical, highly personalized way, without, however, denying the existence of the public realm and its restrictions. In a Tocquevillian mood, intimate relations could be seen as being an integral part of, and tying the individual to, the wider social whole, and therefore facilitating the creative integration of the individual and society, which is the condition of democratic alertness.

Hence intimacy, together with civility and sociability, represents the essential basis for any meaningful reinvention of an individualized and deconventionalized modern society. This argument is followed by an assumption that only a society that sustains all three manifestations of the balance between the informality and formality of interactional practices is in the position to create conditions for a cooperative, integrated and innovative system. To which degree this assertion about the role of civility, sociability and intimacy for the quality of social life is supported by social theories will be discussed in the next part of the book.

Part II

Revealing the significance of informality

4 Explaining cooperation

Society is made up of the reciprocal services, which men do to each other (Mandeville (1729) 1970:349).

THE RENEWAL OF INTEREST IN COOPERATION

Although the issue of cooperation has always been an important topic of sociological debates, in the past decade it has been raised to a new significance. A great many phenomena – from short-termism in stock markets to the growth of Mafia activity in the former Soviet Union and the impressive success of Silicon Valley – have been given explanations in terms of the presence or absence of cooperative relationships. This visible renewal of the interest in the issue of cooperation can be attributed to the search for new ways of protecting against free-riders and therefore increasing competitiveness. With the significance of formal control being undermined by many structural processes of the 1980s and 1990s, cooperative relationships based on trust are increasingly seen as a precondition for competitive success. This widely accepted view assumes that as markets become more volatile and fragmented, technological change more rapid, product life cycles shorter and highly specialized production more dominant, a 'non-contractual element of contract' (Durkheim 1984:162) becomes more needed. It is claimed that in a post-industrial, global, hypercompetitive, knowledge-based economy, relationships of trust and cooperation are essential. A solidaristic structure of industry and a high-trust managerial culture are perceived as necessary conditions to achieve the full involvement and creativity of a newly empowered staff. Consequently, in the last decade it has become extremely fashionable to see cooperative attitudes not just as a characteristic of individuals and their particular relationships but also as the property of society as a whole (e.g. Fukuyama's *Trust* or Putnam's *Making Democracy Work*).

Modernity's cooperation and compatibility problems are the result of the asymmetry built into its three characteristics, namely, expansion of options, specialization and functional differentiation (Offe 1996a). According to the Enlightenment vision of progress, modern society is expected to be rational, reflexive, formalized, relying on the division between politics and the market as well as the separation between public and private interests. The failure of modern attempts to achieve autonomy and to act in the spirit of rational formalism has, however, resulted in blaming modernity for neither promoting all interests equally nor distributing needs and opportunities for autonomy equally. Consequently, 'the modernization of the parts comes at the cost of the modernity of the whole' (Offe 1996a:16). This trend increases the risk that each part, while going about the task of autonomy and the achievement of its own goals, may effectively restrain the free choice of overall social objectives and any attempt to give directions to global social processes. The immediate effect of such a situation is the emergence of problems of cooperation and mutual adjustment of the outcomes of fragmented action. Therefore, today's cooperation problem needs to be seen in the context of the growing complexity, uncertainty and fragmentation of society and the increased autonomy of its parts.

Modern societies ensured their solution to the problem of cooperation by setting their foundations in formal procedural democracy and rational universal administration; however, these attempts to act in the spirit of rational formalism have always been complemented by the practical importance of various informal, non-hierarchical, voluntary negotiated forms of self-coordination and strategies for alleviating contingency and ambiguity. A theory that seeks to explain the construction of networks of cooperative relationships should adopt realistic assumptions about formal as well as informal characteristics of modern social life. Seeing modern systems as incorporating, to a greater or lesser extent, formal rules and informal subcultures is, of course, nothing new. It has been conventional knowledge in organizational studies that official and formal rules are often not those found to be operating in practice. My argument goes a step further by insisting that the present conditions are forcing us to search for a new balance between forms of interaction that can increase the predictability of mutual actions. Assuming that the reduction of uncertainty and the establishment of reciprocal expectations are essential for cooperation means not only arguing that the co-existence of formal and informal elements is the structural property of modern social organizations, but also that these relationships are dynamic ones and shaped by the system's orientation towards predictability.

In order to construct a more convincing argument about the significance of understanding the changing relationships between formality and informality in securing cooperation relationships, a closer look at the leading sociological explanations of the phenomenon of cooperation is required. In what follows I critically evaluate the main approaches to cooperation and try to assess the significance attached to informality in their solutions to the collective action problem. Our main focus will be on the two dominant perspectives. The first of those approaches refers to the utilitarian tradition, recently reinforced by the growing interest in rational choice theory, in which trust is seen as a rational strategy adopted to foster exchange (Gambetta 1988a;

Coleman 1990). The second tradition, inspired by Durkheim, is founded in the recognition that universal solidarity among citizens underpins their very individual and particular existence; and it sees trust as arising out of the internalization of collective values (Fukuyama 1995). Recently there has been a slow convergence of these two approaches and this new, more eclectic stand is represented by Putnam (1993) and Brown (1995). We will start with a discussion of the rational choice theorists' contribution to understanding the phenomenon of cooperation.

RATIONAL CHOICE THEORY

The question of collective action, or the question of how public goods are produced, which is crucial to any understanding of why people choose to cooperate when there are no external mechanisms enforcing their commitment, has always been at the centre of attention of rational choice theorists. Lessons from the rational choice approach, where the problem of collective action, or the free-rider problem (which is analogous to the Prisoner's Dilemma problem in two-person relationships) refers to the problem of cooperation in large groups, is that beneficial cooperation may not occur even when players possess motives for cooperation. Since nobody can be excluded from the consumption of public goods once the good is produced, the question is what motivates rational actors who always choose the course of action that satisfies their most preferred goals with the greatest efficiency, to contribute voluntarily to the provision of collective goods.

The task for rational choice theory has been to prove that cooperation is consistent with the postulates of individualism and self-interest. In order to explain the conditions for cooperation, scholars have turned for inspiration to recent work in theory of the repeated games under uncertainty. Confronted with the limits of rationality, since game theorists point out that strategic rationality alone cannot adequately coordinate interaction, rational choice scholars have restricted themselves to listing options available to players in their attempts to foster cooperation (like making the other players better informed, demonstrating to them that cooperation is in their interest or increasing numbers of their contacts). Being unable to prove that cooperation emerges by itself simply because it is the most rational strategy, rational choice theorists have realized that there is a need to include some lubricant that can foster the process of cooperation. They notice that 'repeated games need some form of friction to generate predictable outcomes' and, since 'moral codes are a form of friction' (Dasgupta 1988:71), the concept of trust has been incorporated to explain how cooperation is possible. Trust facilitates cooperation because it is a kind of precommitment, a device 'whereby we can impose some restraint on ourselves and thus restrict the extent to which others have to worry about our trustworthiness' (Gambetta 1988a:221). In this way, rational choice theorists avoid relying on the

Hobbesian solution to the problem of order by opting for the notion of trust as a collective asset, which can be accumulated or exhausted over time. By viewing trust as a social lubricant, which makes possible production, exchange and cooperation, trust is assigned the status of a public good, which solves the problem of collective action.

Since the predisposition to trust 'can be perceived and adopted as a rational pursuit even by moderately forward-looking egoists' (Gambetta 1988a:228), rational choice theorists can argue that systematic and long-lasting cooperative relationships may be possible between self-oriented, rational individuals. To trust in trust is more beneficial than any non-cooperative strategy because the latter may, by spreading distrust through the system, introduce the unpredictability of sanctions. This, in turn, can lead to uncertainty in agreements, stagnation in commerce and industry as well as to a general reluctance towards impersonal and extensive forms of cooperation. It is assumed that rationally acting people choose to cooperate – that is, to put their trust in trust – because it is the most rational strategy and because it is in their interest, especially in a long-term perspective. By looking at the presentation of the issue of cooperation in the writings of James Coleman, one of the main representatives of rational choice theory, we will be able to scrutinize the rational choice account of the notion of trust and how cooperation is related to rationality and interest.

According to Coleman, the key requirement for overcoming the free-rider dilemma is group solidarity, which, he claims, depends upon all the group's members being consciously able to monitor and sanction each other. Mutual trust, which reduces the cost of monitoring and sanctioning activities and which itself is a result of rational calculation, is seen as a device for policing free riders. Consequently, an analysis of trust is constructed on the basis of simple relationships between a person's expected gains and expected losses from another person. By assuming that both trustor and trustee are rational, Coleman shows that the trustor's decision to place trust is based 'not simply on his estimate of the probability of the trustee's keeping the trust, but also in part on the use of negative sanction' (1990:115). Rational individuals only trust when both potential gains are bigger than potential losses and when trust relations are supported by sanctions. Sanctions, such as mistrust, for example, reduce the volume of exchange in a system, and can therefore be seen as 'a public good' (Coleman 1990:116). Mutual symbolic sanctioning – such as encouragement, discouragement, approval and disapproval – is seen as not so costly to produce and as more effective than negative sanctions.

Coleman (1988) rejects the extreme individualism of rational action by linking purposive activity at the micro level to systemic interdependencies at the macro level. By conceptualizing social capital as a resource for action, seen as a complex and interactive event, Coleman aims to introduce social structure into the rational action paradigm. The forms of social capital, namely, obligations and expectations and social norms, are dependent upon closure and continuity because these features of social structures provide a form of social control on which the effectiveness of norms and obligations depends. In the past, primordial social organizations were strong because '[i]nformal consensus could generate norms, and rights could be allocated and enforced via that social capital' (Coleman 1993:9). The ability of primordial organization to ensure the existence of effective norms and mutual obligations was born of continuous informal social processes that depended on dense and relatively closed social structures. According to Coleman, today the closure of social networks has been destroyed by the technological changes that have expanded social circles and erased the geographical constraints on social relations. In the modern world, which consists mainly of formal large-scale organizations and where our responsibility for others shrinks, our opportunities to accumulate social capital becomes increasingly lower. In today's societies technological changes and the emergence of big institutions have undermined the natural process of spontaneous social organization with its informal relations. Consequently, as the primordial structure disappears, sanctions that proliferated in the primordial social structure have become ineffective. For example, writes Coleman, with the reduction of the family functions, parental control has weakened. Hence, in a massive social system based on purposive organizations, those sanctions and norms ought to be replaced by constructed organizations aimed at sustaining individual responsibility in relation to others. However, those constructed social organizations and narrow-purpose corporate bodies, which now cover some functions once served by the family and local communities, can never completely replace primordial social capital. Nonetheless, Coleman (1993) hopes that the loss of social capital is correctable through such a design of purposive organization, which creates informal incentives and informal relations able to compensate for the loss of primordial social organization.

Coleman's attempt to overcome the division between interest and norms, based in the argument that rational choice theory can provide the underpinning for a normative theory, failed, because he did not address the problem at the heart of rational choice explanations, that is, 'the question of how temporally embedded actors actually reach decisions that can retrospectively be interpreted as rational' (Emirbayer and Mische 1998:966). Instead, Coleman supplements the communicative action approach, within which he positioned the argument that solidarity is produced by explicit communication about joint interests and joint sanctioning, with an economic perspective, which argues that symbolic sanctioning is very cheap to produce (Barnes 1995:79–81). Consequently, Coleman 'has had to reinvent the state of primordial nature' (Alexander 1992:216) in which purposiveness means rationality and calculation. Hence, his concept of solidarity moves away from the rational actor model without, however, becoming closer to the Durkheimian perspective whereby solidarity is produced unconsciously through shared emotions and interactions. Therefore, the main problem with Coleman's theory of solidarity is that it does not shed new light on the subject, nor does it improve on accounts of shared meaning as developed in the Durkheimian concept of solidarity (Collins 1994:161–3). Furthermore, Coleman's assumption that actions are caused by their anticipated consequences did not allow him to theorize 'the interpretive process whereby choices are imagined, evaluated and contingently reconstructed by actors in ongoing dialogue with unfolding situations' (Emirbayer and Mische 1998:966). Finally, Coleman's polarized vision of the private and the public and his too strong emphasis on the role of primordial groups led him to recommend remedies for the loss of informal control which do not take into account the process of individualization or the possibility of a more diffuse management of the problem of trust.

Hechter's conceptualization of solidarity also runs into the same type of problems. Hechter (1987:10–15), a representative of a moderate wing of rational theory, stresses the importance of the size of the group for the understanding of the problem of solidarity. While trust can be a spin-off of the participation in small and informal groups which do not need formal control to secure communication and common understanding (e.g., family, friends), it needs to be secured in larger groups where common knowledge, needed to sustain cooperation, is not easily available. In larger groups cooperation may be possible only when such groups have a highly developed system of formal control and when they offer to their members access to common goods (Hechter 1987:181–3).

Yet, at the same time, cooperation or group solidarity is viewed as 'the degree that its members comply with corporate rules in the absence of compensation' (Hechter 1987:39). This circular definition of solidarity 'leads to a peculiar tension, if not contradiction, in the very concept of solidarity', since both joining and membership depend on the group's capacity to satisfy its members' needs (Lechner 1990:103). Consequently, inability of rational choice theory to solve the 'normative' side of solidarity and its exclusion of other than opportunistic behaviour diminishes the appeal of this theory's explanation of cooperation.

The evaluation of the rational choice account of cooperation suggests that a sociological explanation of cooperation cannot be formulated wholly in 'economic' terms since in order to understand collective action we also need to acknowledge the role of social relations and the obligations inherent in them in the production of trust. It also points out that rational choice theory wrongly identifies the importance of trust solely in terms of cooperative relationships and that it makes the too simplistic assumption that trust is a synonym of rational expectations. Furthermore, seeing cooperation as a by-product of trust automatically equates distrust with a lack of cooperation (Gambetta 1988b:162–8). However, while it is possible that cooperation can be a result of trust (although it is worth remembering that in some situations distrust can only be a healthy sign), it is also possible that a lack of cooperation can be an outcome of other factors (such as lack of sufficient information) rather than the absence of trust. Equating the concept of trust with cooperation forces this approach not only to opt for a 'strictly behavioural interpretation of the concept of trust', which operationalizes trust as trusting (i.e., cooperative) choice of behaviour (Lewis and Weigert 1985:975), but it also limits a cognitive basis of trusting attitudes to fixed, stable images of partners in exchange. Moreover, although trust may lead to cooperative behaviour, it is not a necessary condition for cooperation to occur because while trust is the willingness to assume risk (Luhmann 1988), 'cooperation does not necessarily put a party at risk' (Mayer *et al* 1995:712). Therefore, the rational choice vision of trust as a factor reducing risk, rather than a factor describing the situation where risk is recognized and assumed, directly connects trust with rationality.

In the rational choice approach trust is defined as a purposive behaviour aimed at the maximization of utility under risk. By assuming that both trustor and trustee are rational, it is shown that the trustor's decision to place trust is based on his or her estimate of the probability of the trustee's keeping the trust (Coleman 1990:115), which is a too narrow an understanding of trust since trust is not a means that can be chosen for a particular end (Luhmann 1979:89). Furthermore, trust cannot be treated as synonymous with rational expectations because it can be based on familiarity and passion, and as such it can be enabling and also disruptive (trust, as love, is blind) (Dunn 1993). Although trust can rely on rational expectations, as our trust in money illustrates, 'the relationship between trust and rationality is complicated and uneven' (Dodd 1994:137). The complexity of this relationship is nowhere more visible than in the difficulties faced by all rational attempts to build trust.

The rational choice efforts to convince us that to induce cooperation between self-interested individuals, who, under most circumstances, have an incentive to defect rather than cooperate, are based on the assumption that iterated interactions between self-interested individuals produce norms. According to this perspective, people, motivated by self-interest, reciprocate exchange because they fear that others, who are seen as concerned with protecting their own self-interest, would distrust them, and, consequently, it could mean their exclusion from any further beneficiary exchange. The social disapproval that would follow nonconformist behaviour costs more than giving in to social pressure. In this framework, norms, such as trust, are not 'extrarational', they are produced consciously, by explicit communication about joint interests and joint sanctioning. Although the rational choice approach is more realistic than the Parsonsian perspective in not arguing that demand for a normative system is a sufficient condition for bringing it into existence, it still relies on positive sanctioning as a less expensive solution for policing agents. Seeing norms as a more profitable way to induce cooperative behaviour among self-interested individuals means that norms are not really contrasted with self-interest since the pursuit of self-interest exploits social norms to punish untrustworthiness. In these circumstances, therefore, group norms and self-interest are seen as identical. However, this does not reflect 'the reality of social norms'. In contrast to rationally optimal actions, social norms are not instrumental, they are not conditioned upon future states of affairs and they have their own emotional, independent 'motivating power' (Elster 1989). Due to seeing trust and solidarity as less emotional, more calculating devices for policing free riders, the rational choice perspective fails to provide a successful explanation of the 'normative side' of solidarity and its exclusion of other than opportunistic behaviour diminishes the appeal of its explanation of the process of accretion of trust.

Nonetheless, the fundamental reason for the failure of this approach is not that people are assumed to be self-interested and rational, but that they are perceived to be acting independently and acting without taking into consideration their dependence on others. Rational choice theory, because it underestimates human interdependence and fails to see the importance of the mutual interacting, learning, reflecting and constructing shared meanings (Barnes 1995:29), cannot explain why genuine collective action by rational self-oriented and independently acting individuals is impossible. In a real situation people are tied together and are dependent on each other and sometimes are even able to reflect on their mutual dependence. Unlike in the Prisoner's Dilemma game, they are not coerced into acting independently. Assuming that interdependence is a more reliable way of understanding social life means that problem solving in public life is seen as a more social rather than cognitive effort. During their search for a solution to social problems, people learn that cooperation is necessary to produce a satisfactory outcome. People's mutual obligations towards each other are not outcomes of their individual separate calculation but the fruit of their daily interaction, in which by negotiating, organizing and reflecting on their relationships with others, as well as by reconciling their needs with the needs of others, they construct their expectations. Expectations in relationships between patients and doctors, lawyers and clients, employers and employees, husbands and wives, citizens and politicians, students and teachers – are all constructed in the process of gradual learning by establishing levels of shared understanding and mutual obligations. For instance, the issue of involuntary unemployment is better explained by levels of mutual obligations and understanding between employers and employees than by the rational choice model (Akerlof 1984:145–71).

At the end of the day, the simplicity, abstractedness and unrealistic assumptions on which the majority of the models proposed by this approach are built do not allow this approach to take account of all factors responsible for cooperation. These models seem only to demonstrate what individuals will do when they are in a situation in which they cannot communicate and when they are without the capacity to change the rules. People are seen as incapable of long-term reflection about joint strategies to improve their common fate. It is also assumed that individuals have no autonomy to craft their institutions and that people cannot affect each other's norms and benefits. Since the rational choice approach is not capable of noticing the incremental, self-transforming nature of organizational change, it also does not appreciate the possibility that trust relationships established in a small-scale organization can be used as initial social capital allowing the organization to expand and successfully solve new problems and foster change. There is no space in this perspective for the observation that cooperation can be enhanced or obstructed by the structures of the institutional arrangements of the surrounding political regime.

To sum up, although rational choice theorists are increasingly taking into account the contingencies and uncertainties involved in choice making and although they are now interested in the role of values and norms, rational choice theory is still at its best while analysing situations involving instrumentally rational action. Because of its lack of conceptualization of the interpretive process of the construction of choices, this approach is less successful in dealing with a variety of more contingent and complex actions motivated by passions, emotions or pro-social orientations. It also does not explain traditional actions arising out of habit and the routine of everyday life. Furthermore, since rational choice is applicable to situations in which actors' identity and goals are established and the rules of the interaction are precise and known to the interacting agents, this theory does not help us much in more transitional situations where actors' goals become fuzzy or as the rules of the interaction become more fluid and imprecise. It also does not help in understanding people's behaviour in a less structured context, where 'social structures in which it is to the potential trustee's interest to be trustworthy rather than untrustworthy' (Coleman 1990:111) are disappearing. In modern societies, with such a diffused and fragmented culture and with the decreasing role of social disapproval, the growing number of exchanges with strangers, with the lack of a monitoring system and with the increased opportunity for 'free riding', many parameters of rational actors' calculation of whether to cooperate or not cooperate are absent.

THE NORMATIVE APPROACH

The normative–collectivist approach has also attracted a wide range of criticisms. Nonetheless, it has not lost its appeal for those social scientists who think that disintegration and a lack of cohesion in modern societies are to be blamed for the cooperation problem. As they try to provide solutions for the growing fragmentation and absence of a clear collective interest, they seem to assume that informal means of cooperation based on trust gain visibility because we live in a transitional period characterized by the decline of traditional institutions, which served control and moral functions. In such transitional periods, when neither traditional certainties nor modern probabilities hold, 'trust is central to social life' (Hart 1988:191). The feelings of uncertainty and ambiguity, resulting from the retreat of morality from the institutions of the social structure and the erosion or 'the decentering of some of our most important institutions' (Wolfe 1991:462), are assumed to increase the importance of informal bonds and group solidarity. By placing its hopes in the 'synthesis between collective solidarity and individualism' (Seligman 1992:169), this approach asks if a liberal society, characterized by individualism and pluralism, can constitute practices of involvement and cooperation. The normative–collectivist approach, in contrast to rational choice, sees society as a 'moral bond' that subsumes the individual. By relying on Durkheim's definition of society as a 'system of active forces' operating upon individuals, this perspective stresses solidarity and trust as integral to social order and undermines the role of other interactional exchanges. The representatives of this perspective are unable to reflect upon the experience of society in various forms of social interaction in which people engage.

Solidarity, as the commitment that subordinates individual interest to a larger social whole, was at the centre of attention of all classical writers who believed in the progressive triumph of social and economic integration. In the Parsonian–Durkheimian perspective, an individual's moral commitment and obligation towards others are a source of 'non-contractual elements of contract'. Durkheim, who criticized the utilitarian model in which social order is produced automatically out of the self-interested actions of rational individuals, saw solidarity, that is trust, reciprocity and moral obligation, as possible only to the extent that individuals share their values and norms. Durkheim's 'precontractual' trust was based on 'the governing terms of social solidarity, which in modern, organic society was based on the ethical valuation of individual personhood' (Seligman 1992:121). Also Parsons, assuming, like Durkheim, that social order which rested on self-interest cannot be stable, rejects individualistic accounts of society and argues that normative structures are the only route to collective order. Solidarity is identified by the institutionalization of shared values, while trust is seen as residing in the individual's belief that others will put self-interest aside in favour of collectivity-orientation (Parsons 1951:193). This normative constitution of social order is secured by 'properly' carried-out socialization, which produces comfortable conformity. People can be trusted to meet their obligations and responsibilities and show 'other-orientation' because as members of the same collectivity they share a common culture based either on kinship, shared intimacies, familiarity or common background. The moral mechanism also solves the main problem of cooperation, that is, the need for a large amount of information, by assuming that people are self-monitoring agents, thus there is no need for external control.

Parsons' concept of trust does not explain how compliance with norms is generated nor how institutions promote solidarity. It seems that the assumption that solidarity is a result of the development of affective ties generated during socialization allowed him not to problematize the issue of trust and, consequently, the concept was left underdeveloped. Furthermore, explaining solidarity by norms alone, without making clear how the norms are enforced, 'amounts to a tautology' (Hechter 1987:23) and makes this perspective guilty of too 'oversocialized' a conception of human beings. Consequently, this approach does not answer the question of how cooperation is produced in other than relatively small and homogeneous communities based on personal ties. Parsons' representation of order neglected the facts that it had been constructed through intense struggles in the relatively recent past (Wagner 1996:105) and that, moreover, the observed coherence and the stability of social systems do not last forever.

One of the most recent examples of this approach is Fukuyama's book *Trust. The Social Virtues and the Creation of Prosperity* (1995), where he argues that the problem of free riding can be mitigated if the group possesses a higher degree of social solidarity. He assumes that a society's endowment of social capital is necessary to permit the proper functioning of modern rational economic and political institutions. Fukuyama's central argument is that social capital has major consequences for the nature of the industrial economy because 'ethical habits, such as the ability to associate spontaneously', are crucial to 'organizational innovation and therefore to the creation of wealth' (1995:37). Nations differ in their propensities to trust due to historically rooted cultural differences. Hence it can be said that social capital is created and transmitted through 'cultural mechanisms like religion, tradition and historical habits' (Fukuyama 1995:26).

Fukuyama does not develop an elaborate theory of trust or corporation. He believes in a particular cultural attribute, the extent to which people can deal with others on a basis of trust, rather than depending on extensive regulations to prevent others from cheating, is critical to economic performance since 'people who do not trust one another will end up cooperating only under the system of formal rules and regulations' (1995:27). All low-trust countries (France, Italy, China, South Korea) rely on centralized control, state intervention, hierarchical, centralized and legally defined authority and people cooperate there on the basis of formal rules. In high-trust countries (the USA, Japan and Germany) the existence of a supportive culture of 'spontaneous sociability', that is a readiness to cooperate with others in an economically productive way, results in the flourishing of numerous institutions and associations, seen to be a good in themselves. As many reviewers were quick to point out, low-trust China with its double-digit growth, Italy with its fast growth, Japan and Germany with their new economic problems, hardly support Fukuyama's thesis about trust as a wealth producing factor.

Although, according to Fukuyama, the neoclassical model of rational, self-interested human behaviour 'is eighty per cent correct' and his interest lies in explaining only 'a missing twenty per cent' (1995:13), he wants to prove much more. His book is full of statements suggesting not only that culture matters but that 'culture is what really matters' (Fallows 1995:8). This strong cultural determinism seems to be the only way in which Fukuyama has been able to connect his argument that the most effective organizations are based on communities of shared values with his other assumption that the inability to create large organizations harms the long-term growth potential of countries. Seeing trust as the key and fixed ingredient in economic success not only lowers the importance attached to self-interest and coercion but also makes Fukuyama 'oddly morally blind' since he cannot appreciate the role of mistrust in the functioning of a healthy society (Mulgan 1997:124). It also does not take into account actors' ability to use, shape or change institutional arrangements. Fukuyama, too much like Parsons, views people as 'cultural dopes' being under the control of a mysterious and all-embracing culture. Fukuyama's lack of understanding that social relationships cannot be explained simply in terms of the role expectations prescribed by the culture, that action is not merely adherence to learned norms but that it is much more complicated and requires negotiations of meanings, also contributes to his inability to pay serious attention to the conditions of the emergence of cooperation. In the normative approach, trust and cooperation enjoyed by some countries are simply explained as these nations' historical good luck. It is assumed that for reasons rooted in a common history, belief in the same god, dedication to the same political ends, or a common ethnic or cultural heritage, parties may come to see themselves as members of a community of fate. Since implicit conditions of the membership in such a community exclude exploitation of economic vulnerabilities of their fellows, its members come to trust each other. The possibility of social change is rather limited since change can only be perceived here as an incremental and very slow process of cultural transformation. Furthermore, although Fukuyama argues that solidaristic communities are not so easily copied because they are examples of the historical fusion of a collective national identity and particular economic ambitions, he also assumes that by limiting the role of the state, the intervention of which is seen as threatening a society's endowment of social capital, the level of trust can be increased. Finally, Fukuyama's emphasis solely on the beneficial outcomes of informal sociability and his assumption that 'the more trust, the better', overlooks the possibility of various types of social capital and their consequences, which are not necessarily only beneficial for the quality of life (see our discussion of types of social capital in Chapter 3).

TOCQUEVILLE-LIKE APPROACHES

While neither of the two main perspectives offers a satisfactory explanation of cooperation, they have been, as a consequence of the mutual criticism and exchange of ideas, slowly converging on some basic issues. Subsequently, rational choice theory incorporates the importance of social norms and accepts the central role of social communication and mutual sanctioning as mediators of modern individualism. The collectivistic perspective, on the other hand, replaces the traditional criteria of solidarity with the modern values of individual rights, universal citizenship and the idea of the morally autonomous person and recognizes the role of interest in stabilizing cooperative relations, without, however, giving up on stressing the social aspect of individual existence. The best example of this more eclectic approach is Putnam's book *Making Democracy Work* (1993). Putnam, while stressing the importance of community, solidarity and mutual bonds, argues along the lines of the Durkheimian perspective. On the other hand, he borrows from rational choice theory its emphasis on methodological individualism, actors' rationality and the concept of norms seen as securing the transfer of the right to control and action from the actor to others.

According to Putnam, the basic problem of a democratic society is the creation of voluntary associations because only their dense networks of interpersonal trust and cooperation can overcome the free-rider dilemma. In a Tocqueville-like way, he suggests a direct connection between the increased quality of social life, on the one side, and civic engagements and norms of reciprocity on the other. Putnam emphasizes the existence of networks of interactions in the civic community, whose citizens, in a proper Tocquevillian tradition 'though not selfless saints, regard the public domain as more than a battleground for pursuing personal interest' (1993:88). Moreover, he argues that social capital, which is generated by civic political culture is at its strongest when rooted in an old tradition. Consequently, Putnam's reformulation of the question of civic culture, by stressing that social capital is 'path dependent', assumes that a society is indifferent to government action, and this leads this perspective to overlook the role of the state (Woolcock 1998:157).

Personalized, informal and close relationships are presented as the most fundamental form of being together, thus the family is seen as a first and neighbourliness as a second 'aspect of informal social capital' (Putnam 1995:73). However, social connectedness can also manifest itself 'in formal settings, such as the voting booth, the union hall' (*ibid*). Recent evidence of the erosion of formal civic organizations and the loosening of the bonds within the family and local community has made it clear that social capital cannot be taken for granted. At the same time, social capital is not produced automatically; it must 'often be produced as a by-product of other social activities' (Putnam 1993:170). To illustrate how dilemmas of collective action can be overcome by drawing on social capital, Putnam uses the example of rotating credit associations, which combine 'sociability with small-scale formation' (1993:168). The functioning of this type of organization depends upon the reliability of its members and consequently it is very important to know the individual candidates' reputation for honesty. Thanks to informal social contacts, which can be seen as the feature of a small community with personalized social relations and personal information as the basis for trust, some groups are able to overcome their reputational uncertainty and create rotating saving associations. This reputational uncertainty is 'minimized by strong norms and by dense networks of reciprocal engagement' (Putnam 1993:168). Consequently, it is argued that in order to overcome problems of imperfect information and enforceability, there is a need to draw on external sources of social capital, such as pre-existing social connections between individuals. However, as Putnam acknowledges, this issue is more complicated in larger, more complex, more impersonal settings.

Seeing the existence of trust within a given community as the basis of cooperation focuses Putnam's attention on the importance of the norm of reciprocity. However, unlike Coleman who sees norms, trust and reciprocity as characteristics of a specific group in the context of social closure, Putnam defines these norms as characteristics of individuals acquired through social networks (Edwards and Foley 1998). The most important norm, that is the norm of reciprocity, together with networks of civic engagement, is the main factor in creating and maintaining trust as social capital. 'Social trust in complex modern settings can arise from two related sources; norms of reciprocity and networks of civic engagement' (Putnam 1993:171). Informal contacts and personalized information are seen as the main factors behind both norms of reciprocity and the role of networks. Generalized reciprocity, as the important factor in reconciling self-interest and solidarity, is associated with dense networks of social exchange. Similarly, networks of civic engagement, which foster communication and norms of reciprocity and cooperation, rely on informal, local contacts and assure that 'the informal solution to the exchange problems in the past carries over into the present and makes those informal constraints important sources of continuity in long-run social change' (North 1990:37). The ability of networks of civic engagement to bring various groups together is seen as the consequence of the 'informal' nature of exchange within these networks. Therefore, the success of any network of civic engagement, such as a political party (seen as networks of interpersonal communication and exchange), is a direct result of the party's ability to plug into a local stock of social capital (e.g. into other civic networks). In contrast, a party dominated by vertical networks, which link 'unequal agents in asymmetric relations of hierarchy and dependence', is unable to sustain social trust and cooperation (Putnam 1993:173). Only those informal relationships that consist of networks of interpersonal communication, and which bring agents of equivalent status together, are free of dependence and formal control. Hence, the patron-client relationship, as an example of an interpersonal relationship where the exchange is vertical and asymmetric, is seen as not helping to solve the dilemmas of collective action because it does not develop norms of reciprocity between clients and does not facilitate feelings of solidarity between patrons and clients.

Putnam provides a description of various forms of dense networks of civic engagement, norms of reciprocity and generalized trust but he fails to supply 'a theory that identifies the mechanisms of production, maintenance and growth of social capital' (Levi 1996:46). This is a result of his inability to prove that trust emerges as the outcome of membership in civic associations or that these networks of civic engagements produce generalized trust. Putnam's theoretical agenda resembles the normative perspective because it 'harks back to a Parsonsian vision of social theory, emphasizing value integration as the source of liberal-democratic stability, and rejecting Hobbes' solution to the original Hobbesian dilemma' (Favell 1998:219).

Putnam's romanticized image of community precludes him from seeing that certain networks of civic engagement are a source of both trust and distrust (Levi 1996:51). Furthermore, the argument that civic culture depends on the shared, bounded nature of civic political associations does not take into account the importance of other social situations and settings, such as workplaces, universities or cyberspace chat groups. Moreover, his argument is rather circular: the key condition for overcoming dilemmas of collective action is the existence of a stock of social capital, but at the same time, the fostering of norms of reciprocity and networks of civic engagement requires pre-existing solidarity and collaboration. Putnam's book not only draws the wrong lessons from the history of regional development (Sabetti 1996) but also it does not leave enough space for social change. Putnam's latest argument in which he blames technology for making our social networks 'wider geographically, but shallower sociologically' (1995:60), only reinforces the previous impression that he assumes, although not explicitly, that cooperation arises out of, and is rooted in, personalized, informal face-to-face contacts.

Another attempt to move away from opting for one single model and to adopt a more Tocqueville-like approach to explain the collective action problem can be found in Brown's *When Strangers Cooperate: Using Social Conventions to Govern Ourselves* (1995). Given our interdependence, we are forced to cooperate and therefore the basic problem of a democratic society is the creation of conventions for interdependence between free individuals. Seeing convention as helpful in solving cooperation problems has a long tradition going from Hume and Burke to Oakeshott's understanding of conventions as emerging out of the intuitive understanding of collective good. Hume, for instance, argues that when we perceive the same sense of interest in others, we immediately perform our part of any contract, as being assured that they will meet their obligation. More recently Lewis (1969:208) defines conventions as 'regularities of behavior, sustained by an interest in coordination and an expectation that others will do their part', while Sennett views convention as 'the single most impressive tool of public life' (1974:37). Brown, who follows this understanding of the role of convention, argues that given the limitations of markets and the failure of governments to solve many of our problems, there is a need to explore other forms of social cooperation. To solve the problem of cooperation does not require the overcoming of the contradictions of 'individualism' and 'community' but it demands a mutual agreement of citizens on how to govern themselves by conventions.

Social conventions are 'neither market-driven nor codified in law' but – by being taken for granted 'in living together and governing ourselves' – they help us to negotiate uncertainty and unfamiliar situations (Brown 1995:17). The spontaneous coordination of behaviour, as the example of forming a queue illustrates, is often prompted by conventions. When waiting in a line, for example at a bank, we are willing 'to go along to get along' because it is our understanding that everybody else does the same. As the convention of a line 'endures because it works for everyone ... eventually', this established regularity of behaviour becomes a public good (Brown 1995:23–4). Therefore, the solution to public problems depends upon various kinds of social organizations; some being spontaneous, *ad hoc* and voluntary, others more permanent and disciplined. Diverse cultural and social traditions as well as the proliferation of voluntary associations are important societal assets, which should be coordinated through mutually agreed conventions.

Brown's and Putnam's perspectives are consistent with Tocqueville's emphasis on voluntary associations and as such they offer some interesting insights into an explanation of cooperation. Both of them offer an interpretive frame that draws a line between public virtues and private individualistic behaviour and upholds the necessity of a common culture seen as expressed in conventions and shared values. In their approach trust is seen as a systematic quality that cannot be generated by referring to people's psychological characteristics and cannot be reduced to or derived from these characteristics. Institutionalized trust, or social capital, is viewed as an important determinant of economic and political performance. This rediscovery of culture prompts Putnam and Brown, like earlier theorists, to rely on normative assumptions about the need for coherence and consensus of values. Nonetheless, in contrast to both normative and utilitarian approaches, which tend to believe that not much can be done to create trust and solidarity, these more eclectic approaches at least specify more clearly the conditions for the creation of cooperative relationships.

LINKS BETWEEN INFORMALITY AND COOPERATION

For both main sociological approaches, rational choice theory and the normative perspective, trust is a preferable solution for the collective action dilemma; however, each strand proposes its different definition. In the individualistic approach, cooperation raises the issue of sanctions and benefits; in the collectivist approach the concept of solidarity (defined as social bonds or as resulting out of interdependence, which keeps us entangled) is perceived as the main source of cooperation. Modern society is seen as either being in search of a solution to tensions between closeness and distance or as trying to balance hierarchical and non-hierarchical ways of negotiating social expectations.

In the discussed theories difficulties in reconstructing cooperation and trust are presented as depending upon the existence of a densely interacting community whose members share common interests (rational choice theory) and norms (normative approach). Rational choice theorists, seeing an appeal to the utilitarian self-interest of organizational members and a reorganization of the structure of control as the way to secure cooperation, implicitly presume the existence of links between closure of a community and cooperation. On the other hand, the normative perspective, which sees solidarity as a product of the cultural context and stresses the existence of networks of interaction, indirectly assumes the existence of links between social integration and social cooperation. Although these two perspectives differ in their views of social capital, with the normative approach adding moral and ethical values to what rational choice theorists perceived as a neutral resource, they both limit what constitutes cooperation to either the specific type of context (closure) or the specific nature of the group (integration). Closure means the situation of co-presence and proximity in which partners share the same location in time and space. Integration, which describes cohesive relations between individuals and groups, is also seen as context specific because the majority of the normative perspectives assume that shared norms and values are acquired through social networks, above all, through horizontal, informal and personalized links. Hence, what both rational choice and the normative approach have in common is an underlying assumption about the connection between cooperation and the nature of interaction. Both rational choice theorists' insistence upon closure, continuity and density of social interaction and Putnam's accent on horizontal relations and on personal information suggest that they do not assume that all types of interaction produce cooperation. These two perspectives rather allow us to believe that it is the informality of the process of interaction and co-presence that creates mutual obligations and relations of cooperation. Thus, the common final conclusion is that only informal personalized interaction allows us to overcome reputational uncertainty. Therefore, the informality of face-to-face interaction, presented as granting partners with the needed information about their mutual trustworthiness, is implicitly assumed to be solving the free-rider dilemma and facilitating cooperation.

Both integration and closure, according to their respective perspectives, are capable of producing mutual obligation and cooperation because each of them is seen as enhancing opportunities for informal interaction, that is, personalized, face-to-face and frequent exchange. Both approaches' attempt to solve the problem of collective action by granting enormous significance to informal face-to-face encounters runs into a number of problems. Firstly, they do not recognize the possibility of reciprocities between absent agents. They also do not clarify on the basis of what kind of presumptions the social capital perspective assumes less attractive characteristics of modes of articulation in the interaction between absent agents. In other words, what are the connections between informality, closure and social capital? Secondly, these approaches do not pay enough attention to the possibility that informal face-to-face interaction can also be a source of distrust as well as trust. Thirdly, seeing informal face-to-face interaction as the key condition for overcoming the dilemma of collective action is often accompanied by the assumption that morality has a place in face-to-face interaction. In many ways this line of thinking has recently been reinforced by the widespread conviction that traditional institutions which served moral functions are in decline. This belief that in modern societies morality can be found in the processes of moral communication rather than in specific moral institutions is represented, for instance, by Luckmann, who claims that although morality retreated from the institutions of social structure, it has not disappeared from the interaction order and that co-present interaction is still one of the most important settings where people demonstrate 'the *persistence* of traditional forms of moral evaluation' (1996:76, 78). However, an emphasis on the moral dimension of social interaction can only be sustained if we accept that all people have a need for inclusion. As Turner (1987) notes, informal encounters generate solidarity only when people's needs for inclusion are strong. Since the need for integration revolves around the need to trust others, we need to consider whether we become involved because we need to feel the trustworthiness of others or whether we are involved because we trust others. In other words, what are the connections between informality, integration and cooperation?

Both approaches also face complementary problems when they explain the coordination of actions. For Coleman, like other rational choice theorists, the coordination mechanism is self-interest, and so he focuses on purposive, strategic action, which he equates with economic rationality. Expressive, non-rational, psychological and meaningful actions are excluded from his discussion. In the normative approach it is assumed that social norms influence actions and communication sustains social networks, while purposive or instrumental action's capabilities to enhance the production of social capital are not noticed. It could be said that while the rational choice proposition neglects the communicative nature of collective action, the normative perspective overlooks the strategic side of collective action. Thus, their proposed solutions to cooperation seem to be based upon an overly firm dualism between instrumental and non-instrumental action. This results in overlooking the fact that although cooperation can be a result of coercion, common values or personal bonds, unless cooperation also serves an egoistic motivation, it will be unstable and less predictable (Williams (1988:11).

If we exclude from further discussion the threat of the use of force, as an unacceptable and unnecessary way of securing cooperation in today's societies, we are left with various structures (institutions, networks and conventions) as means of reducing the complexity or uncertainty of the context. Furthermore, taking into account that the presently occurring social reorganization, by increasing the need for the coordination of individuals' and corporate actors' choices, enhances the practical importance of various non-hierarchical, voluntary negotiated forms of self-coordination, we are forced to focus our attention on a new combination of formal and informal modes of coordination. This new mixture of formal and informal, as seen in various interdependent interaction networks, may 'strain the capacity of the modes of coordination that have dominated the modern world – hierarchical coordination within firms and public-sector agencies, market coordination between firms and households, and again, hierarchical coordination exercised by the state over organizations and individuals within its territorial domain' (Scharpf 1993a:125). While in all interactions the uncertainty of others' choices and the vulnerability to others' opportunism is a fundamental problem (Luhmann 1988), in the conditions of worldwide economic and cultural interdependence, the cost of actors' opportunism and generalized caution, which destroys chances of cooperation, is such that it puts a 'huge premium on the capacity for trustworthy communications and commitments among interdependent actors' (Scharpf 1993a:149). In order to reduce the cognitive complexity, and hence uncertainty associated with real-world interactions (high-gain or high-risk relationships), there is a need for structural preconditions for coordination. These preconditions seem to be increasingly provided by network-like relationships, emerging within as well as across the boundaries of hierarchical structures. Formal rules continue to play a role in the development of network structures by enhancing the density of communication; 'the informal, emerging patterns of interaction which create interorganizational networks cannot be completely separated from formal structures of decision making and governance' (Benz 1993:171). A recognition of the multilevel character of coordination highlights the dialectical nature of relationships between formal and informal modes of arrangement. 'Actors who are not able to coordinate informally can therefore switch to formal mechanisms in order to reach a solution. The availability of this opportunity is often a necessary prerequisite for the working of informal interactions' (Benz 1993:171). Furthermore, successful cooperative relations are often facilitated by the fact they are conducted 'in the shadow of hierarchical authority' (Scharpf 1993b:13) and they often bring together the global and the local ties. These hybrid networks, which combine formal and informal modes of coordination and organization, highlight the distinctive features of the contemporary period, that is, the new nature and shape of relationships between formal and informal aspects of various social systems.

Since in order to cooperate people need to overcome a lack of predictability of others' behaviour as well as an uncertainty of the environment, the problem of uncertainty seems to be a convincing starting point in the search for links between types of interaction and cooperative attitudes. By accepting that all forms of exchange are inherently embedded in social relationships and that this embeddedness can take several distinct forms, such as social ties, cultural practices and political contexts, we will be able to understand 'why economic behaviour is market driven as well as rule driven, without assuming that actors do not intend to maximize in economic context' (Beckert 1996:829). Following Sabel (1993), I would argue that while the deliberate creation of social capital is not impossible, the question of cooperation should be formulated as an empirical question about people's perception of their mutual relationships. If we assume that collective goods need to be imagined, debated and agreed upon by a group of people before they can join forces to act collectively, it becomes clear that the production of a public good is a contingent process dependent upon many factors. The development of self-organizing and self-governing forms of collective action needs, for example, to overcome problems such as 'lack of predictability, information, and trust as well as high levels of complexity and transactional difficulties' (Ostrom 1990:25–6).

Therefore, the question whether and under what conditions any collective action is likely to occur is an empirical question, the answer to which depends on the prevailing economic and political conditions and their history, as well as on agents' skill in reinterpreting these circumstances. In order to sustain cooperative relations, people need to make a commitment to rules which describe their mutual rights and obligations. These rules are developed internally in the process of interactions, and trust relationships help to monitor and sanction them (Ostrom 1990:185–6). While shared norms can reduce the cost of monitoring and sanctioning, in some empirical settings, long-term commitment can be undertaken with 'only modest investment in monitoring and sanctioning', although in other cases just the opposite may be needed (Ostrom 1990:36).

Generally speaking, people, knowing uncertainty and ambiguity of social scenes, tend to utilize contingent strategies in relating to one another. This contingent rule-following commitment facilitates monitoring others' conduct, since people adopt their tactics on the basis of obtained information about others' conformity to norms. At the same time, monitoring enhances the probability of cooperation because with the assistance of sanctions, 'initially for their information value and eventually for their deterrence value', it helps to solve the problems of commitment (*ibid*:187). In the same vein, Barnes argues that 'the key to understanding collective action lies in the existence of mutual symbolic sanctioning considered as an aspect of communicative interaction, that is normal and natural to us as social beings' (1992:263).

So, the problem of what factors encourage collective action can be restated as the issue of how people in a particular group come to see one another as following the accepted rules or as trustworthy, which subsequently can be translated into three empirical questions. First, how do people create new rules that describe their mutual rights and obligations? Second, how do they secure voluntary compliance with those rules? And, third, how do they monitor compliance with the rules?

Answers to the questions can only be provided by empirical studies that analyes conditions under which cooperative relations are established or common-pool resource problems are solved. For example, Ostrom's (1990) analyses of governance and management of common-pool resources in Switzerland, Japan, Spain and the Philippines demonstrate how, in this type of situation, people, who are dependent on each other, develop a strategy of cooperation. Such studies of the development of self-organizing and self-governing forms of collective action suggest that there are many different solutions to these dilemmas but that all of them require the removal of institutional obstacles to open deliberation and the establishment of institutional support for their creation. Moreover, all these positive solutions demand the recognition of collectivities based on people's reinterpretation of themselves and their history in such a way as to make trust the natural outcome of their common experience.

From the heterogeneity of different sociological approaches to the collective action problem we have learned that our ability to predict others' behaviour is connected with the opportunity for monitoring and sanctioning others' actions (rational choice theory) or with the existence of shared expectations and values (normative approach), or with the reality of power (Hobbesian perspective) or the institutional structures being put in place (Toquevillian approach). It can be said that the broader the scope of institutionalization and the wider the social networks, which serve both instrumental and non-instrumental motivation, and the dense system of conventions, the stronger the group identity and the more predictable the context, the higher likelihood of cooperation. Therefore, systems, where people are free to govern themselves, this means where civility allows them to preserve mutual respect, where they can use social networks (sociability) to limit the power of formalized structures, where there is enough space for individual autonomy and the development of intimacy, can secure voluntary compliance with the rules of cooperation. Cooperation would be at its best where there are conditions conducive to the development of civility, sociability and intimacy, that is, three styles of interaction practices, which express the optimal balance between informal and formal elements in different types of interactional settings.

5   Making music together

... making music together is an event in outer time, presupposing also a face-to-face relationship, that is a community of space ... Such a close face-to-face relationship can be established in immediacy only among a small number of co-performers. Where a large number of executants is required, one of them ... has to assume the leadership, that is, to establish with each of the performers the contact which they are unable to find with one another in immediacy (Schutz 1964:176–7).

INFORMALITY AND PROXIMITY

The title of this chapter comes from Schutz's article in which he stresses that the mutual tuning-in relationship, that is, the experience of 'we', is established by the reciprocal 'sharing of the other's flux of experience in inner time, this living through a vivid present in common' (Schutz 1964:173). 'Making music together' describes something more than merely the process of coordination of human action. It refers to the relationships that are established by the reciprocal sharing of others' experiences and experiencing togetherness. Schutz's remarks are directed only to communication within face-to-face relationship where performers' and listeners' 'tuning-in' to one another is founded upon the common experience of living simultaneously in the same dimension of time.

While all communication is unavoidably sequential and needs time to get accomplished, communication at a distance, in contrast to face-to-face inter-action, is less determined, requires different means of monitoring and develops its own forms of coordination. As the current development in electronic means of communication spreads a new indeterminacy with regard to expressions referring to time and distance, a question arises: which characteristics of 'getting together' are essential for 'making music together'? Schutz suggests that with the growing size of the group, new channels of monitoring are needed and they are provided by the establishment of leadership. Furthermore, he insists that the emergence of hierarchical structures does not necessarily mean the reduction of performers' autonomy or the bureaucratization of their relationships, since the leadership is merely to help to 'establish with each of the performers the contact which they are unable to find with one another in immediacy' (1964:177). This requires the introduction of a type of monitoring that will reduce performers' suspicions of the inequality of burdens without, however, infringing on their autonomy. If we assume that in the case of small groups, their 'making music together' depends upon the balancing of proximity and individual autonomy, in the case of larger groups, it seems to require the balancing of control and autonomy. However, to balance both proximity and autonomy as well as control and autonomy is a difficult task, and its essence is best expressed by the creation of the condition for negotiating everybody's acceptance of restrictions on their autonomy. Following on our discussion in Chapter 2, it can be said that the accomplishment of a negotiating process depends on the balance of the backstage and frontstage work (Friedman 1994). Consequently, 'making music together' can be successful only when distinctions between formalities of the frontstage and informalities of the backstage are drawn in a flexible manner, allowing for specific adjustments required in particular conditions. It can be argued that a more promising way of living in modern societies requires dealing successfully with the shifting of boundaries between visible, private, emotional and informal, on one hand, and formal, public, distant and inaccessible, on the other. Assuming that an absence of any sharp and consistent way of drawing distinctions between formalities of the frontstage and informalities of the backstage is the main factor explaining a given group's achievements in making music together, moves us away from a dichotomous vision rooted in a preference for either co-presence and intimacy of backstage regions or for formalities of frontstage regions. Writers who still share the conviction about the importance of proximity and the primacy of face-to-face interaction assume, more or less implicitly, that only co-presence creates the conditions conducive for 'making music together'. The second perspective reveals a preference for system integration, which focuses on the compatibility of relationships between the institutionalized parts and roles of the social system (Mouzelis 1997).

In what follows I shall examine both approaches' explanation of the phenomenon of 'making music together'. Firstly, various ways in which informality via proximity is connected with mutual tuning-in relationships will be examined. This will be followed by a discussion of the contrasting view, which sees hierarchical integration between actors in specific roles as being responsible for order and integration. In the last part we will conclude that the establishment of collective identities, as the most significant factor responsible for 'making music together', should be seen as rooted in both the interlock of objectively definable relationships and informal interaction.

Many studies draw our attention to the persistence and importance of situations of co-presence. Co-presence, proximity or face-to-face informal interactions are still identified as fundamental to social order because the quality of everyday life is seen, for example by practitioners in conversational analysis or ethnomethodology, as dependent upon actions that constitute the setting as a real and practical place. Precisely because of this temporal and sequential enactment of social order and embeddedness of all social conventions in particular contexts, proximity and locality are perceived as important phemenona in shaping and organizing actions and their outcomes. While the growing space-time distanciation becomes one of the key characteristics of modern societies, changes in our experiences of presence and absence and changes in the timing and spacing of interaction are acknowledged, but they are not seen as leading to a deeper transformation of social relations.

The concept of proximity or co-presence in ethnomethodological studies or conversation analysis seems to overlap, if not actually be synonymous with, informal kinds of interaction. To some degree this is the result of the fact that mundane, ordinary conversations and situations have always been central to both ethnomethodology and conversation analysis. When adopted by other sociological studies, the empirical statement about the informal nature of co-present interaction takes the form of a more theoretical presumption about links between informality and proximity. This supposition is based on the incorrect assumption that informality is the direct result of, and can be reduced to, the time-space proximity of agents. In reality, the relationships between informality and proximity are complicated because of the existence of a difference between situations of co-presence and 'presence availability' (Giddens 1987). Co-presence is 'a form of experience, characteristic of large parts of most people's lives, in which others are directly "available", and, in which the individual *makes* him or herself "available", that, demonstrates agency in Goffman's sense' (Giddens 1987:136). Presence-availability does not refer solely to the time-space proximity of agents, but to the fact that they must be situated in such a way as to be able mutually to monitor and align their conduct with one another. 'Therefore, in addition to the time-space proximity of agents, the concept of presence-availability incorporates a concern for the conjunction of material circumstances and social procedures that is involved in the constitution of social locale' (Cohen 1989:97). However, even presence-availability only tells us about the constraints affecting the course and conduct of social activity without determining how face-to-face interaction is conducted, so it cannot be seen as synonymous with informality. Moreover, the difference between situations of co-presence and 'presence availability' is more blurred than is usually assumed (Giddens 1987:137).

This too simplistic identification of the concepts of co-presence with informality is also sustained by many other misleading assumptions concerning the notion of proximity. Firstly, proximity usually refers to the sharing of the same physical space, therefore it overlooks the fact that the situation of co-presence of strangers has a different quality from the situation of co-presence of friends. In addition, since in all situations of co-presence people 'are inherently vulnerable to one another' (Giddens 1987:135), this view excludes 'mediated' types of interaction (for instance, telephone conversations), which can be of an informal nature. Secondly, proximity is often contrasted with absence but, as Giddens (1987:135–6) notes, presence is always mediated by what is absent. Thirdly, proximity is often seen as the characteristic of small groups, whereas in fact there is no limit to the number of people who can share physical proximity and there is nothing to prevent small groups from being formalized. Fourthly, situations of co-presence are usually described as constitutive of mundane aspects of everyday life and involving people of equal status. However, for example, the face-to-face encounter between Churchill, Roosevelt and Stalin at Yalta 1945, which led to a crucial decision for the whole world, indicates that a co-present situation cannot solely be linked to the micro level (Mouzelis 1993). Furthermore, face-to-face interaction routinely brings together subordinates and superordinates, thus our search for conditions that enable an enhancement of social capital should be expanded to include broader institutionalized structures and the hierarchical organization of modern societies. Keeping in mind that the identification of co-presence with informality is too much of a simplification, which is sustained by many other misleading assumptions concerning the notion of proximity, let us look at how various writers argue for the importance of proximity – and, indirectly, informality – for the quality of life.

The significance of proximity or co-present interaction for the quality of social relations, it is argued, relies on three types of argument. Firstly, co-present or face-to-face interaction is identified as the fundamental or primary type of interaction because this type of interaction is the most common and because informal interactions are 'rooted in certain universal preconditions of life' (Goffman 1983:3). There is 'every reason to suppose that the basic forms of mundane talk constitute a kind of benchmark against which other more formal or "institutional" types of interaction are recognized and experienced' (Heritage 1987:257). Ordinary conversation, therefore, represents a framework necessary for the study of all types of interaction. It is argued that 'naturally occurring conversation is a kind of "bedrock" out of which all other forms of interaction are built' (Boden and Zimmerman 1991:18). This is due to the fact that we were all, as childern, first exposed to this primary form of interaction through which socialization proceeds. In a similar vein, co-present interaction is assumed to be the primary type of interaction because 'copresence is biographically and historically prior to other forms of communication: infants first communicate through touch and copresent sights and sounds' (Boden and Molotch 1994:258). Consequently, all people always aspire to the personalized, informal contacts of face-to-face interaction. This preference for 'upgrading' towards more personal forms of communication or the 'compulsion of proximity' (Boden and Molotch 1994) makes informal interaction dominant and more frequent than other forms of communication. People's desire for the informality of face-to-face interaction can be seen as their search for authenticity because, as Goffman (1959) argues, the real function of informality and intimacy of the backstage is connected with the fact that only there can people really be themselves. Secondly, it is assumed that striving towards co-presence is also functional since informal face-to-face exchange is not only preferred but also necessary across a wide range of tasks.

This latter argument, which points to the crucial role of the proximity of interaction in carrying out daily duties and tasks, is supported by much evidence of the efficiency and superiority of this type of exchange over more distant and formal types of communication. Not only are the most important actors in organizations continuously involved in co-present interactions (e.g. managers spend seventy per cent of their time talking: see Boden and Molotch 1994), but this type of interaction is essential if we want to take full advantage of all opportunities in complex situations. The significance of proximity or co-present interaction is also supported by arguments suggesting that proximity permits the monitoring of partners' behaviour, that the most important tasks depend upon the proximity of interaction and that proximity provides additional information (such as a reading of so-called 'body language') as well as an increased probability of cooperation. Simmel notices that people in physical proximity give each other more than just words: 'Inasmuch as each of them sees the other, is immersed in the unverbalized sphere of his mood, feels a thousand nuances in the tone and rhythm of his utterances, the logical or the intended content of his words gains an enrichment and modification' (Simmel 1950:353).

Not only does proximity allows us to monitor our partner's behaviour and to acquire additional information ('body language'), but it also increases the opportunities to 'display commitment and to detect a lack of it in others; hence, it adds substantive and nuanced information' (Boden and Molotch 1994:264). Thus, intrinsic to every face-to-face interaction is mutual informal control or what Garfinkel terms 'practical ethics' (Boden and Moloch 1994:266). Heritage's analysis of various strategies used by speakers (such as delays, acceptance, accounts and so on) to maintain social order, leads him to conclude that 'the institutionalized timing features of preference design maximize the tendency for social solidarity actions to take place. The preference system itself is intrinsically "biased" towards solidarity actions' (1984:276). Seeing the organization of co-present talk as showing the routine preference for solidarity brings us back to Goffman's argument that by attending and responding to what our co-partner says, we contribute to the establishment of solidarity; consequently, the interaction order ought to be seen as a moral order. From this perspective, proximity, as it enhances the mutual co-ordination of interaction through tact and respect for the needs and demands of others, is an essential factor in sustaining trust, cooperation and solidarity.

This connection between proximity and morality provides the third argument in support of the fundamental importance of proximity. Goffman is not the only social scientist who calls our attention to this phenomenon. The moral significance of proximity was exposed in the experiments carried out by Stanley Milgram (1974). By manipulating the space and physical barriers between subjects and their victims, Milgram was able to observe the difference it makes to the subject's performance whether she can see, hear or touch the victim. He shows that it is difficult to harm a person we touch, but it is easy to harm a person who is 'remote and barely visible', thus, 'the victim is truly an outsider, who stands alone, physically and psychologically' (Milgram 1974:39). The connection between spatial location and readiness to inflict pain is also suggested by Bauman to whom morality is 'inextricably tied to human proximity' (1989:192). Following Milgram, he concludes that there is 'the inverse ratio of readiness to cruelty and proximity to its victim' (1989:155). Since the moral attribute of proximity is responsibility, physical or psychological separation leads to a lack of moral relationships, that is, to the diffusion of responsibility, which is the 'building block of all moral behaviour' and which 'arises out of the proximity of the other' (Bauman 1989:184). Arguing that proximity means responsibility, and responsibility is proximity, Bauman says that '[r]esponsibility is silenced once proximity is eroded; it may eventually be replaced with resentment once the fellow human subject is transformed into an Other' (1989:185). The shrinking of morality with the distance is explained as a result of the growing immunity to the influence of traditional, spontaneously formed and communally sustained attitudes towards the victims. Bauman argues that only personal images that are formed within 'proximity-cum-responsibility context' belong within the realm of morality. These personal images, in contrast to abstract categories, reside 'in the semantic universe of good and evil, which stubbornly refuses to be subordinated to the discourse of efficiency and rational choice' (1989:188). Therefore, the spread of anti-Semitism first of all required overcoming the images of 'the Jew next door' (Bauman 1989:187). Not surprisingly, Bauman worries about the danger of the increasing moral indifference in our modern, rationalized, industrial technologically proficient society, where so many violent actions can be effective at a distance.

However, while it is true that with the progress of science, technology and bureaucracy the importance of distance declines, it does not necessarily have to mean the shrinking of morality. New technologies can help us to become less indifferent, as many examples testify. Thompson (1995), for instance, shows how new media technologies can 'transform visibility' by making those who exercise power, rather than those over whom power is exercised, subject to a certain kind of visibility, therefore making the abuse of power more apparent and forcing us to be less indifferent. Well-known episodes of amateur video cameras registering brutal conduct by people in uniform raised questions of justice and fairness as the problem of national and even international concern. The most famous was the assault of Rodney King by police in Los Angeles in 1991, which was captured on home video and showed across the globe; another example is the case of Palestinian detainees whose very rough treatment in the hands of Israeli soldiers was also registered by an amateur camera. The public outcry following the viewing of those videos indicates that responsibility does not always equal proximity. The same argument is raised by researchers of new communication technologies who show how these technologies have freed interaction of the requirement of co-presence and have generated virtual communities, which are for some people real and morally involving (Cerulo 1997). This suggests that proximity is a rather ambiguous concept and that its significance can be expanded beyond a geographical connotation of the term into a more 'spiritual' meaning. Hence, it seems that the concept of morality, as limited to proximity, is too narrow, because it does not include instances of moral proximity.

Precisely this new definition of proximity is developed in Bauman's more recent writings. While presenting the tourist as a manifestation of the 'age of contingency', Bauman (1996) argues that the essence of tourist freedom expresses itself in the fact that she, although being physically close to the 'locals', is at the same time spiritually remote. The tourist is extra-territorial, moves through space and other people's lives without really touching them. The formula for the tourist's life is attractive because 'it holds a solemn promise that the physical closeness will not be allowed to get out of gear, let alone out of control, and slide into a moral proximity' (Bauman 1996:54). The tourist has paid in advance to avoid the physical closeness being developed to a moral proximity. This new concept of moral proximity refers not to geographical proximity but rather to sharing moral obligations and duties. The tourist is free from moral obligations because she herself is depersonalized, made into a faceless number and provided with the homogeneous adventure-tour kit by a mass-oriented tourist industry. Having her individuality removed, the tourist becomes part of the standardized mass, which does not have any moral responsibility. 'Nowhere as much and as radically as in the tourist mode is the uniqueness of the actor – that condition *sine qua non* of all responsibility – disavowed, erased, blotted out' (Bauman 1996:54). Seeing tourists as all being and doing the same, leads Bauman to argue that the tourist is 'bad news' for morality since the moral subject should be characterized by moral proximity, responsibility and uniqueness. The uniqueness of the actor is the condition for responsibility and therefore moral responsibility vanishes when 'everybody does it'. Only when the other is for us a unique, irreplaceable individuality do we feel responsible. With the role of geographical proximity played down, the notion of proximity becomes more ambiguous.

Like Bauman, Vetlesen (1994:273) also notes that proximity is an ambiguous concept and that apart from a strong 'spatial' connection, proximity also has a 'non-spatial' dimension, which refers to our sense that something is close to us, that we know it. While observing that one of the causes of large-scale immorality is the distance created between perpetrator and victim, which sets them emotionally apart, he, however, notes that the suspension of emotional bonds is not a direct outcome of sheer distance but rather is mediated by our familiarity with the other. Seeing familiarity, which does not necessarily have to be based on the immediacy of co-presence, as having an important moral impact since it can increase our reluctance to harm the person we know, leads to the assumption that the factor of familiarity over-rides the factor of physical proximity. However, the feeling of familiarity itself can be easily eroded (for example, by the passing of time) or replaced with resentment as the result of stereotyping or other techniques of neutral-izing attitudes, such as, for example, quantification or 'a technology of dis-tance', which imposes rigour and uniformity and reliance on numbers and quantitative methods, minimizes the need for intimate knowledge and per-sonal trust, therefore substituting moral feelings in favour of rigour and impartiality (Porter 1995). Moreover, everyday cognition relies heavily and uncritically upon culturally available schemata, as people always enter situa-tions of co-presence 'carrying an already established biography of prior deal-ings with other participants' and with a 'vast array of cultural assumptions presumed to be shared' (Goffman 1983:4). This, together with the fact that the 'objectification of people' and standardization as well as stereotyping are strategies well suited for communication that goes beyond the boundaries of locality and community, means that in order to understand people's moral conduct we need to know their images of others, who these others are for them, how the perception of the others was constructed and what influenced it or who shaped it. Since face-to-face interaction does not necessarily break down boundaries or facilitate communication, it is not enough to assume that proximity 'makes a difference', it is also necessary to include an analysis of existing stereotypes, discriminations, the spread of propaganda messages, types of communication technologies and hierarchical structures.

Proximity does not by itself account for cooperative behaviour or the lack of it; however, it is a crucial perspective in any account of individuality or locality. The degree of closeness, physical co-presence and visibility also ought to be taken into consideration while discussing the level of social capi-tal because informality can function as a substitute for formal ties and formal control. Effectively, claims that proximity and the immediacy of social inter-action contribute to commitment and cooperation should be treated at least with some caution. By the same token, the same caution is necessary when considering the links between informality and proximity as well as in discuss-ing the impact of informality or proximity on social relations. The assertion that there is no necessary correlation between informal interaction, proxim-ity and type of social relationship, nonetheless, does not necessarily override totally the importance of informal encounters or proximity for establishing cooperative relationships. Co-presence is an important factor in reducing the ability of co-partners to exploit the situation to their own advantage since face-to-face interaction helps to reduce the ambiguity of communication and to increase mutual knowledge. Studies of game theory testify, for instance, that the lower the degree of ambiguity in communication, the more beneficial the outcome of the interaction (Gambetta 1988a).

The ability of co-presence to reduce ambiguity and increase familiarity will preserve the significance of face-to-face interaction even as the spatial and temporal distance between partners in communication continues to increase. Hence, although new communication technologies have freed interaction from the requirement of co-presence, modern systems still rest on micro-orders and are marked by 'the compulsion of proximity' (Boden and Molotch 1994:258). In some situations, proximity can be a functional substitute for formal interorganizational interlocks, while in other cases distance can allow us to avoid limitations brought by more localized ties. At the same time, we need to comprehend changes to the nature of tension between presence and absence, changes that have been brought about by the increased split between the sphere of localized, closed human relationships and the world of large-scale organizations. This new tension and the new type of relationship between proximity and distance characteristic of the modern experience is in some way symbolized by the social figure of the stranger, seen as a synthesis of proximity and distance, and therefore as never again being able to signify a kind of complete otherhood (Stichweb 1997:4). With the modern experience of strangeness, that is, our experience of others as being neither friend nor stranger, becoming constitutive of everyday life, the threat of spreading specific modern attitudes of indifference has been increasing (Stichweb 1997). In order to reduce this suspending or suppressing of reciprocity, we should be rethinking the basis of obligations and responsibilities in such a way as to increase people's motivation to abandon their indifference and to enter interaction. Because of their complex nature, modern systems demand a delicate balance of co-presence and absence as well as hierarchical and non-hierarchical ways of arranging social positions. This balance requires a new institutional design, which – without solely relying on co-presence – would enhance the symmetrical, horizontal and cooperative links between people. Hence the search for a solution to tensions between closeness and distance or co-presence and absence has become an integral part of modern society.

INFORMALITY AND INTEGRATION

The formal–informal distinction, apart from being implicated in the dichotomy between proximity and distance, is also at stake in the micro–macro split. For a sociological analysis to be satisfactory, it must demonstrate a connection between micro, that is face-to-face, interaction and the organized pattern of role relationships that constitute the social system (macro-level). Among various versions of simultaneously handling large-scale processes and face-to-face situations, Lockwood's distinction, as proposed in 1959, has provided the most useful framework for this type of conceptualization (Mouzelis 1997). Since Lockwood's proposal to distinguish between social integration, which concentrates attention upon 'the orderly or conflictual relationships between *actors*' and system integration, which focuses 'on the orderly or conflictual relationships between *parts*' (1992:400), all sociological perspectives have tried to link these two types of integration. In order to analyse the connections between the two dichotomies, informal–formal and micro–macro, the most ambitious reformulations of Lockwood's distinction, namely Giddens' and Habermas' theories, will be discussed.

Following Lockwood's classification, Giddens (1984:28) links social integration with face-to-face interaction, while system integration refers to connections between those who are physically absent. Actors' interaction, defined as a face-to-face interaction of two or more people where each partner, by virtue of her or his physical co-presence, has to handle problems of self-presentation and has to interpret the meaning of the self-presentation to others (Giddens 1987:106–135), distinguishes social from system integration. This physical co-presence of interacting actors enhances the negotiation of an agreed definition of the situation, thereby ensuring a higher degree of social integration, which can be characterized as the 'reciprocity of practices between actors in circumstances of co-presence, understood as continuities and disjunctions of encounters, while system integration refers to 'reciprocity between actors or collectivities across extended time-space, outside conditions of co-presence' (Giddens 1984:376–7).

According to Giddens, in traditional societies, where much of daily life was conducted on a face-to-face basis, there was high 'presence availability'. Modernity, however, 'breaks down the protective framework of the small community and tradition, replacing this with larger, impersonal organisations' (1991:33). As societies become more complex, institutionalized and centralized, people are influenced not only by localized face-to-face interaction but also by those more diffuse social relations (such as class, ethnicity and economics) that stretch away in time and space. Thus, interaction always involves actors who are 'positioned' to one another and is patterned by actors' identities, which are resources provided by each position. The positions that actors occupy within institutions and collectivities involve the specification of a definite 'identity' within a network of social relations. Since they are responsible for defining the identities of the occupants of the positions, these positions determine the nature of interaction (Giddens 1981:88–90). Changes in a particular range of normative sanctions relevant to a given position would lead to a crucial modification in styles of interaction. For example, if my position as a university lecturer involves helping and advising students and if it is defined in a very open-ended way, my relations with students can evolve into an informal and more flexible type of interaction. However, if my position was to contain a strong emphasis on supervision and administrative duties, it would sanction my more formal and restricted interactions with students. Also, the possibility of exercising an individual choice between various identities offered by various positions increases the probability of more flexible and informal interaction. Having the opportunity to depart from the official 'identity' of a restricted role and being able to draw upon other identities, enables more flexible relations in which boundaries between 'frontstage' and 'backstage' behaviour are not so pronounced.

The massive centralization of authorities and allocative resources, combined with the development of new means of communication, has resulted in the expansive time-space distanciation (Giddens 1984:171). Even though face-to-face encounters continue to be crucial for social grouping, they are now enmeshed in systems of far greater time-space extension. The significance of electronic communications is that for the first time in history the embodied agent is not the only means for conveying reciprocities of practice across time and space. However, although electronic means of communication can create possibilities for an expanded range of contacts, this development does not, Giddens (1981:40) thinks, come without a price as some intimacies of face-to-face interaction are being lost.

With the growth of large-scale systems and the expansion of electronic means of communication, we can expect that the sense of impersonality and anonymity will increase (Giddens 1981). These trends can be attributed to the nature of new types of relations, namely, to the fact that in the exchange between absent agents constraints characteristic for face-to-face interaction do not apply. Thus, as the volume of such interactions increases, reciprocities between absent agents become increasingly impersonal, egoistic, instrumental and specialized (Giddens 1981:150–2). This type of argument assumes that the interaction between absent agents has formal, impersonal characteristics and does not constitute a basis for solidarity and it also does not consider that interaction in circumstances of absence cannot simply be reduced to the impersonal or to processes with an enormous space–time impact. However, whether 'reciprocal practices are macro or micro has nothing to do with whether or not actors are physically co-present' (Mouzelis 1991:33). By not considering that the face-to-face or micro type of interaction may entail macro rather than micro processes of reciprocity, Giddens' approach encourages criticism. His identification of face-to-face interactions with actions the consequences of which do not stretch widely in time–space is seen as not logically compatible with these reciprocity-achieving mechanisms. Furthermore, linking social integration with co-presence, associated with reciprocity in microsocial contexts, does not eliminate the misleading connection of micro with agency. Neither does it permit recognition of the existence of a whole range of qualitative differences and consequences in time and space between various interactional processes (Mouzelis 1991:31–3).

Giddens' framework also does not really allow him to define analytically the domain of sociability, which is located somewhere between the institutionalized, macro and public region and the more private, personalized and micro sphere. Institutionalized personal ties, which – because of their nature – are both abstract and personalized, can be seen as synonymous with sociability, and are, according to Giddens, restricted only to pre-modern societies. This assumption underlines his contrast of the conditions for trust in pre-modern societies, where personalized trust is based on 'institutionalized personal ties and informal or informalized codes of sincerity and honor', with the framework of abstract trust in modern societies, which is characterized by the dominance of trust in impersonal principles and anonymous others (Giddens 1990:114). When discussing formal bureaucracy, Giddens defines informal relations as existing 'in groups and organizations developed on the basis of personal connections; ways of doing things that depart from formally recognized modes of procedure' (1989:727). This traditional way of seeing informal relations does not permit him to grasp and examine how social networks contribute to the activation of collective identities in contemporary life.

While Giddens' structuration theory attempts to combine the analysis of action and structures, Habermas seeks to construct a model of social life in which the relations between the subjective and objective levels are explicitly incorporated. The dualism between the subjective and objective points of view is overcome by their synthesis provided by the theory of communicative action. The action-coordination mechanism referring to social integration is based on 'a normatively secured or communicatively achieved consensus' since, according to Habermas, to communicate is the same as to reach agreement considering that 'communicative action' is oriented towards 'shared understanding' (Habermas 1984:117). On the level of system integration, coordination is based on the systematic steering media of money and power. Habermas' conceptualization of society as constituted by two structural components which are analytically independent – that is by the lifeworld, linked to social integration mechanisms – and the system, connected to system integration mechanisms, together with his evolutionary scheme, is the basis of his diagnosis of the deficiencies of modernity.

The first element, the lifeworld, can be seen as a focus of 'everyday practice', 'everyday communication' and interactions between people who share a background of linguistic and cultural resources. The lifeworld is a 'culturally transmitted and linguistically organized stock of interpretative patterns' (Habermas 1984:302) used by actors during interaction. In this way, the lifeworld is seen as 'a community of communication', where communicative subjects tend towards agreement. The second element, the system, is oriented towards purposive and strategic action and it enhances the capacities of a society to reproduce itself and to guide its activities in relation to the complexities of its environment. The advance of the process of differentiation results in the emergence of differentiation between social and system integration, unheard of in less complex societies. As traditional normative regulations decline, communicative coordination is replaced by steering-media coordination, resulting in 'colonization of the life-world' (Habermas 1984:45). The state and the market destroy communicative processes by pushing the moral elements of communicative action into the background. Habermas' perception of the colonization of the lifeworld by modern society's rationalized systems is the result of his definition of instrumental-strategic action as involving neither shared understanding nor the intent to communicate, which depends on such understanding (Alexander 1985:414). System integration, thus, 'works over the consciousness of the actors' and through the operation of markets and power, thus it 'subdues action orientations', while system integration points to an externist perspective, which 'reaches through and beyond action orientation' (Habermas 1984:117).

This conflation of a methodological distinction (externist, internist perspective with a substantive one, i.e., steering media) leads to the assumption that only the externist perspective is appropriate for studying the economic and political subsystems, and the internist one for the examination of the lifeworld (Mouzelis 1997). Not stressing the importance of communicative forms of coordination outside of the lifeworld results in Habermas' underestimation of the fact that shared understanding is 'just as much a feature of socially organised labour as are instrumental or strategic motives' (Layder 1994:200) and that members of formal organizations also have a need to achieve consensus by communicative means. Thus, Habermas does not see any role for face-to-face, including informal, encounters in the 'formally organized domains' of the economy and administration. Although he admits that in these subsystems 'informal organization is also invariably found' and that in organization members in fact act communicatively and non-strategically, he nonetheless assumes that members know 'that they can have recourse to formal regulations, not only in exceptional but in routine cases' (Habermas 1987:310–11). Commenting on this statement, Barnes (1995:215) argues that Habermas' decoupling of these two types of action results in an empowerment of formal rules, which contrasts with the lifeworld's dialogical conversation. It can be added that it also leads to the underestimation of human creativity.

The argument that purposive rational action is encroaching more and more into areas of social life and the assumption about the importance of impersonal rules are related to Weber's concepts of rationalization and the ever-increasing bureaucracy with its technical superiority. Although Habermas' vision is less tragic than Weber's myth of the iron cage, his instrumental reading of modern institutions points to nostalgia for the past, a 'cozy, communicatively oriented lifeworld', which is not threatened by 'the cold calculating' systems of purposive-rational action (Alexander 1985:412–13). The main pathology of modernity resides in 'the lifeworld being colonised by steering media that are "appropriate" only to the economic and political spheres' (Mouzelis 1997:115). As much as Habermas laments 'the passing of a world in which individuals could be more autonomous and self-directed by looking within themselves for authenticity' (Wolfe 1997:185), he also wants to protect a public sphere in which rational communication and critical discourse can take place. It is in need of protection because, as the private sphere is colonized by the invasive force of the market, the public sphere is taken over by the administrative logic of the state.

Here again Habermas' theory unnecessarily re-introduces a dichotomous vision of society, which does not provide an adequate empirical description of the major contemporary institutions (Wolfe 1997). In reality, we 'are not faced with a contrast between, on one hand, constraint through institutional coercion (established via media like money and power) and, on the other, voluntary cooperation freed from constraint altogether' (Alexander 1985:422). In reality, the public is not separated from private, as it was assumed in the eighteenth-century model of the liberal public sphere on which Habermas' ideal-typical construction is based (Calhoun 1997:82). Furthermore, Habermas, by characterizing his concept of publicness as spatial and dialogical in character, does not provide a satisfactory understanding of the nature of modern public life. This type of interpretation of the public sphere, 'obliges us to interpret the evergrowing role of mediated communication as a historical fall from grace' (Thompson 1995:132). Habermas' notion of publicness is still constructed around the traditional concepts of co-presence, locale and the idea of a dialogical conversation. In his description of the rise of the bourgeois public sphere, Habermas attributes the central role to face-to-face conversation. Furthermore, because he interprets the impact of new means of communication wholly in negative terms, he 'has deprived himself of the means of understanding the new forms of publicness created by media', the development of which has resulted in a new phenomenon of publicness 'detached from the idea of dialogical conversation in a shared locale' (Thompson 1995:132).

Although Habermas' conception of the public sphere represents some of the more significant efforts to characterize this domain of life, for many writers Habermas' treatment of public activity in terms of rational-critical discourse rather than identity-formation or expression, subjective feelings and emotions reduces the meaning of plurality and fails empirical and normative tests (Scheff 1990; Vetlesen 1994; Calhoun 1997; Wolfe 1997). Habermas' concept of consensus is seen as too limited to describe the complex process of observation and inference that leads to varying degrees of mutual understanding and misunderstanding. By referring only to cognitive consensus, thereby neglecting emotional aspects, it excludes the sphere of privacy and underestimates the importance of emotions in many encounters. Habermas' model of public discourse guided by rational and universal criteria is seen as lacking a realism or 'a feel for the nitty-gritty of actual interaction' (Wolfe 1997:187) since in real situations motivations hardly resemble Habermas' discourse ethics with its formal-procedural and universal intentions. Furthermore, Habermas underestimates the fact that discourse itself can be directed by selfish or manipulative intentions, that the outcomes of communication are frequently insignificant and that accepting imperfection, private interests, irrationalities and striking deals is a part of being human (Wolfe 1997:187). Hence we need to recognize that the shifting of boundaries between the public, that is, collective, visible and formal, and the private, that is, inaccessible, emotional and informal, as well as the shifting of boundaries between various roles and identities has become a natural and more promising way of living in modern societies.

Habermas' concept of consensus does not allow him to realize that determining whose 'speech is more properly public is itself a site of political contestation' (Calhoun 1997:85). It follows from Habermas' concentration on rational discourse that formal-procedural ethics – seen as the necessary protection against the concretization of the other – leads to the bracketing of differences and undermining of the self-reflexive capacity of public discourse. Consequently, the working of the public sphere depends upon the private sphere's capacity to motivate citizens to rise above private identities, prejudices and concerns rather than on the process of the recognition and open expression of differences. However, the process of transcending differences can be undemocratic and, moreover, the process of identity formation cannot be reduced to the private sphere (Calhoun 1997). Habermas' concept of consensus also does not allow him to realize that in pragmatic political conversation the achievement of understanding, which preserves plurality, is often a more effective goal than the achievement of agreement. Partners in relations such as these are aware of the locality, context and plurality of their respective claims, so they are not necessarily rationally devoted to a search for consensus. Such encounters rely upon certain intuitive communication competencies and their participants are not necessarily concerned with universality or impartiality. Seeing people as an abstract, faceless and 'formal' other can also bring about other dangers, such as being unable to tune into other people's needs and failing to grant any significance to emotions. Being aware that favouring universality over contextuality results in seeing practical discourse as a purely cognitive accomplishment, Habermas tries to grant some role to emotions by introducing the concept of solidarity. Solidarity, as presupposing empathy, is rooted in the experience that each person must take responsibility for the other because as 'consociates all must have an interest in the integrity of their shared life context the same way' (Habermas 1992:244). By defining the concept of solidarity as referring to our feeling for community, Habermas, however, fails to notice that with the growing abstractedness of our experience of the community, our indifference towards it also increases. As a consequence his theory cannot bridge the gap between the individual and the community. In other words, this approach does not explain how concern for our neighbour arises, why we perceive her as one of us, or how it is that the absent and unknown other can become a part of 'us'. 'It is precisely the nonpresence of the addressee that necessitates the assistance yield to empathy by the faculty of imagination. Hence, in the many cases where the other is absent and unknown, there can be no question of my "feeling" how the other feels; what happens here is rather that my empathy capacity is guided by imagination to the place of the other, to the particular context in which his or her wealth is at stake' (Vetlesen 1994:329).

Habermas is criticized for idealizing 'communicative action' by considering it to be oriented towards 'shared understanding', for grounding critical rationality in ordinary language and for the elimination of understanding from strategic action (Alexander 1985; Ajzner 1994; Layder 1994). His dichotomous vision of society does not reflect the complex reality of the modern world with its shifting boundaries between visible, private, emotional and informal, on one hand, and formal, public, distant and inaccessible, on the other. Living in modern societies requires a successful way of dealing with this phenomenon. This proposal is in line with Wolfe's (1997:188) argument that 'the world would be a richer place if people can both live in Goffman's backstage territory and still come forward to Habermas's frontstage to work out their common lives by commonly agreed to, even rational, standards'. Any realization of such a vision needs first to address the question of how valued identities and collectivities are constructed. The role of boundaries in the process of the creation of distinctions, negotiations of rules of inclusion or establishing rules of cooperation, will be our next topic.

BOUNDARY MAINTENANCE

As it has been argued in the Introduction, managers travel because their experience leads them to perceive the situation of co-presence as the solution to the problem of precommitment and, thus, as a way of reducing risk. In the following chapter, it has been assumed that as the demarcation line between the public and the private becomes fluid and less visible, the unpredictability of social life increases. In the first part of this chapter, the argument has been developed that although proximity can reduce the indeterminacy of interaction, it is neither a necessary nor a sufficient condition for cooperative relationships. Therefore, being partners in face-to-face interactional practices, while it reduces indeterminacy and imputes familiarity, which in modern societies is increasingly difficulty to maintain, does not necessarily lead to consensus and shared understanding. Since the reducing of uncertainty and unpredictability of social life relies on the mechanism of consensus formation, we need to look at theories searching for explanations of the problem of collective agency or boundary maintenance. These theories tend to stress the nature of interaction and argue that in informal interaction people have some chance to face others not only as independent calculative strategists but as interaction partners, with whom they can establish cognitive and emotional attunement, mutual understanding and behavioural interdependence.

The notion of attunement, identified in terms of the cognitive and emotional mechanisms of consensus formation, is in the centre of Scheff's theory of the relationship between individual and group. According to Scheff, social bonds, which are established through the mechanisms of the distribution of status and prestige, are the basis of social solidarity and it is through the network of these bonds that people acquire 'a sense of belonging'. Scheff's discussion of social bonds is essential for our understanding of the relationship between informality and reaching agreement, not only because he argues that social bonds presume both a cognitive and an emotional connectedness, but also because he suggests that it is not only words but also the manner and style of utterance that are important for enhancing solidarity and the creation of social capital. Hence, in order to understand modern societies, 'one may need to conduct detailed studies of discourse because only such studies will show intricate mixtures of understanding and misunderstanding, self-knowledge and self-deception' (Scheff 1990:181).

Since the bond-relevant signals are carried for the most part by manners and since our modern culture is characterized by a very complex and not very coherent system of signalling bondedness, ambiguity and confusion are frequent. In Scheff's explanation of the achievement of consensus in interaction, a central role is given to pride and shame, which are also essential factors in sustaining self-identity. Scheff constructs a 'deference-emotion' model of social interaction in which people are seen to be motivated by the maintenance or enhancement of their standing in the eyes of others. Codes of deference, which are built into everyday interactions, ensure that people conform to social norms as they are motivated by a concern for status or prestige.

The deference-emotion system, made up of a subtle system of social sanctions, may take formal and public forms, but the majority of conformist behaviour occurs in the absence of formal sanctions and in private situations where public sanctions are inappropriate. Because the informal deference-emotion system is 'virtually instantaneous and invisible, and cheap as dirt', while formal sanctions are 'slow, unwieldy and expensive', Scheff argues that informal, interpersonal sanctions are frequently more important (1990:75 and 74). Sanctions, such as interpersonal deference and derogation, produce internal sentiments of pride and shame. A development of Goffman's treatment of impression management enables Scheff to propose that, in effective social interaction, people observe, imagine and constantly check one against the other and that this process 'enables participants to accomplish the incredibly complex process of understanding *in context*' (1990:31).

Scheff's theory is used by Barnes in his attempt to develop his own social theory of boundary maintenance and to resolve the problem of collective agency. However, Barnes does not accept Scheff's nativist account of the deference-emotion system as organically rather than culturally transmitted. According to Barnes, the structure of communicative interaction occurs through the symbolic sanctioning of action, and these sanctions are used to motivate people to engage in collective action. Looking at Weber's status groups, Barnes argues that in order for status groups to exist and to carry out their exclusionary and monopolistic strategies, that is, reserving specific goods and opportunities to members and denying them to outsiders, the most typical problem of collective action, the free-rider dilemma, needs to be solved (Barnes 1992). Since it is individually irrational for members of the group to support its exclusionary and monopolistic strategies, the group needs to facilitate the collective action of members. 'If status group is to persist, and hence to exist, its members must generate a stream of collective action directly oriented to that objective. Such a stream cannot be sustained by "economic" arrangements, and must rather be secured by processes of honouring and dishonouring embedded in ongoing communicative interaction' (Barnes 1992:264). In Weber's account, 'special honour' functions as a symbolic reward, which is allocated by members themselves and 'distributed among the membership and inalienable from them: action related to such honour is autonomous group-oriented action, decoupled from the influence of outsiders' (Barnes 1992:265). Individuals of the same status may cooperate to further shared ends due to the ability of the membership to withdraw recognition and deny 'the special honour' to disobedient members. Status groups as groups with specific characteristics may generate a stream of collective actions because of their ability to communicate their approval and disapproval, praise and blame, recognition and rejection, and honour and contempt to its members. Many of these sanctions are interpersonal and as such are sustained by informal interaction, which generates moral expectations. This task of boundary-maintenance, while at the same time conveying to members whom to trust and whom not to trust, makes the group's continuing existence possible.

Barnes' mixing together of paradigms of Weber, Goffman and Scheff seems to point towards interesting developments in resolving the problem of collective agency. The main difference between Scheff's and Barnes' approach is that Scheff makes the connection between emotion and motivation, while Barnes focuses on the connection between networks of interaction and actions. Like Weber, Barnes is aware that the instrumental dimension of action is secondary insofar as the explanation of the operation of status group is concerned. He stresses, unlike Marx, that group organization is prior to the emergence of shared interest. 'What comes first, as it were, is being together, proximity, social relationships, social intercourse, ready opportunity to intensify and organize interaction. Then comes shared interest; and then comes action' (Barnes 1995:144). While, according to Weber, it is a distinctive lifestyle that identifies members to each other, Barnes sees as crucial the role of interaction. For instance, only the role of informal interaction 'will account for recruitment and the retention of members' to new social movements (Barnes 1995:168). To summarize, in networks of social interaction in which people communicate freely and where the instrumental dimension of action has a low priority, the process of negotiation of a shared conception of collective good and sanctioning of it will depend upon the distribution of informal sanctions, such as affirmation or denial of social status.

Since this type of sanction is distributed by relatively informal, personalized interaction, at the risk of simplification, it can be said that the informality of interaction is an essential element of the mechanism of consensus formation.

In contemporary circumstances, as many sociologists with some exaggeration argue, a generally obligatory and specific deference code is absent, the threat of public shame does not work and status is losing its fixed attribute quality. Furthermore, we are more dependent on trust and less on familiarity because 'the division of labour under late-modernity has been characterized by an exceptional growth in number of roles we fulfil in society, but at the same time, it has seen an increasing difficulty in maintaining a sense of familiarity with others in similar roles' (Seligman 1997:162–3). It leaves people less able to trust each other in the situation when the certainty of status and familiarity with others are gone, thus encounters with unknown others are seen as 'a risky intersubjective undertaking' (Luckmann 1996:81). They are risky because every such interaction puts our status under continuous review and calls for distrust, making consensus possible only after evidence. This perception of new risk provides the impetus for attempts to search for the basis of consensus, thus co-presence is perceived as one of the most significant ways of securing pre-commitment. It also assumes that face-to-face informal interaction generates consensus and solidarity by matching people's common interests, their understanding of the situation and by interlocking them in a more stable network-like relationship of sociability (Barnes 1995).

Therefore, being partners in face-to-face, indeterminate and flexible interactional practices imputes familiarity, which in modern societies, due to the division of labour and the differentiation of roles, is increasingly difficult to maintain. Familiarity, relying on shared experiences, does not however exclude the existence of some conflictual interests or strategic considerations. This means that we should analyse both the process of communication through which group identity is reproduced and the structural conditions necessary for reflective processes to take place. This proposition of an approach able to explain the process of the construction of networks of relations and able to eliminate the macro–micro divide, should incorporate the strategic side of interaction, a factor neglected by communicative action theories, as well as the communicative nature of collective action, which is ignored by the rational choice approach. In such a perspective, social networks, or sociability, should be seen as appealing not solely to the sense of emotional bonds but as being sustained on the basis of self-interest, mutual understanding and consensus attained on the basis of convincing others. By bringing interest and solidarity together, we can conceptualize sociability as contributing to socio-cultural constraints on self-interested behaviour and as playing an important part in open, widespread networks connecting people in their formal as well as informal roles. Since the boundaries of such a group are firmly grounded in shared meaning, they are sufficiently strong to confer relative value to collective identities (Lamont 1992). At the same time, what is unique to our modern sociability and collective identities is the multiplicity of affiliations, which not only changes the nature of human experiences but also increases the human scope of creativity and innovation. To what degree informality contributes to the development of more innovative and reflexive ways of thinking will be the topic of our next chapter.

6   The dynamics of innovation

Network relations and linkages represent natural responses to situations where the sharing of tacit knowledge is a prerequisite for the successful production of new technological knowledge (Radosovic 1991:33).

FROM GENIUS INVENTORS TO NETWORKS OF FLEXIBLE INNOVATION

The growing international concern for technological innovation as a stimulus to economic growth has resulted in an impressive number of publications dealing with the issue. Until recently the two dominant ways of approaching the problem have been inspired either by the economic theories of Schumpeter or by social science studies of technology. In the first type of perspective researchers of innovation focus either on the macro processes, such as the development of government technology policy and industrial policy, or on micro-level phenomena, such as the innovation strategies of industrial companies. In the second type of perspective, analysts focus on the micro level and explain technological innovation in terms of individual actions (Sorensen and Levold 1992). The more recent interests tend to look at innovation not in terms of characteristics of either individuals or government but by adopting the network approach, which, I would argue in what follows, provides a very promising context for discussion of the role of informality in the process of innovation.

In casual observation, invention is still perceived as a social phenomenon that is somehow mysterious and surrounded by myths. Until the nineteenth century the dominant myth of the inventor was the notion of the hermit genius, 'spinning inventions out of his intellectual and psychic innards' (Burns and Stalker 1961:21). Before methods of organizing inventiveness had been devised and applied, inventions were seen as accidental, random, uncontrollable and unplanned products of a creative mind. Technological advances, seen as simply 'happening', were attributed to individual and isolated amateurs. However, even if 'the myth of accident and inspiration did go some way towards accounting for the nineteenth century facts' (Burns and Stalker 1961:24), it still left out of the picture much significant information about inventors' social conditions and about informal ties that connected many of them. Presenting the important inventors (such as Watt, Black and Roebuck), Burns and Stalker (1961:25) stress that these eighteenth-century Scots were members of a small and closely integrated society, which served as a social medium of technological development. However, by the beginning of the next century, there was a clear awareness of the need to institutionalize these informal connections. The establishment of various learned societies, which were 'at the same time friendly and scientific' (Smiles, 1865, quoted in Burns and Stalker 1961:25) meant that for some time the responsibilities for scientific advance and for technical innovation were passed to them. However, very soon, due to the rapid expansion of science and technology, there was a need to institutionalize personal links between scientists and technologists; consequently, science and industry evolved into two distinct systems.

With industrial concerns increasing in size, ever greater administrative complexity brought a wide range of bureaucratic positions and careers into being and introduced the separation between owners and managers; further changes occurred in the social circumstances affecting the production of innovation. During the second part of the nineteenth century, institutional barriers between science and industry and between 'pure' and 'applied' science were established. 'In the twentieth century the new and elaborate organization of professional scientists has been eventually matched by one of technological innovators into groups overlapping teaching and research institutions, Government departments and agencies, and industry' (Burns and Stalker 1961:36). While the typical industrial entrepreneur of the nineteenth century was the owner and manager of a company who put into practice a novel method of production by embodying it in a new firm, later, according to the Schumpeterian interpretation, a radical transformation took place as innovative entrepreneurs were becoming 'mere managers'. Moreover, Schumpeter, who thought that the entrepreneur was the driving force in the process of innovation, assumed that this trend towards the routinization of innovation was an irreversible process.

Schumpeter's thesis about the unfitness of bureaucracy for innovation, and his argument about the essential role of innovative entrepreneurs in giving birth to a new technical paradigm for future growth, rely on the conceptualization of innovation as referring to 'simply the different employment of the economic system's supplies of productive means' (Schumpeter 1991:68). His presentation of innovation as the formation of a 'new combination of material and forces' stresses that it is quite immaterial whether new production is done by making use of a new invention or not. Because Schumpeter was interested in the transformation of the economy by the development of new technology, his concern was only with innovations that could produce a continuous effect in the market, not with inventions that remained visions of isolated inventors. Successful innovation is 'a feat not of

intellect, but of will. It is a special case of the social phenomenon of leadership' (Schumpeter 1991:65). Through technological innovation, new products and processes are created, assuring firms a temporary monopoly, and
the associated high profits.

Although Schumpeter, by distinguishing those new ideas that revolution-
ized the economy from those that did not, stresses that it is appropriate to
keep 'invention' distinct from 'innovation', he seems to play down the element of invention since the innovation carried out by entrepreneurs need
not necessarily be inventions (1991:222–5). Schumpeter conceptualizes the
innovative entrepreneur's main function as 'simply the doing of new things
or the doing of things that are already being done in a new way (innovation)'
(1991:223). Although entrepreneurs may be inventors, they are not inventors by nature of their function. An inventor is different from an entrepreneur because the inventor produces ideas; the entrepreneur gets things
done which may but need not embody anything that is scientifically new.
Besides, inventions result in very significant consequences for the economic
history of capitalism (Schumpeter 1991:224).

Innovations produce an effect in the market; they transform the economy
and monopolies produced by innovations set in motion a cycle of profits,
investment and in turn business cycles. Since according to Schumpeter
(1991:222), the 'mechanisms of economic change in capitalist society pivot
on entrepreneurial activity', progress and its cyclical 'waves', which ensure
long-term transitions from one to another historical stage, are presented as
dependent upon the quality and creativity of entrepreneurs. However, on
one hand, Schumpeter stresses that it was the nonroutine character of innovation that produced the economic effects of monopoly, profits, business
cycles and economic progress, while, on the other hand, he points out that in
order to have these economic effects innovation must be produced by efficient – which means routinized – production processes and must reach the
market in routinized channels. The temporary monopoly over a valuable
product or service produces profits from innovation only when the innovation is produced on a larger scale by bureaucratic organizations. The problem is, however, that this inevitable routinization of innovation destroys the
entrepreneurial function and, therefore, as innovation becomes routinized,
many of its economic effects disappear. Hence, seeing innovation as only a
bureaucratic routine undermines Schumpeter's main argument in favour of
capitalism, namely, that it allows innovative entrepreneurs enough autonomy to produce economic progress (Stinchcombe 1990:191). Schumpeter's
empirical observation on the capacity of larger firms to 'routinize' innovation and the need for it to get profits out of the monopoly of innovations is
therefore in contrast with his theoretical argument about the necessity of an
individual heroic entrepreneur. To some degree this contrast also reflects
the difference between two historical stages of the development of
capitalism.

Innovation in competitive capitalism is typically embodied in the formation of new firms, seen by Schumpeter as the result of the rise of industrial families. However, in the second stage of capitalist development, innovation occurred within big units largely independent of individual persons. 'Progress becomes "automatised", increasingly impersonal and decreasingly a matter of leadership and individual initiative' (Schumpeter 1991:71). For Schumpeter, who saw the role of industrial family interest in capitalist society as the guardian of the nation's economic future, the decline of the importance of the entrepreneurial function, as time went on, was a very worrying signal. He viewed the concentration of ownership and absentee ownership as leading to the progressive bureaucratization, 'mechanization' and impotence of the class of industrial warriors (1991:230). Subsequently to this new environment offering less resistance to new methods and new goods than used to be the case, 'the element of personal intuition and force would be less essential than it was: it could be expected to yield its place to the teamwork of specialists; in other words improvement could be expected to become more and more automatic' (Schumpeter 1991:231). Schumpeter's association of the elimination of family industrial enterprises with 'the loss of those attitudes and aptitudes of industrial leadership or alertness that enter our picture of the entrepreneurial businessman' (1991:231), contrasts the first stage of capitalist development, where personal initiatives, intuitions and passions were so essential, with the second stage where bureaucratization and 'divorce of the success of the concern from the success of the man' (Schumpeter 1991:71) are dominant.

The contrast between the spontaneity of the first phase of technological advancement and the highly structured formalistic nature of the second stage of industrial management has been translated in many empirical studies of innovation into a contrast between the first stage of the process of innovation and its final stage. In this type of research, innovation is defined in the broadest way 'as a process starting with the recognition of a potential demand for, and technical feasibility of, an item and ending with its widespread utilization' (Zaltman, Duncan, Holbeck 1984:7). In discussions of the relationship between spontaneity and formalization, it is argued that formalization is beneficial only in the particular stage of the innovation.

Defining formalization as 'the emphasis placed within the organization on the following specific rules and procedures in performing one's job' (Zaltman, Duncan, Holbeck 1984:138) leads to an argument that the highly creative initiation stage of the innovation process requires less formalization or the expansion of informality, whereas formalization appears to aid the implementation of innovation. This argument is based on several assumptions. Firstly, it is assumed that the strict emphasis on rigid rules and procedures may prohibit organizational decision makers from seeking new sources of information. The rigidity of existing procedures might restrict access to both the appropriate sources of information and channels of communication, therefore lowering the opportunity for members to become more aware of potential innovations or to identify sources of problems in organizational performance. Secondly, it is argued that formalization in the initial stage can cause role conflict, while the lack of it in the implementation stage can be the source of both role conflict and role ambiguity. For instance, when members of an organization identify the problem, but the rules and procedures prevent them from taking corrective (innovative) action, they can experience role conflict. Hence during 'initiation a broad set of operating guidelines could be established that reduce formalization and give individuals more autonomy in seeking solutions to decision problems' (Zaltman, Duncan, Holbeck 1984:161). However, in the final stage of the process of innovation, some formalization of rules is welcome because clear rules can reduce the potential ambiguity surrounding new roles and new demands. For instance, the need to formalize the final result of informal cooperation in the process of innovation is shown by Steward and Conway (1996) in their case study of the relationships between an industrial firm and a university. This cooperation began informally, when a friend of the founders of the company put them in contact with two professors from the university. 'They became friends ... the link was totally informal and friendship based'; however, in order to secure the efficiency of the product implementation – the relationship 'became formalized and a contract was drawn up between the university and the company' (Steward and Conway 1996:216).

The contrast between the spontaneity and routinization within the process of innovation is also reflected in other dilemmas faced by organizations, namely, the dilemma of flexibility and stability and the dilemma of uncertainty. It is commonly understood that the organization has to show in its functioning both flexibility and stability, so it is able to preserve continuity and to adapt to new circumstances. In order to be able to modify its practices or accept new innovations, the organization needs to be flexible, which is often prevented by the structure and processes securing its stability. However, these two requirements do not need to be mutually exclusive. The organization 'can solve this stability–flexibility dilemma by altering and simultaneously expressing these two forms in different parts of the organizations' (Zaltman, Duncan, Holbeck 1984:129). It can be done by increasing flexibility and, therefore, lowering the level of formalization and bureaucratization within those parts of the organization that are facing a higher level of uncertainty. Following Burns and Stalker's (1964) assumption that different types of organizational structures might be effective in different situations, it can be argued that when organizations face a high level of uncertainty, thus when organizations' information needs are high, such organizations should adopt more flexible and more decentralized organic types of structures with open channels of communication. The fact that more flexible, decentralized and less formalized organizational structures are better suited for rapidly changing environments and for innovation is confirmed by the results of empirical research, which has found, for instance, that the organization units experiencing the highest uncertainty have the least formal structure, while the units within a more predictable context tend to have the highest level of formalization of their structure (Lawrence and Lorsch 1967). These studies also point out that the higher level of uncertainty faced by some parts of organizations, as for example by research units, the greater differences in organizational routine and nonroutine decision-making structures, openness of channels of communication and more organic types of organization are required. Therefore, research groups, that are responsible for the initiation of innovations would develop a different type of organizational structure than other subunits of organizations that are important in the implementation stage of the innovation process.

A similar argument is developed by Stinchcombe (1990) in his elaboration on Schumpeter's examination of the relation between economic innovation and routine administration. Stinchcombe argues that an innovation involves a higher level of uncertainty than producing old goods and that it poses the administrative problems of differentiated information collecting and decentralized decision making. Therefore, innovation creates pressure for decentralization and because 'the level of uncertainty of the work involved to introduce an innovation will ordinarily be higher than that of other production, such a division is likely to have a higher skill mix than a division with an equally complex product or service that is no longer an innovation' (Stinchcombe 1990:24). Making innovation an ongoing concern for any organization means the creation of a new social system, which is not routinized and which has some autonomy. Therefore, according to Stinchcombe, building a social system around innovation can be successful only if larger social orders would allow considerable autonomy to this new not routinized social unit (1990:153–91). To sum up the discussion thus far, in debating the relationship between formalization and innovation as well as the relationships between flexibility, uncertainty and innovation it is necessary to consider the stages of the innovation process, the role of various parts of the organization in the process of innovation and the nature of the organizational environment.

And finally, the contrast between the spontaneity of the first phase of technological advancement and the highly structured formalistic nature of the second stage of industrial management, seen as the consequence of the application of required solutions for historically specific problems, seems also to be replicated in the contrast between the formalized, highly bureaucratized system of Fordist mass production and the new more flexible, lean, globally oriented mode of post-Fordist production. Post-Fordism can be seen, within the neo-Schumpeterian approach, as the fifth of Kondartiev long waves or technical paradigms for future growth. In neo-Schumpeterian analysis, post-Fordism is claimed not only to introduce new products or industrial processes but also to induce new forms of work organization and management and new communication technologies. Moreover, the widespread diffusion of the benefits of innovation across the economy is supposed to increase industrial productivity and induce changes in institutional rules and social norms. This understanding of the nature of the main waves of technological change as composed of a 'cluster of radical innovations', which introduce 'the best practices' at the frontier of industrial development (Freeman and Perez 1988:47–8), offers, however, too deterministic a definition of innovation (Amin 1994). Many recent studies of the causes of the significant increase in productivity achieved by new types of industries undermine this perspective and argue that social innovation is equally important as the technical one, that there is a need to examine 'the less tangible social innovation' and that the character of qualitative change should be seen as 'actively *negotiated* as well as passively accommodated' (Elam 1994:47, 49). Adopting the perspective that is concerned not only with technological innovation but also with social innovation, and which therefore looks at social relationships in specific workplaces, networks and interactions between various social agents involved in the process of innovation, means the rejection of neo-Schumpeterian technological determinism.

Not only does post-Fordism depend more than the previous regime on innovation, but this new wave is supposed to be innovation and knowledge intensive and centred around information technology. In Fordism the goal was to make employees' activities more predictable and thus more controllable, which has resulted in the widening of the information and knowledge gap between people employed at various levels of management because the system that ensures control and conformity also inhibits creativity and initiative. In contrast to Fordism, which gives top management control over information flows and which depends upon the existence of mass markets for standardized products, in post-Fordism, functioning in a fast-changing, competitive and global environment, diffusing knowledge is a source of competitive advantage. Since, unlike capital, knowledge is most valuable when those on the front lines control and use it, organizations' capacity to create an environment in which employees can exploit information more effectively is crucial (Bartlett and Ghoshal 1995:140–2).

In the present context of opening markets, the arrival of new competitors, the shortening life cycle of products and processes, increased economic turbulence, and when knowledge is the most fundamental resource, a higher level of innovation is essential. Furthermore, since cooperation can lower the cost and risk of introducing new technologies, there is widespread recognition that 'successful innovation calls for cooperation' (Chesnais 1996:21). Such cooperation often has a strong social basis, involving affinity and loyalty. Besides, with the growing cost of innovations, companies collaborate even with their competitors; their strategy is to 'collaborate with some rivals, in order to compete with others' (Niosi 1996:105). Moreover, not only do today's firms 'recognize that the diversity of human skills and the unpredictability of the human spirit make possible initiative, creativity and entrepreneurship' (Bartlett and Ghoshal 1995:142), but they also try to plan and organize it, albeit in very flexible and informal ways. All these facts, together with the growing awareness that innovations of the economy depend on the external environments' characteristics (that is, on the degree of coherence and linkage between education, research and investment-related institutions as well as with other firms), mean that the quality of cooperation and linkages between these interacting units becomes very important. Moreover, since in the modern economy knowledge is essential and since, accordingly, the most important process is learning (Dogson 1996:61), firms develop new forms of collective learning that are mostly localized due to the fact that technologies are more specific to particular industries and products (Niosi 1996:102).

It is increasingly clear that, in our electronic global world, innovation is still guided by local processes. The conditions of local economies, especially 'clusters' of suppliers, customers, producers and technological organizations, are crucial factors for innovation (Porter 1990). Many studies of successful economic regions also stress that the social relations of successful innovation are largely local. They emphasize the importance of opportunities for face-to-face encounters between partners in economic activity, which are seen as helping to solve information problems and as producing trust, which is a necessary precondition of the development of flexible specialized local economies (Sabel 1989). Informal communication is the primary way that new information flows into and through organizations, especially in large projects and developments marked by uncertainty. Ongoing informal and formal communication permits different aspects of a project to be carried out in parallel rather than sequentially, allowing the development to proceed rapidly, while preventing mistakes and securing the quality of the product (Sproull and Kiesler 1991:132–3). Informal encounters, by bridging gaps between different networks, allow for the circulation and appropriate selection of information and resources and help to build pre-commitments for further cooperation. Furthermore, since learning, which is a central activity in the system of innovation, is a social activity that involves interaction between people, learning-by-interaction is essential in the production of innovation (Lundvall 1992). Hence there is growing recognition that innovation should be seen as 'a socially embedded process which cannot be understood without taking into consideration its institutional and cultural context' (Dogson 1996:61).

This recognition of the importance of the social basis of innovation and the process of interactive learning paints a totally new picture of relationships between firms and innovation. In these new relationships the accent is on the role of networking in acquiring and sharing tacit knowledge, seen as essential in the process of technological innovation. The new nature of these relationships manifests itself in the blurred boundaries between research, production, universities and firms. Technological collaboration among firms, and between firms and universities and state laboratories, has been rapidly increasing in the 1980s and 1990s (Niosi 1996). Many firms put together commonly defined Research and Development (R and D) projects, often with the help of universities and governmental laboratories. Likewise, many universities, especially in the USA, have established 'informal', creative and intimate partners with corporate science. In the past innovation was thought to follow 'a straight line from basic research (conducted mainly at universities) through applied R and D (conducted mainly by firms) and then into the wider economy. Now analysts have at last noticed that innovations meander into the economy along a much more circuitous path, and often in a form (such as the content of people's heads) that cannot be codified and is therefore impossible to measure' (*The Economist*, 4 October, 1997:14). These various new forms of alliance and collaborative research secure a higher level of 'flexible innovation', which increases the transfer of complementary knowledge and speeds the innovation process, while at the same time reducing costs and risks (Niosi 1996:103).

The more recent interests, as discussed above, tend to look at innovation by adopting the network approach. Therefore, in some way, we have moved around the whole circle and we are back at the stage where again creativity, tacit knowledge and networking are seen as crucial in the process of innovation. Moreover, while previously innovation studies were either assuming 'the fluidity of sociotechnical relations (constructivists) or the lack of such fluidity because of structural limits (economists), today's approach argues that mezzo-level arrangements (networks) involved in technological innovation are 'neither fluid nor determined' (Sorensen and Levold 1992:12–13). Since networking is presented as a part of innovation activities, in order to understand the nature of innovation we need to look closer at the role of social networks and at the characteristics of the knowledge flowing through these channels.

TACIT KNOWLEDGE AND NETWORKS

Today it is commonly agreed that the network model provides a more realistic representation of the diversity and frequency of interaction between participants in the process of innovation (Coombs *et al* 1996). Many empirical studies of innovation since the 1950s have demonstrated 'the importance of both formal and informal networks' (Freeman 1991:500). The fact that a new industrial order is characterized by continuous innovation and collective learning, together with the fact that success in innovation depends upon the quality of knowledge flow, makes the role played by personal networks in facilitating access to knowledge essential. Now to be 'part of a network has become even more valuable than being able to generate knowledge autonomously' (Gambardella 1992:394). The growing importance of knowledge in the process of production and the increasing complexity and interdisciplinarity of knowledge also point to the necessity to look closer at innovative networks, especially within the realm of science.

Studying this type of network already has a long tradition. It started with investigations discovering the collegial interdependence of researchers involved in the informal exchange of information, which secures the distribution of rewards, prestige and ideas. An impressive number of studies have tried to show that workers in scientific specialities are organized in social circles (see, for example, Barnes and Edge 1982). These investigations argued that informal networks among scholars in both the past and present attest to the importance of personal contacts in constructing the community and that scientific knowledge is tacit knowledge, embodied in human beings. An exemplary illustration of the interplay of formal and informal elements, for instance, was displayed in the functioning of the Republic of Letters, which case we have already discussed in Chapter 3. While modern scientific knowledge is based more on anonymous scientific expertise rather than on scientists' reputation for being 'men of honour', personal contacts, informal exchange and reputation for credibility and truthfulness, for instance, are still important factors, which contribute to 'a legitimate sense in which modern science is much more trusting' (Shapin 1994:417).

The importance of informal networks in the community of contemporary scholars is demonstrated by Crane (1972) who uses for this purpose Price's (1963) concept of the invisible college. Locating the central process of communication and control within science in research networks, she stresses that within these networks credibility is earned and directions of research strategy determined. Informal networks are also seen as useful because they are valued sources of information about relevant literature or experts who can help solve difficult problems (Senker and Faulkner 1992). Networks, however, are non-stable, their membership changes over time, their boundaries are not fixed but rather overlap, they disappear and new ones emerge. Collins (1982) complicates this picture further by arguing that it is necessary to go beyond treating informal communication as merely a more flexibly packaged version of formal communication. His study suggests that in new scientific fields little of tacit knowledge is learned during scientists' apprenticeships and that the systematic transfer of new knowledge is sometimes impossible because 'skill-like knowledge' travels best through accomplished practitioners. He stresses not only 'the informality of some information exchange, but also its necessary capriciousness – a symptom of the lack of organization of unarticulated knowledge into visible, discrete and measurable units' (Collins 1982:49). Informal channels of transmission of knowledge can enhance or limit the passage of knowledge due to such processes as competition, leading to 'the overt concealment of information by scientists', or the adaptation of a 'reasonable degree of secrecy' (Collins 1982:63). Informal networks can be constructed around various types of activities and have different characteristics. Stressing the importance of informal networks in the transfer of technology, Steward and Conway (1996) describe five informal networks, which are distinguished on the bases of five shared commonalities; leisure activity, profession, scientific and technical speciality, user or potential user of innovation and friendship. The cohesion in each of these five informal networks results from the mutual sense of attachment to the specific type of activity, sharing of which allows for plugging into others' views and ideas in an informal way. In all cases, the transmission of scientific knowledge, which is informal and partly tacit, involves many complexities and uncertainties.

This type of science study shows that scientific research demands a range of skills and tacit knowledge. It also demonstrates how much 'tacit knowledge' is involved in the building of new knowledge and what role is played by weak ties. Another tradition in network analysis that has contributed enormously to our understanding of the interplay between formal and informal is networks analysis of technology and technological innovation. This approach looks at the processes of the circulation of information and resources and often stresses the advantages and even the necessity of informal processes, the importance of unstructured communication and cooperation-based exchange for the effective, flexible and innovative functioning of any formal organization. These studies reveal that 'nonhierarchical coordination often offers solutions to the problems when hierarchical intervention and control fail' (Benz 1993:168). Informal networks perform a very significant role in larger official systems because they provide their participants with access to better information, enhance the possibility of learning and promote trust (Kudushin 1995). Building wide networks with different organizations, subcontractors and even with customers enlarges a firm's knowledge and opportunity for more innovative and experimental solutions. These networks are 'simultaneously development, design, marketing and learning', which can be seen as 'disorderly problem-solving negotiations, in which different kinds of knowledge are contraposed and checked, and where the outcome also depends on the persuasive ability of the engineers involved' (Sorensen and Levold 1992:27). Within this type of network, participants are human carriers of not easily transferable knowledge. Senker and Faulkner's study (1992) found that firms' innovation activities involve a lot of informal interaction with external sources of scientific and technological knowledge, and that much of the knowledge so acquired is tacit in nature. Hence, accessing technological knowledge requires tacit knowledge; some would even argue that it requires more tacit knowledge than in the case of scientific knowledge (Collins 1984). 'The very tacit nature of technological knowledge complicates the transfer of technology and demands mobility of engineers' (Sorensen and Levold 1992:28). Nonetheless, both science and technological discoveries cannot be explained wholly in terms of explicit knowledge.

The importance of tacit knowledge was put forward by Polanyi, who took – as the starting point for developing a theory of non-explicit thought – an assumption that the pursuit of science is determined at every stage by 'unspecifiable powers of thought' (1969:153). This theory, which he calls 'an informal logic of science and of knowledge in general' (1969:153), says that 'tacit knowing is the fundamental power of the mind, which creates explicit knowing, lends meaning to it and controls its uses' (1969:156). While arguing that 'we know more that we can tell' (1967:4), Polanyi points out that tacit knowing provides coherence and integrity to our observation and that 'this act of integration, is the tacit power' (1969:140). We cannot tell how to recognize faces or how to ride a bicycle because we internalized this knowledge by practice and experience. 'By contrast "articulated knowledge" is transmittable in formal, systematic language. It has many forms, but a main constituent is the general principles and laws acknowledged by the scientific and engineering communities as supplying a foundation for further practices' (Senker and Faulkner 1996:77). However, while tacit knowledge is opposed to explicit knowledge, the two are not sharply divided. 'While tacit knowledge can be possessed by itself, explicit knowledge must rely on being tacitly understood and applied. Hence all knowledge is either tacit or rooted in tacit knowledge. A wholly explicit knowledge is unthinkable' (Polanyi 1969:144).

Moreover, knowledge is always personal because our knowledge of reality – due to the fact that the indeterminacy of reality can only be discerned by personal judgement – is personal. Since personal participation is the universal principle of knowing, 'all tacit knowing requires the continued participation of the knower, and a measure of personal participation is intrinsic therefore to all knowledge' (Polanyi 1969:152). Meaningful knowledge can only be acquired by an act of comprehension which is 'necessarily personal' and can never be replaced by a formal operation (Polanyi 1948:44). This means that information formalized in instruction, standards or textbooks is nothing more than 'empty talk' until it is brought to life by practising individuals (Dosi 1988:1130).

Although the formalization of tacit knowing 'immensely expands the powers of the mind, by creating a machinery of precise thought', it can however also reduce possibilities for intuition and coherence of our thoughts (Polanyi 1969:156). Attempts to depersonalize our knowledge would, consequently, result in an alienation 'that would render all observations on living things meaningless' (Polanyi 1969:152). Therefore 'any attempt to gain complete control of thought by explicit rules is self-contradictory, systematically misleading and culturally destructive' (Polanyi 1969:156). Hence, only the pursuit of formalization that does not undermine tacit knowledge can be viewed in positive terms.

To sum up, tacit knowledge is an essential component in both scientific and technological innovation. The continuing importance of tacit knowledge and skills in innovation is a result of the fact that new science and technology 'in themselves, necessarily involve the use and creation of tacit knowledge' (Senker and Faulkner 1996:83). The tendency for advanced knowledge and techniques to rely on and generate tacit knowledge is further reinforced by the complexity of the systems, which are impossible to model in a laboratory, and therefore the only hope of the reduction of their complexity is by 'open-loop feedback processes using human intelligence in learning-by-doing mode' (Kline, quoted in Senker and Faulkner 1996:84). Hence, while some knowledge can be formalized and shared through textbooks, patents or instruction, tacit knowledge continually proves itself to be successful practice. Moreover, in sharing such knowledge the role of informal and personalized interaction is crucial, to such a degree that, for instance, Senker and Faulkner, after examining studies highlighting the relative importance of informal networks, say that 'we would suggest that some types of tacit knowledge are quite extensively shared through interaction between competitors' (1996:88).

However, small personalized networks can also produce conflictual relationships and tensions with the imperatives of its wider corporate context. Their operation can generate problems for companies due to difficulties in appropriating benefits from their innovation. Born (1996) illustrates that the information transfer behaviour of researchers is not always in accordance with the economic interests of the employer. She describes the existence of 'informal discourses and practices' between researchers and uses the concept of 'sociality' to identify these informal networks generating innovation. 'The dominant informal ethos in IRCAM's software research culture centres on concepts of collaboration and sharing of knowledge ... . They constitute the sociability of the research culture and this sociability is in itself a source of social gratification' (1996:107–8). Because of the centrality of knowledge flow and tensions connected with property rights, such a research culture which lacks any formalization and documentation of innovation prevents the circulation of new programs due to researchers' ambivalence and anxieties with regard to their ownership of projects. For example, by 'neglecting documentation, programmers protect their work from others and retain intellectual, material control and social control over it' (Born 1996:114). This internally oriented sociability can, therefore, result in the guarded closure or 'bounded circulation of information', which creates locally the structure of protection. 'The gift of microsociability' in the research culture, as described by Born, puts light on the group's capacity to construct boundaries and control the distribution of technological innovation and shows the difference between this type of network and the economic type of network. While commodity logic enforces closure and realism in the research process as well as the wider distribution of knowledge, the research culture based on sociability is 'free' and only locally assessable, which contributes to researchers' feelings of job satisfaction (Born 1996:113–5).

Another problem for the organization generated by the functioning of informal networks is connected with the fact that these networks can also result in information leakage (Steward and Conway 1996:216). However, the main difficulties faced by the organization in its relations towards informal networks is connected with the fragility of the bridges between the organization and external information networks and with the unpredictable nature of the interaction patterns within the external informal networks (Steward and Conway 1996:217). There is an increased attempt on the part of various companies to overcome these problems in novel ways. In the past, the importance of personal contacts in technology transfer was consistently ignored, despite the fact that their role was 'replicated in study after study' (Allen *at al* 1983:208). Now, however, building cooperative networks becomes a conscious effort of many companies trying to increase their capacity for innovation by utilizing tacit knowledge. The growing understanding that the transfer of tacit knowledge requires an essentially non-contractual or cooperative relation permitting a process of close interaction and dialogue between individuals (Yamin 1996), therefore, results in a new appreciation of the information potential of weak ties because they are more likely than strong ties to link members of different small groups (Granovetter 1973:351). These weak ties, although fragile, are strategic links for innovative organizations because they 'are likely to be more important than strong ones for the transmission of influences over long distances and between groups which are not densely connected' (Collins 1982:47). Even though they often are not the most important ties in the eyes of participants, they could for some innovative networks be the most important because, as network theory argues, they provide bridges between various circles (Granovetter 1973).

In general terms, it can be said that an informal network of relations affects the distribution of resources to individuals. The links that connect people in the system of informal relationships, and which have been called 'weak ties' (Granovetter 1973), are channels through which vital information about the system passes. Their boundaries are only loosely defined by the ramifications of indirect contacts. The cohesion of these chains of indirect connections is not necessarily founded in face-to-face interaction. While researching how information about job availability travels along social networks, Granovetter not only found that employers preferred to hire people through personal contacts, but also that many people find their jobs through people they really did not know so well. Arguing that certain forms of network allow for the easier transmission of information, Granovetter demonstrated how the networks serve to structure the flow of information to actors.

Granovetter shows that the importance of weak ties is not an accidental occurrence but it is due to the fact that the people you do not know well are probably moving in circles that are different from your own and therefore less likely to have the same information as you. It is argued that strong ties tend to form cliques, while weak ties tend to bridge cliques and bring everyone into the same network, so that weak ties are a better basis for collective action. Weak ties can be seen as bridge ties because they provide indirect access to a greater diversity of resources and other circles, thus, they increase the diversity and size of networks (Granovetter 1973). Bridges, as weak ties or 'the channels through which ideas, influences, or information socially distant from ego may reach him' (1973:357), are fragile. Hence any attempt to strengthen them may, paradoxically, reduce the freshness and uniqueness of the input for the network (Steward and Conway 1996:217).

Granovetter's idea of contrasting the role of weak and strong ties, and therefore assigning different functions to cohesive and more loosely coupled groups, runs against the early sociological literature's identification of social cohesion as being an important social factor driving innovation. Seeing interpersonal influences, created on the basis of cohesion and proximity, as responsible for the diffusion of information, was a part of the studies of small groups. They were based on the assumption that people, while adopting an innovation, which always entails an uncertainty and a lack of knowledge about costs and benefits, rely on others to help them to identify and manage this risk. The early post-war studies show how innovation, not only a technological one, becomes efficacious only to the extent that it is assimilated by informal networks. Katz and Lazarsfeld's (1955) study looked at small groups as a medium of change and demonstrated how messages were assimilated into the existing personal networks of primary groups. When confronted with a new question people, it was argued, turn to the members of their groups with whom such issues are discussed. These opinion leaders were seen as responsible for the diffusion of mass media information, while their social relations were defined as a form of social capital, which provides information that facilitates action. Likewise, Coleman (*et al* 1966:118) argued that confronted with the need to make a decision in an ambiguous situation – a situation that does not speak for itself – people turn to each other for cues as to how to interpret the situation. The authors of *Medical Innovation* showed that, when a new drug appears, doctors would start prescribing it only after arriving at some shared way of looking at it, achieved by seeking advice from their colleagues.

However, the importance of cohesion and strong groups in the process of innovation is undermined by new studies carried out in light of recent developments in network theory. These investigations provide a strong support to Granovetter's assertion that weak ties are better than strong ones for the transmission of novel information. For example, Burt's (1987) reanalysis of a sociological classic, *Medical Innovation*, demonstrates that doctors were not following the behaviour of the people from whom they sought advice or with whom they discussed the case. By showing that cohesion fails to predict adoption of the drug by prominent doctors, while, however, the same physicians conformed to the adoption norms of their structurally equivalent peers, Burt (1987) suggests that structural equivalence should be seen, more than cohesion, as a factor responsible for generating social pressure to conform. The study by Campbell, Mardsen and Hurlbert (1986:98), which expands Granovetter's arguments about the importance of weak ties as sources of fresh information, shows even more directly how valuable weak ties are as channels of novel information. Also Meyerson's (1994) study confirms that weak ties are more likely than strong ones to link an actor to information that is new and not otherwise available. Novel information flows through weak non-redundant ties, while strong ties, which are characteristic of overlapping contacts and cohesive groups, restrict members' access to new information. Thus, weak non-redundant ties are conducive to carrying novel information, while strong ties in cohesive groups have enormous power of mobilization because they are a source of norms. Furthermore, 'you can not have both information-oriented and mobilization-oriented networks in a stable equilibrium' because cohesion restricts novel information accrual in at least two ways (Meyerson 1994:385).

The argument that while cohesive groups made of strong ties can become increasingly self-sufficient, thus increasingly isolated and closed to outsiders, members of loose-knit networks are more likely to be exposed to information sources that provide novel information, is based on several assumptions. Firstly, it can be said that strong ties are time consuming since the more cohesive the group, the greater amount of interaction it demands (Meyerson 1994:385–7). Secondly, following the cognitive dissonance thesis, which states that individuals are prone to expose themselves to information that is consistent with their beliefs, it can be argued that members of strong ties groups would reject information that disturbs their group norms and cohesion. Thirdly, there is historical reason to believe that the maintenance of closed networks blocks innovation and reinforces traditionalism, generally in the form of the closed economy (Levi 1996).

In short, in light of recent developments in network theory it is clear that weak ties rather than cohesion should be seen as responsible for innovation. The rejection of the myth about the innovative role of cohesive groups and the rejection of the myth that whole knowledge is 'articulated' and transmittable in formal and systematic language, leaves us with an assumption about the role of weak ties and tacit knowledge in the process of innovation. Furthermore, arguing that weak ties and tacit knowledge are not mutually exclusive options, brings into the picture the role of informality.

INFORMALITY AND INNOVATION

It is commonly believed that nothing great has ever been accomplished without 'enthusiasm' or 'passion'. Writing about the relationship between enthusiasm and passions, Passmore points out that what people achieve is a 'consequence of their remaining anxious, passionate, discontented human beings' (1979:326). Even more, human projects can be dehumanizing and alienating when they are done without emotions. In contrast, the love of one's work, the passion for works of art, the enthusiasm for scientific and technological achievements would shape the nature of one's achievements in such a way as to help people to become more human (Passmore 1979).

The role of emotions in the process of creativity is appreciated in a variety of works trying to grasp what is the essence of creativity. Although it is impossible to generalize about creativity and the creative personality, there is some shared understanding that a creator should be seen as having 'emotions and aesthetic feelings as well as social awareness of the relation of his or her work to the world's work, its needs, and feelings' (Gruber 1989:5). Creative works, because of being innovative, can be risky and disruptive of the existing arrangements. Thus, in order for 'wild' ideas to become effective, 'the creator must be in good touch with the norms and feelings of some others so that the product will be one that they can assimilate and enjoy' (Gruber 1989:14). This means that emotions are an important component of the process of creativity in more than one way.

The argument that emotions are not useless has recently gained strength due to the popularity of Daniel Goleman's book *Emotional Intelligence.* It argues that emotional intelligence, which includes 'self-control, zeal and persistence, and the ability to motivate oneself' (Goleman 1996:xii) helps people to excel and secure job success. Goleman's book is interesting for our discussion because, behind his main attempt to teach people how to manage their emotional life with intelligence, there are assumptions about the predominance of weak ties in our society and about the role of less-explicit knowledge. The need for this new type of intelligence is increasing, according to Goleman, because people become more lonely, because primary groups do not provide a grounding in the basics of emotional intelligence, and because the market forces that are reshaping our worklife are creating an unprecedented demand for emotional intelligence. As electronic networks, e-mail, teleconferences and informal networks are emerging as new functional entities in organizations, emotional intelligence and 'the virtuoso in interpersonal skills' is the corporate future (Goleman 1996:146–60). As a third of the American workforce become 'knowledge' workers and work teams dominate the work environment, the skills that help people to be innovative and to harmonize social relationships become increasingly valued. According to Goleman, the single 'most important factor in maximizing the excellence of a group's product was the degree to which the members were able to create a state of internal harmony, which lets them take advantage of the full talent of their members' (1996:161). He argues that what makes somebody creative and successful is not their academic IQ but their emotional IQ. This different way of being smart relies on one's ability to motivate oneself and one's ability 'to work their informal networks into *ad hoc* teams' (*ibid*). This argument is supported by a study of 'star performers' at Bell Lab (Kelley and Caplan 1993).

Successful work performance depends on a rapport with a network of key people (Kelley and Caplan 1993). The existence of informal networks, that is, 'the networks of relationships that employees form across functions and divisions to accomplish tasks fast' (Krackhardt and Hanson 1993:104), are especially important for handling unanticipated problems. While networks of knowledgeable people are crucial for highly productive work, the high achievers and innovators do the work of building reliable networks before they actually need them (Kelley and Caplan 1993). People who cultivate good relationships with others whose services might be needed in crucial moments as part of an instant *ad hoc* team to solve a problem or handle a crisis, are able to carry out the most interesting and innovative projects. The role of the formal organization is to handle easily anticipated problems, however, 'when unexpected problems arise, the informal organization kicks in [...]. Highly adaptive, informal networks move diagonally and elliptically, skipping entire functions to get things done' (Krackhardt and Hanson 1993:104). Furthermore, what matters, since there are various types of informal networks and not all of them are equally beneficiary for the company (for instance, Krackhardt and Hanson (1993) identified three types of informal networks: communication webs, expertise networks and trust networks), is the 'fit' between the type of informal networks and the company's goals. As companies become less hierarchical and rely more on teams, the role of informal networks increases and therefore there is a need for a more sophisticated view of informal networks.

However, the most important context for facilitating the innovation process are the so-called 'hot groups'. They are unplanned, spontaneously emerging groups, not respecting the existing segmentation of roles and the existing hierarchies and they are inspired by the dedication of their members to solve impossible problems. 'When hot groups are allowed to grow unfettered by the usual organizational constraints, their inventiveness and energy can benefit an organization enormously' (Leavitt and Lipman-Blumen 1995). These types of group thrived at Bell Labs and at the beginning of Apple computers. Looking at these two success stories illustrates that hot groups generate excitement, chaos, joy and that this type of culture is 'exciting, urgent, flamboyant, defiant, using its own emotional symbols' (Leavitt and Lipman-Blumen 1995:113). Hot groups are rare, especially within traditional organizations that do not show a strong commitment to scientific values: but their fluid structures and small sizes, their members' total preoccupation with the group task, and their participants' intensive intellectual and emotional involvement make them very successful. In setting up hot groups what can also be helpful, apart from the organization's dedication to scientific investigation, is the openness and flexibility of organizational structures and the adoption of a people-first, not task-first, approach.

Crisis, competition or unexpected or new developments may also generate high energy and dedication, and when formal hierarchies and status systems are suspended in attempts to restore equilibrium hot groups may become an essential force in the organization. Hot groups, as highly achieving, creative small circles, which combine intense intellectual and emotional involvement, bring together both high expertise and the chance of insight or intuition. Members of hot groups 'pump up ideas and possibilities at an astonishing rate. From the outside, many of their ideas look wildly absurd and impossible to achieve' (Leavitt and Lipman-Blumen 1995:111). Such a description of the process of creation, when 'wild' ideas emerge with enormous speed, sheds new light on the nature of creativity. Instead of dismissing the elusiveness of creativity, it can be said that creativity involves several elements, which depend upon the existence of the conditions for informality.

The relationship between insight and creativity has been widely discussed in the literature. Some theorists develop approaches to creativity that rely heavily on unconscious processes (Kostler 1964; Simonton 1997). In such accounts the role of sudden insight is enormously exposed. Others look at creative processes as fully accessible and not qualitatively different from other forms of reasoning (Perkins 1981; Weisberg 1986). The third group argues that creative achievement is accomplished mainly through purposeful work (Wallace and Gruber 1989), which, however, does not exclude the role of insight, especially as part of a protracted creative process. These researchers also point out that the occurrence of an insight indicates a certain degree of mastery of a domain and that insights represent a moment of consolidation of what one has already known (Gruber 1989:17–19). Following William James, they argue that at 'a certain stage in the development of every science a degree of vagueness is what best consists of fertility' (Osowski 1989:127). Likewise, they agree with Einstein's statement that knowledge arises from sense impressions that are 'irregular, confused' and with his comment that 'clear ideas' emerge through observing the world, until finally intuition helps to solve the problem (quoted in Miller 1989:173). Thus, the process of creation is seen as the constant interplay among purpose, play and chance, which evolves over long periods of time. What is essential in this process is that the conditions for innovation must secure both short-term flexibility and long-term consistency (Gruber 1989:14).

The longevity and durability of creative work, together with the increased cost and complexity of today's scientific investigations, which require team work and long-term investment, combined with the fact that the final stages of the innovation process demand formalization, means that the innovation process should be seen as a successful venture of informality and formality. Seeing innovativeness as an interplay of informality, which is a necessary aspect of creativity because of the role of tacit knowledge in human cognition (Polanyi 1967), and formality, which reflects the institutional framework of the innovation process, also suggests that until organizations unblock the daily routine put in place for the preservation of the equilibrium between formally structured groups and privileges, innovation will only be a result of the 'irresponsible creativity of individuals' (Crozier 1967:289).

Since innovation is 'about taming uncertainty' and since a new industrial order is characterized by continuous innovation, 'the resources you draw upon to achieve this end must themselves be reasonably certain' (Elam 1993:35). This, together with the growing importance of knowledge in the process of production, means that a new productive challenge depends more and more on 'managing the non-contractual elements in contract' (Elam 1993:35). To make sure that all participants in complex innovative endeavours have good reasons for trusting each other is a very difficult task in today's context because of the nature of the modern system of production. Modern organizations, which operate in such a way that roles are open to negotiation and interpretation, face the increased demand for trust because '[t]he more the negotiation, the more the need for trust because the less the boundaries and content of specific role expectations can be explained according to rigid or formalized codes' (Seligman 1997:41). The connection between the increased division of labour and the increased demand for trust brings with it a higher degree of indeterminacy, which – as it cannot be stabilized any more through members' mutual familiarity – should be achieved by relying on some regulations that are 'formal and visible in character rather than informal and invisible' (Elam 1993:35). It is difficult to think about any other way of achieving this task than by providing the opportunity for the development of networks, which allow participants to join forces with others in the collective process of learning. Hence, the growing appreciation of informal networks, seen – because of their role in the creation of trust – as the essential condition to maintain interaction and the flow of tacit knowledge.

While an opportunity for the open-ended negotiation of trust depends upon free negotiations of the boundaries of interaction and free-of-rules interaction, the practical results of the creative process are connected with the existence of limits to openness and with the introduction of coherent rules and formalized procedures. In this view, the innovation process can be successful only when people involved in it are, on one hand, relatively free from rules and regulations, while, on the other hand, they function within wider formalized structures able to provide them with some codes of behaviour. Networks, by enlarging the chance of communication and commitment, while, at the same time, functioning within the formal patterns of regulation, are, therefore, a significant aspect of any process of innovation. Hence, both informality and formality should be seen as the crucial and dynamic aspects of the process of innovation, the success of which depends upon finding the optimal balance between these two styles of interaction.

Part III

Informality in the changing world

7 Technology and informality

A connected world: towards a digital Utopia?

Interactive telecommunications – telematic technology ... speaks a language of cooperation, creativity and transformation. It is a technology not of monologue but of conversation. It feeds fecund open-endedness rather than an aesthetics of closure and completion (Ascott 1991:115).

In this part of the book we look at some empirical evidence of the importance of informality in the contemporary world. Nowadays the concept of informality is most frequently used in relation to forms of interaction on the Internet and in relation to forms of social life in communist and postcommunist societies. We will start our discussion with an examination of informality online and its role in enhancing the Internet's function as 'the most powerful driver for innovation that the world has ever seen' (Cairncross 1997:118). In the following chapter, we look at various strategies of informalization as responses to the structural characteristics of communist and postcommunist states.

The effects of electronic computerized communication on the nature of interaction are difficult to overlook. Many new studies focus on the growing importance of communication based on electronically mediated interaction and show how it changes our social life. The introduction of electronic devices makes a substantial difference in the nature of communication mainly by liberating exchange of information from constraints of space and time. It is also argued that electronic media create a very special category of communication able to provide participants with an experience of an informal and intimate interaction. Since '[t]he informality of electronic messages is heightened when the medium is bidirectional and interactive' (Meyrowitz 1985:109), we will focus here not on one-way communication media (although the role of television should not be underestimated) but only on what de Sola Pool labelled 'technologies of freedom'.

In what follows we will briefly describe the explosive growth of the Internet, the development of which is often presented as exemplifying 'the death of distance' and promising a more democratic world, and hence revitalizing discussions of a vision of a global electronic community. The impact of electronic computerized communication on the nature of interaction will be further discussed by examining civility, sociability and intimacy online through a closer look at the network society, virtual communities and the main features of the relationships resulting from electronic proximity. Since each new technology is – as Marshall McLuhan argues – initially understood in terms of its predecessors, in order to comprehend the impact of new communication technologies on society, we start with an examination of the changes brought by the telephone. Although the telephone was the first 'technology of freedom', even today its role cannot be underestimated because it has inspired so many changes to societal structures and institutions and because recent innovations (mobile phones, the decline of the cost of international calls) are still reshaping the nature of societal interaction.

The telephone, like other new means of electronic communication, is an agent of effective action and serves society's many varied, and even contradictory, needs. It is 'a facilitating rather than a constraining device' because it 'adds to human freedom' by transforming our relations to space and by allowing us to use this new freedom however we choose (de Sola Pool 1977:3–4). Unlike electronic mail, but like face-to-face contact, telephone conversation is 'real time' and synchronous. However, telephone contacts differ from traditional face-to-face encounters in two ways: they transcend distance and they transmit only audio information (Thorngren 1977). On the other hand, the telephone conversation tends to be more informal, while 'asynchronous communication, like letter writing, has tended to be more formal and less off-the-cuff exchanges' (Negroponte 1995:167). Because telephone conversation includes informal, moment-to-moment, backstage region experience, it facilitates personal, intimate and very casual types of conversation. Hence, the liberating impact of the telephone manifests itself in its contribution to the expansion of informality in our relationships.

Because of its informality and intimacy, the telephone is an important instrument sustaining the already established bonds of friendship and family relations. The telephone networks, especially the early ones that favoured local over long-distance conversation, enhanced the existing social networks of communication and reinforced community social habits (Fischer 1984). However, since telephone conversation does not create a totally different and new set of relations, but only reinforces existing networks of contacts, it is not a substitute for face-to-face contact but rather an additional channel for communicating with friends, family and co-workers (de Sola Pool 1977; Thorngren 1977). This function of the phone, that is, talking to friends and family, is gaining importance with the increase in geographical mobility and tourism, and with the declining cost of international calls. The advertising slogan of Britain's BT – 'It's good to talk'– suggests that business or instrumental calls become a less essential part of telecommunication companies' operations, while social calls, which tend to last longer than the typical business calls and which are made for the most part by women, are an important source of profit. For women the telephone is a valued substitute for personal contacts and ongoing telephone communication between female family members constitutes an important part of women's support structure and contributes significantly to women's sense of well-being, security, stability and self-esteem (Moyal 1989:12). The main group of users of Australian telephone lines are young professional women, born in another country, making long social calls to friends back home (Cairncross 1997:241). Since the telephone enhances key female relationships and creates a 'psychological neighbourhood for women', it can be defined as a form of care-giving, provision of support and friendships (Moyal 1989:15).

The introduction of the telephone did more than enable people to communicate over long distances. It made possible the separation between production and administration, as well as the creation of national markets in stocks and commodities. It had an impact on urban structures and caused mass migration to suburbia; it challenged existing class relations by extending the boundary of who may speak to whom. It reduced isolation and danger for rural families, while city dwellers used it as a babysitter. It led to new social and occupational roles, it reinforced the teenage peer group and it also altered modes of courtship and possibilities of romance (Cherry 1977; Poster 1990; Sproull and Kiesler 1991). Recently the enormous expansion of mobile phones (now more than half of all new telephones worldwide are mobile and within five years almost one in three telephones will be mobile; *The Economist*, Survey of Telecommunications, 13 September, 1997:16) allows for better use of time and helps to overcome the rigidity of our timetables as we now communicate even when we are walking to work, driving a car or shopping. This new convenience, which makes possible the crossing of past divisions between various locations and activities blurs the difference between the public and private and that 'makes people feel that the private lives and messages of others are their private property as entertainment' (Woollacott 1998:7). The mobile phone can also change definitions of our roles and our duties as well as raise 'productivity by using previously idle time' (Cairncross 1997:7). Furthermore, new inventions, such as answering machines and voice mail, have helped to overcome the rather interruptive or intrusive nature of the telephone. Consequently, it can be said that the telephone has been steadily overcoming its limitations and that it has been transformed from a medium of exchange of information into a medium with the potential for meeting a wide range of needs. Moreover, fibre-optic telephone lines are an essential aspect of the communication revolution because their capacity and digitization enable images to be broken down into computer codes and sent down telephone wires with enormous speed. Consequently, further advancement in the process of reducing the constraints of physical proximity has led to a new phenomenon of electronic proximity.

With the development of electronic communication McLuhan's 'global village' is now not only a seductive image but it is technically feasible (Woolley 1992). Enthusiasts see the promise of a digital Utopia in the convergence of computers, telephones and television sets and in a rapidly expanding system of networks, collectively known as the Internet. The Internet, unheard of a decade ago, was being used in early 1997 by an estimated fifty-seven million people around the world, with another thirteen million using it for electronic mail (Cairncross 1997:2). In 1997 alone over 95 billion e-mail messages were transmitted around the world, 10 billion more than the number of letters (Woolley 1998:11). The Internet, with the explosive speed, becomes not only a new global means of communicating but also the universal source of instantaneous knowledge.

The Internet is a physically decentralized constellation of computers linked to vast stores of information. The invention in 1989 of the World Wide Web has brought to the Internet hypertext and multimedia, while with the Netscape browser, the use of the Internet 'seized the public imagination' (Brown 1997:97). Since 1993 the Internet has had many uses: from finding information and providing electronic mail services to carrying telephone calls and television programmes as well as facilitating newsgroups and mailing lists. The Net, which is an informal term for the loosely interconnected networks that use computer mediated communication (CMC) technology, is broader than Internet since it includes all interconnected, interoperating computer networks including commercial services such as Prodigy or America Online, CompuServe and bulletin board services. Since the early 1990s the number of Internet commercial hosts has been increasing rapidly (while in 1991 there were about 9000 commercial domains, by the end of 1994 this had increased to 21 700; Castells 1996:355; Wellman *et al* 1996:215). In particular the last few years has seen a dramatic increase in the density of Internet hosts, which is the best indirect indication of the amount of Internet-based economic activity. The number of Web sites worldwide rose from 55 million to 230 million in the first ten months of 1997 (*The Economist*, 21 February, 1998:116). The Internet has rapidly become an important marketing tool for large multinationals and there is much evidence that these companies, by gaining a profile of their customers and by monitoring their clients' behaviour – which allows them to create special products and address niche markets – have increased their profits.

The commercialization of the Net is problematic not only because it raises questions of pricing, access, censorship and copyright as well as how and by whom the Internet will be managed and mediated, but also because of its relatively low profitability due to the still small number of users. Even in the USA, the most wired society in the world, less than seven per cent of the population was connected in 1995 (*The Economist*, Survey of the Internet, 1 July, 1995:12). By contrast Algeria, at the same time, had 16 registered users of the Internet (Wellman *et al* 1996:216). With one American home in five having a PC with a modem, Americans made up over half of all world users in 1997 (Cairncross 1997:111 and 95). Moreover, the spread of this technology is not only uneven between countries but also within countries. For instance, in American society the gap between information technology haves and have-nots, even in the context of the declining prices of computers, has not been closing. In 1989, nearly 6 per cent of the lowest income households in the USA had a computer, and close to 2 per cent of the lowest income households used network services at home, whereas nearly 35 per cent of the highest earning quartile had computers at home and over 11 per cent of the highest income individuals used them. Four years later, the income gap in household computer access was even wider, with respective figures 7 per cent and 3 per cent for the lowest income group and 55 per cent and 23 per cent for the highest income individuals (Bikson and Panis 1997:414–17).

The average user of the Net is a 'largely politically conservative, white man, often single, English-speaking, affluent, residing in North America, professional, manager or student' (Wellman *et al* 1996:216). Although trends suggest an increasing participation of women (in 1995 making up only around 20 per cent of users), non-English speakers and people of lower socioeconomic status (Wellman *et al* 1996:216), we are far away from universal access and there is a danger that the new communications revolution may exacerbate rather than meliorate this inequality. Many realists remind us that only a fifth of the population currently have even telephones, that only one per cent of the world's population enjoys a connection to the Internet (Brown 1997:17), that computers are still costly, and that around the world there are still relatively high levels of adult illiteracy (in the USA 20 per cent; Doheny-Farina 1996:144). Therefore, the idea of a digital world is simply 'laughable' (Stallabrass 1995:19).

Despite pessimistic predictions that the information highway may leave many 'stranded in the technological version of inner-city ghettos' (Reich 1994:19), nobody doubts that the digital revolution will inspire enormous social and cultural changes. Optimistically oriented writers, who see the Net as evolving into an open, global forum to which anybody can contribute, in which information is shared and important problems discussed, insist that it is only an issue of time, that young people have symbiotic relationships with the Net and that for them it is a means of empowerment, which, moreover, they use as they want (Rushkoff 1994). Furthermore, according to this line of argument, there are so many people on the Net, using it in so many different ways and for so many different purposes (from therapeutic to criminal) that no one can really keep track of, or effectively censor, its context. Another hope connected with the Net's liberatory potential is based on the fact that it is not dominated by a single large industry. Not only is the Internet still largely outside of the control of the mass media (Rheingold 1993) but it is still a largely decentralized constellation, without core power, therefore promising democracy. However, although today the Internet has 'no central command' and 'nobody owns the Internet, runs it, maintains it, or acts as gatekeeper or regulator' (Cairncross 1997:95), new trends for decentralization and commercialization are opening new gaps and bringing new threats to these celebrated features of the Net. When evaluating the Net's character we should remember that the unique and exclusive position of the Net is

fragile and to some degree connected with the initial stage of its development. Furthermore, while acknowledging that computer-based technologies, as all technologies, are neutral, we should be aware that it is very
difficult to characterize the Net's nature because it still continuously evolves,
is complex, sophisticated and often indeterminate (Doheny-Farina 1996;
Stallabrass 1995).

This indeterminacy and continuously changing nature make the Net a
special phenomenon. The Net is unique because it is 'a new domain of
human activity', because it is 'not technology *per se* but the social interaction
it is inspiring' (Kiesler 1997:x). It has been called the superhighway, frontier,'
virtual community, the third place, Agora, the wired neighbourhood.
Travelling on the Internet is frequently characterized as being chaotic, confusing and fragmented. This is attributed to the Net's formlessness, consisting in 'its potentially limitless plasticity in supporting or implementing
different forms of communication media. It makes communication possible
without being a medium for communication itself' (Shardlow 1996:14). This
means seeing the Internet not as a new medium but as 'something that
makes possible a collection of new media – e-mail, newsgroups and the
'World Wide Web' (*ibid*). Apart from its formless, chaotic and changing
nature, the Net's accidental development is another of its unique features.

It started with *Accidental Empires*, which were built by groups of 'kids wear-
ing jeans and T-shirts' who developed personal computers and the personal
computer industry while searching for 'adventure, not business' (Cringely
1992:264 and 47). The big, traditional computer companies for the most
part rejected the microprocessor because 'they just did not have the vision
needed to invent the personal computer [...]. They didn't understand the
idea. These were intelligent men, but they had a firmly fixed concept of what
computing was supposed to be' (*ibid*:42). Therefore, the personal computer
was invented by hobbyists, people who were not limited by formal organizational goals. 'Only those who aren't trying to make money can afford to
advance a technology that does not pay' (*ibid*:45). The computer for these
people was 'a talisman of a new kind of war of liberation' or the latest battle
in the counterculture campaign (Rheingold 1993:48).

The Internet has emerged almost by accident and its spread has been a
result of spontaneous demand from millions of users (Rheingold 1993).
Although computer mediated communication networks are a spin-off of
American military research (Cairncross 1997), the use of the communication capacities of networks emerged 'somewhat unexpectedly' and mainly in
the world of universities. These grassroots parts of electronic networks have
been growing explosively ever since, although now the use of the Internet
also rapidly expands to the business world. 'For the past two decades, teenager hackers and pony-tailed ex-hippies have been labouring in American
university computer labs to build the Internet. Now it is the turn of smartly
besuited young men in gleaming corporate offices to take it over' (*The Economist*, Survey of the Internet, 1 July, 1995:14). Having the university world as

the common ground for the development of the Net has consequently shaped the process of its diffusion and the habits of electronic communication. It has also helped to preserve a relative openness and innovativness of the system. The new electronic systems have also helped 'Baby Boomers with computers' to resurrect 'the central tenet of hippie romanticism', which advises: 'Do your own thing' (Seabrook 1997:88).

The first generation of Net users were people committed to the idea of generalized communication, full of 'utopian, communal and liberation' dreams (Castells 1996:357). The case of the WELL (Whole Earth 'Lectronic Link – a computer conferencing system that enables public conversations and exchange of private e-mail), an online service set up by ex-hippies in Berkeley, California, during the mid-1980s, illustrates well this undercurrent (Rheingold 1993). This group consisted of writers, journalists, academics, students and founders of communes from the 1960s as well as many other people with experience of years of living in communes. All of them brought their willingness to participate in communal exchange and many of them also contributed their communal experience to creating an online community. Their involvement as well as the development of 'the cyberdelic wing of fringe computer culture' (with many famous people from the sixties as participants: for instance, one such is Timothy Leary, prophet of LSD who announces that 'PC is the LSD of the 1990s'; in Dery 1996:22) often led to exaggerated media claims that the cyber-hyppie 'reconciles the transcendentalist impulses of sixties counterculture with the informania of the nineties' (Dery 1996:22). Consequently, the return of the culture of the 1960s, the union of scientific and non-scientific cultures, links between cyber and punk culture are often presented as eroding 'the supposed dividing line between bohemians and technicians' in today's America (Sterling 1992:235). However, this pioneering era was soon replaced by the second wave of Net users and 'what remains from the counterculture origins of the network is the informality and self-directedness of communication, the idea that many contribute to many, and yet each one has her own voice and expects an individualized answer' (Castells 1996:357). Looking at the number and the role of many 'countercultural entrepreneurs', for whom the Net offers the possibility of entering into business, we need to admit that the Internet is still rather successful in bringing together those who belong to these two opposite poles.

This ability to diminish tensions between the counterculture and the entrepreneurship culture is a result of the fact that the Net can be used for just about everything; for printing, publishing, marketing, debating, entertainment, education, exchanging information and so on. Within Usenet one can join a thousand newsgroups (which are divided by topic area), or post a message at computer bulletin-board-systems (known as BBSs) or participate in hosted conferences or play interactive computer games, send electronic mail or have an intimate chat within an Internet Chat zone (where people can carry on conversations on-line in real time with the help of various operating systems, for instance the Internet Real Chat). Although the Net's openness, the informality and self-directedness of this form of communication as well as its enormous complexity and formlessness, together with its continuous evolution, make it difficult to evaluate the character of the Internet and the related networks that make up the greater Net, we have enough evidence to assume that it can offer some new opportunities for more flexible, interactive, decentralized and democratic modes of communication. The full realization of this potential depends upon many factors. Among them the most important, I think, is the style of interactional practice on this medium. In what follows we will describe the impact of electronic computerized communication on civility, seen as a style of interaction shaped by the relationships between informality and formality in the network society.

THE NETWORK SOCIETY: CIVILITY ONLINE

> Networks are appropriate instruments for a capitalist economy based on innovation, globalization and decentralized concentration; for work, workers, and firms based on flexibility, and adaptability; for a culture of endless deconstruction and reconstruction; for a polity geared towards the instant processing of new values and public moods, for a social organization aiming at the suppression of space and the annihilation of time (Castells 1996:471).

In many theories of transition from an industrial to a post-industrial society the term 'network' is frequently used to capture the emergence of more fluid, flexible and dense organizational relationships that cut across various inter- and intra-organizational boundaries. In studies focusing on the emergence of an information society, the concept 'network' points to new modes of organization made possible by advances in telecommunication technologies. Recently these two uses of the term 'network' have converged in Manuel Castells' idea of the network society.

The concept of the network society is used by Castells (1996) to describe the main trends shaping contemporary societies. Several elements come together to give rise to the new reality of the network society; among them the most important are: business networks, technological tools (new telecommunication networks), global competition and the functioning of the state. All of them working together have made up a new mode of development that alters capitalism, although it does not replace it. The information technology revolution and the restructuring of capitalism have permitted the increase in flexibility, adaptability and networking in the economic, political and cultural spheres. 'The convergence of social evolution and information technologies has created a new material basis for the performance of activities throughout the social structure. This material basis, built in networks, earmarks dominant social processes, thus shaping social structure itself' (Castells 1996:471). The networks' processes and their dynamics are enacted by the speed of operating information technologies, which in turn affect functions and structure in our societies. As a result of this convergence the industrial era's institutions and organizations of civil society, which were constructed around the democratic state and the social contract between labour and capital, have become 'empty shells, decreasingly able to relate to people's lives and values' (Castells 1997:355).

As the networks' processes are shaped by the speed of operating information technologies, a network-based social structure is a highly dynamic, open system, suiting the capitalist economy based on innovation, globalization, the mobility of capital and the deaggregation of labour. What is new about the network society is not that it is divided – this was always the case in all societies – but that this time there are 'few rules about how to win and how to lose' (Castells 1996:278). As previously well-defined structures are beginning to lose their edges, as seemingly permanent things are starting continuously to change and as past relationships are eroding, labour becomes more dependent on individual bargaining conditions in a very unpredictable labour market. The uniqueness of the network society also expresses itself in the fact that, for the first time in history, the basic unit of economic organization is not the individual or collective subject but the network made up of a variety of subjects and organizations, which are 'relentlessly modified as networks adapt to supportive environments and market structures' (Castells 1996:198).

An organization is not an isolated facility of production but rather a node in the complex network, or a set of interconnected nodes of suppliers, customers, engineering and other service functions. These networks, since they share the same communication codes, are not purely instrumental or accidental alliances. Consequently, although there is no one unifying 'network culture', there is a common cultural code, which expresses the essence of contemporary transformations. This new cultural and institutional configuration underlying the network society's organizational forms of life is 'the spirit of informationalism' (Castells 1996:195–9). The ethical foundation of the networks enterprise 'is a mulifaceted, virtual culture', which consists of a 'patchwork' of diverse, eclectic and ephemeral cultures, speeding through electronic channels (Castells 1996:199). Thus, the consequences of the processes of social transformation summarized under the ideal type of the network society are not only bound to technical or economic dimensions of society. The unavoidable fragmentary, fractured and confused nature of communication also affects the spheres of culture and power. In what follows the nature of relations and ties in the networks of firms and companies functioning within virtual culture will be analysed. Finally, we look at the political expressions and relationships as they become increasingly mediated and facilitated by electronic communication.

Today's economies, due to the process of globalization, the rapid entry and exit of competitors, the unpredictable emergence of new products and technologies, the customization of demand, function in an increasingly uncertain, ambiguous and risky environment. In order to respond to these conditions, firms must be fast, flexible, responsive and knowledge intensive. Thus, it is argued in many new theories, they need to change from vertical bureaucracies to horizontal corporations, adopt not only flat hierarchies but team management, move to measuring performance by customer satisfaction and rewards based on team performance and training and re-training of employees of all levels. Consequently, the globalization of competition dissolves the large corporation into a web of multidirectional networks, which – as the actual operating unit – relies on computer mediated communication.

In theories of post-Fordism and in the flexible specialization thesis, infrastructure of communications and computer facilities are presented as the factors enhancing the process of vertical disintegration, decentralization and as helping to coordinate and control dispersed activities. Now, when 'the strict and regular rhythms and routines of the Golden Age of capitalism have been significantly eroded', we are confronted with 'a chaotic and disordered world' (Elam 1994:65). Consequently, it is the network production, viewed as 'a learning system', which fosters high-trust relations (Sabel 1994:121). It is also argued that flexible specialization induces work to be more information intensive, thus, encouraging higher skill levels and employee participation in all aspects of work, including the design of work. 'Here we have the worker depicted as informationally sensitive, made aware by advanced technologies of what is happening throughout the production process and able to respond intelligently to improve the overall system' (Webster 1995:159). Information technology and electronic networks are seen as transforming hierarchies into networks by reducing the number of management levels, by making communication easier across time and space, by increasing interorganizational links, which consequently contributes to the blurring of boundaries between firms, suppliers and customers, and by enhancing companies' flexibility through helping to reorganize the storage of knowledge, systems of monitoring, controlling and planning (Nohria and Eccles 1992:290–1). Hence, electronic networks are seen as adding to the flexibility of the system, ensuring innovation in a fast-changing environment and enhancing the emergence of 'the horizontal corporation' or 'virtual company' (Davidow and Malone 1992), which is 'a dynamic and strategically planned network of self-programmed, self-directed units based on decentralization, participation, and coordination' (Castells 1996:166).

Electronic networks are also seen as permitting the development of new social and work relations and providing opportunities for developing relatively new forms of work organization. However, there has been contradictory evidence about how the introduction of computer mediated communication really affects relations among co-workers and forms of work. According to one perspective, the informality of organizational relationships is increasing with the introduction of computers as: '[o]lder forms of hierarchy and division of labour are replaced by more informal relations' (Heydebrand 1990:281). Collegiality and individual autonomy are extended, stronger emphases are placed on negotiation and on 'results' and the weighing of interest rather than on the observation of correct procedural forms. For other writers, the introduction of information technologies results only in the reinforcement of existing divisions, the reduction of employment, the increase in casual, part-time employment and the deskilling as well as the isolation of workers and decline of the importance of workers' loyalty and commitment to work (Amin 1994; Webster 1995; Sennett 1998). Although there is not yet a full evaluation of the impact of computer mediated communication on work and organizational relations, it seems that there are, as always, elements of truth in both approaches.

On one hand, new forms of work based on the employment of new tele-communication technologies are driven by new market conditions that are promoting organizational restructuring and downsizing, therefore new work hierarchies emerge and some groups' positions and relationships are nega-tively affected. On the other hand, it is also argued that e-mail, fax machines and computers create the opportunity to move an entire office to the home and that the growing number of people working from their homes can gain more autonomy, flexibility and can better accommodate family obligations. The reality is even more complex as working from home, so-called 'teleworking', is a double-edged sword, and, moreover, it affects differently various groups of employees. While some teleworkers benefit from these new arrangements, others, especially managers, feel their power is threat-ened and that their careers suffer because they are invisible or not present where decisions are taken (Wellman *et al* 1996:228). Other studies suggest that while people enjoy the remoteness of supervision and the flexibility of work schedules and autonomy, they resent the lack of distinct separation between family and work and experience difficulties connected with the con-fusion of codes of behaviour (Gurstein, quoted in Castells 1996:361). Fur-thermore, telework reinforces the gender division of household labour because women teleworkers do more household work. Even more impor-tantly, for some employees teleworking leads to 'more structured and for-malized communication with supervisors and to lesser extent with coworkers' (Wellman *et al* 1996:229). The nature of informal communica-tions by teleworkers appears to depend on the employees' social status, their previous relationships and the support of organizations. For instance, aca-demics and other professionals maintain work-related networks, while ser-vice and clerical workers become more isolated. 'New work force hierarchies that emerge from teleworking segregate those who lack contacts, while those that have benefit richly' (Wellman *et al* 1996:229–30).

The impact of 'virtual companies' on our life is also seen as controversial. Observers vary in their opinion as to whether the introduction of electronic communication, by blurring the boundaries between home and work, decentralizes work or not. While some argue that working time has lost its traditional centrality throughout the lifecycle (Castells 1996), others stress that the loss of work centrality in our lives has not really resulted in making home into the centre of our public and private lives (Doheny-Farina 1996). Still others, like Wellman *et al* (1996), argue that computer mediated communication (CMC), by moving workers home, provides a basis for the revival of neighbourhood life. However, the attraction of the Net can also lead to a total elimination of the centre. 'The result of the omnipresence of the Net is that all centres – work centres, school centres and living centres – become less and less relevant' (Kohn 1997:45). In this way, computer mediated communication may further contribute to the decline of social contacts and the increase of social isolation; subsequently, it can undermine – by reducing encounters between strangers – the role of civility as a social norm.

From one perspective, the network society and its virtual companies are in the process of constant change and shifting roles, in the state of perpetual transformation. Yet from another perspective, virtual companies can be more stable and unchanging than their contemporary counterparts. 'The nature of new business relationships will result in stronger and more enduring ties and based on a mutual destiny, one shared by groups of both suppliers and customers ... . Thus, the virtual corporation may appear amorphous and in perpetual flux, but it will be permanently nestled within a tight network of relationships' (Davidow and Malone 1992:142). This stability, based on a common fate, mutual obligation and trust, is presented in the literature as the necessary features of the new type of relationship in the network society. With the end of the traditional arm's length relationship between suppliers and buyers, customers and manufacturers, and so on, effective network organizations require a kind of trustworthy, multidimensional and stable relationship. However, as we have already shown, these types of relationship cannot merely develop on the basis of distinct electronic communication, a fact not always acknowledged by prophets of virtual companies.

The argument supporting the role of familiarity, face-to-face contacts and common tradition in creating trust relations comes not only from studies suggesting that trust is established by common experience and often 'reinforced by ethnic allegiances or local pride' (Sabel 1994:133). The thesis about the importance of co-presence and familiarity for the generation of trust is also supported by the studies of electronically mediated exchange, which provide evidence that electronic communication cannot replace all face-to-face interaction. Nohira and Eccles, while not suggesting that there is no role for e-mail in the network organization, argue that although electronically mediated exchange can increase the range, amount, and velocity of information flow in a network organization: 'the viability and effectiveness of this electronic network will depend critically on underlying networks of social relationships based on face-to face interaction' (1992:290). Furthermore, McKenney, Zack and Doherty's (1992) study, which focused on the ways managers use electronic exchange in performing different roles and stages of problem solving and organizing, also proved that managers rely not only on electronic media but that they piece together face-to-face meetings, electronic communication and one-on-one exchanges on the phone. Therefore, in order for the networks enterprise to work effectively, it cannot be built on electronic networks alone since electronically mediated communication is not the best medium for constructing trust relationships, mobilization or negotiations (Nohira and Eccles 1992).

Some observers also worry that the elimination of face-to-face contact can have a negative impact on the quality of the decision-making process in organizations. They argue that without the human element, without seeing 'the fear and hope' on the faces of co-workers and customers, managerial decisions might become more logical but not necessarily better or more humane (Husted 1996:33). Furthermore, electronic groups' performance is also described as less civil and more conflictual. In a comparison with other forms of communication in an organization, electronic communication will be relatively less conventional, more risky and, since high-status people will not dominate discussion, more democratic. However, group decision-making via such a medium will be very difficult, conflictual and may not necessarily provide the best results. 'When the group decide via computer, people have difficulty discovering how other group members feel. It is hard for them to reach consensus. When they disagree, they engage in deeper conflict. Conventional behaviour, such as politeness and acknowledgment of other views, decreases' (Sproull and Kiesler 1991:67). Electronic group decisions are not only unpredictable, unconventional and riskier, they also may not be optimal for all types of situations; for instance if a decision requires complex and delicate multiparty negotiations 'face-to-face communication is better than electronic communication because it is hard to persuade subtly in electronic communication' (Sproull and Kiesler 1991:73).

The argument that electronic communication and electronic meetings are not equivalent to face-to-face encounters is also supported by many studies of internal organizational communications. Since electronic mail, compared to other media, requires little effort to add multiple recipients to a message, to send messages to distribution lists or to capture electronic messages for resending, privileged information spreads through corporations, allowing even peripheral members of organizations to be better informed (Kraut and Attwell 1997). The study of the proliferation of electronic communication in large organizations suggests that electronic mail does not just broadcast organizational gossip or jokes, but also spreads organizational information, which increases employees' commitment to its management's goal. Nonetheless, many managers feel threatened by the flow of information because of their lack of control over its content (Wellman *at al* 1996). For instance, the informality of e-mail and its lack of respect for hierarchies were the reasons behind Japanese managers' initial reluctance to accept this medium of communication (*The Economist*, 12 August, 1995:57). Furthermore, informal electronic communication may reduce work stress and integrate peripheral employees; it can also be dysfunctional for an organization because conflictual or subversive messages may be exchanged. For instance, striking Israeli academics used electronic networks to coordinate their action against their employers, the universities (Pliskin and Romm 1994). Electronic mailing can also be a threat to organizational goals because people can, as anecdotal evidence suggests, devote themselves totally to sociability online (still the majority of people are doing it from their offices), subsequently forgetting that they are actually at work. Many companies, assuming that employees' pleasure in chatting on the Net results in a neglect of their official duties, try to regulate the situation.

There are also other consequences of electronic mail's capacity to allow us to communicate with the outside world. It can isolate people as the importance and pleasure of e-mail relationships is valued more than talking to the person at the next desk or the next office. Evidence of the loss of collegiality comes from various types of organizations, with universities especially looking very fragmented and not bonded by common identities. The recent international survey of academics discovered that in every country the largest proportion of respondents attached the highest importance to their academic discipline, with whose representatives they are increasingly in electronic contact. Their department and their institutions are not regarded as such important sources of affiliation and identification (*The Economist*, Survey: Universities, 17 October, 1997:20).

While the increased use of electronic communication blurs the differences between people who are here and people in different geographical locations and confuses the differences between strangers and friends, it raises the need for some regulations or agencies that can govern these situations where there is no mutual embeddedness in social relations, where, therefore, many traditional forms of social control are not available. The combined effects of information technology and globalization are making it easier for businesses to hide their dealings and profits. Since many transactions conducted over the Internet are hard to track, companies may ensure their dominant position in the market place without being subject to any control or rules. Subsequently, as the scope of tax avoidance and cheating increases and as the number of invisible connections between commercial enterprises grows, questions about how to generate trust within electronic networks and how to collectively maintain it over time are becoming central to computer mediated communication.

These dilemmas, however, do not seem to bother the Net enthusiasts. The future of relationships online does not represent a problem for believers in a digital Utopia. For instance, Cairncross (1997:xiv) optimistically ensures that trust will be flourishing in the connected world because it will be easier to check whether people and companies deliver what they promise, thus 'people will be more likely to trust each other to keep their word'. This argument that the new Information Age will spontaneously generate its own morality, because the technology permits us to monitor each other's truthworthiness, goes together with the assumption that the state's responsibilities and intervention will be reduced. Thus, national citizenship in its present form will be replaced by a world in which sovereign individuals contract with one another and with agencies that supply protective services (Cairncross 1997; Davidson and Rees-Mogg 1997). Furthermore, this perspective seems to endorse Apple's claim that: 'digital technology and democracy are two sides of the very same coin'. Electronic communication is seen here as allowing people to communicate their views to government more directly, therefore 'rules and representatives will become more sensitive to lobbying and public opinion polls' (Cairncross 1997:xvi). However, serious criticism can be addressed to the prospects of such electronic democracy, where civility and trust are not a result of a shared culture and civil life but are enhanced by 'cybersociety', where not many can participate and in which political institutions are designed for the national, not for the international, circulation of people, capital, commodities and services.

Hopes for the Net to be a new Agora, where a more decentralized, more direct and more democratic decision-making process takes place, are widely held and they can be attributed to several features of the Internet. Firstly, the Net increases accessibility to and the scope of information, and, moreover, this electronic information is not expensive to obtain. Many countries now follow the American example, where many government documents are open to public scrutiny: for instance, a full text of every House bill since 1992 is published on the Net. It is assumed that electronic availability not only undermines elitism and the culture of bureaucracy, but it can also – because of a lack of censorship or governmental control over the flow of information – 'help to keep governments honest' (Cairncross 1997:260). Secondly, new communications technology provides citizens with voices not only because electronic communication makes it easier and faster to send views to politicians. It also increases citizens' power because electronic communication can encourage the further transformation of political debate in direction of direct democracy, where voting from home and frequent referendums will lower the importance of representative aspects of democracy. However, while agreeing that broad access to computers and electronic networks might help to reduce, if not reverse, the trends towards disengagement in civic and political affairs, we need also to be aware that it might be an illusionary promise.

Many of these ideas about the Net being a new Agora can be seen as the result of people's fascination with the new medium and their too optimistic faith in technological solutions to social and political problems. Rheingold (1993:288) notes that the notion of putting powerful computers in the hands of citizens would shield the citizenry against totalitarian authorities echoes the beliefs of eighteenth-century revolutionaries that placing firearms in the hands of people was crucial to overthrowing autocrats. Furthermore, electronic democracy advocates do not always confront the facts and are not always willing to admit that the practical realization of the democratic potential of electronic communication does not always look very promising.

Singapore, where Internet providers and producers need licences and must purge material that is politically, religiously and sexually offensive (*Guardian Weekly*, 14 April, 1996:22), illustrates that 'cybernetic technology can happily coexist with the centralized political grip' (Brown 1997:84). Singapore is not the only country that tries to control material on the Internet. While in some nations the main focus is on banning pornography, provocative and hateful messages with criminal intent, in others state laws prevent the free exchange of political ideas. For instance, in China, governmental rules bar users from doing anything on line to harm national unity or incite the overthrow of the system (*The Australian*, 17 February, 1998:8). However, the Internet is inherently resistant to censorship and a race between regulators and campaigners for free speech online will continue and it will depend upon individual users' responsibility and accountability whether or not there will be a threat to democracy. Thus, the importance of cybercitizens' civility cannot be overlooked. This urgency for a clear message about the need for civility has recently been realized by an American court, which convicted of hate crime a student charged with harassing Asians on the Internet (*The Australian*, 4 February, 1998:10). The growing number of hate crimes committed online sends a timely warning that respect towards other users of the Net cannot be taken for granted.

Another threat to the democratic potential offered by the Internet is the result of a lack of real socio-technical visions among the world's ruling elite. This lack of vision not only erodes the development of the true potential of the digital world but also permits corporate bodies to jump ahead not only of tax collectors but also of social responsibilities in general (Brown 1997). When regulators and world leaders do not have knowledge and vision, the concentration of power in the new information order may undermine the checks and balances of representative democracy. The search for human accountability and transparency of the decision-making process is an important step towards an electronic Agora, where isolated but well-informed individuals come together to debate and where egalitarian, not monopolistic, relationships are dominant. Another step towards democracy online, where a wider, deeper and more egalitarian citizen involvement in matters of state can be realized, should lead us to rethink how to revitalize public discourse and how to protect it from commercialization and commoditization. Taking into account the advancement of the process of commercialization of the Net and noticing that the greatest weakness of the idea of electronic democracy is 'that it can be more easily commodified than explained' (Rheingold 1993:289), do not allow our hopes for wide and free public communication to be raised too high.

It is often argued that the success of commercial television contributed to the loss of citizens' interest and participation in the political process. Now, when politics has to be framed in the language of electronically based media, we can expect changes in the nature, aims and organization of political processes, political actors and political institutions. 'Ultimately, the powers that are in the media networks take second place to the power of flows embodied in the structure and language of these networks' (Castells 1996:476). It seems that the Internet, by spreading a peculiar brand of news, politics, showbiz and gossip, where it is very difficult to distinguish what is a lie, gossip or genuine information and where it is very difficult to establish the reliability of sources of information, has pushed the process of the personalization and scandalization of politics even further. It was on this new medium that Monica Lewinsky's allegations against President Clinton were first made public. American news organizations were forced to admit that it amounted to the Internet's coming of age as a media news force and that from now on the public gets to read not only 'all news that's fit to print' but also the worst gossip 'of quality not seen', based on nothing else than on 'Washington and Hollywood insiders' chatter' (Cash 1998:25). After breaking the Clinton sex scandal, Matt Drudge's *Report*, which has more than 1 000 000 online subscribers, received over 400 000 'hits' a day. Drudge, the most widely read columnist in America, gets at least 450 tips a day, making his e-mail address 'the favoured dirty laundry chute of the political and media elite' (Cash 1998:26). Drudge's online programme does not only lower the level of reporting and spread tabloid culture, it also undermines the opportunities for rational dialogue because this type of politics is abstracted from any ideological content, history or geography. Although even politics through and by the electronic medium cannot be reduced to any media effect, the fact that political actors 'exist in power game through and by the media' (Castells 1996:476), indicates that technology impacts on power and culture.

The vision of a democratic future as achieved by technological progress stresses new opportunities for direct connections of citizens with politicians through electronic mail. While it is true that the increasing numbers of political leaders, members of parliament, political parties and governments now have 'public mailboxes' open to voters, this does not provide people with real exchange. If you send an e-mail to any American congressman or senator, writes Moore (1995:122), what you will get back is a rapid letter from an auto-responder, which is a software that receives messages, takes notes of return addresses and responds, all without human intervention. This 'robotics federal clerk' sends standardized bureaucratic answers limited to the acknowledgement of e-mails. The effectiveness of e-mail communication with politicians is best illustrated by an anecdote about President Clinton's lack of response to an e-mail even from Carl Bildt, then the Swedish prime minister (Cairncross 1997:261). Furthermore, not only can politicians not really be reached via the Net, but also they use it for posting their press releases and official statements. Therefore, although the Internet plays an important role in diffusing information, although to rather selected, better educated and better off groups, this information is tightly controlled and can be a one-way communication. 'Thus, as long as political parties and organized campaigns control the political procedure, electronic citizen participation will take a back seat in informational politics, as it refers to formal elections and decision-making' (Castells 1997:351).

Nonetheless, the Internet can mobilize participation and group formation in conflictual situations and therefore can be used as a vehicle to enhance struggle. Among many examples, listed by Carnevale and Probst (1997:241), of how the Net helped people to get involved and develop their own grass-roots strategies, the most interesting and widely known is the case of the Zapatista National Liberation Army from southern Mexico, in the state of Chiapas, whose leader was continuously in communication through the Internet with the whole world. This extensive use of the Internet to diffuse information not only increased circles of their supporters but also produced their protection since its international visibility made it impossible for the Mexican government to use repression on a wider scale. We should, however, notice here not only the empowering potential of the Net but also that Zapatista-type 'netwars' present a new challenge to the global order, as rebellious groups, using advanced technology for communication, will be able to threaten national governments (Castells 1997:78–81).

To sum up, the network structure of the Internet, by permitting autonomous, spontaneous networking of various people and groups, provides us with some possibility for debate and mobilization in a free electronic forum. However, the immediacy and volatility of the medium and the threats of commercialization and commoditization of exchange means that it cannot simply be left to technology to solve our problems. Although electronic networks may expand our possibility for the re-vitalization of democracy, it is not an automatic process. The assumption that electronic communication, as inherently free of imposed hierarchies, would foster free speech has turned out to be a half-truth. After experiencing the flame wars, that is, verbally violent fights and vendettas online, one shocked user concludes that 'even when egalitarianism is forced on users by the technical limitations of a medium, people find a way to be just as cliquish and exclusionary as they ever were' (Seabrook 1997:255). His disappointed encounter with the Net is shared by many, who are discouraged from posting by the lack of a standard of decency online. In particular, many old timers, who think that there should be a role for decency online and who were actively involved in efforts to exclude certain newsgroups about sex and drugs, are leaving the Net. One of them, Eugene Spafford, condemning cruelty and flaming online, says that in 'any other kind of medium, the reality of the two people talking would prevent a lot of ugliness from happening, but with nothing but bits between them, people feel they can say anything they like – it's not a human you're talking to, it's just a machine' (in Seabrook 1997:119).

At the same time as new technologies create new opportunities, they also generate new problems, such as the increase of invisible transactions on the Net, threats to privacy and further uncertainty about the truthfulness of information. Although there have been several attempts made by computer scientists to construct software which will allow entities on a computer network to reason about the trustworthiness of other entities they interact with, in reality these programs only provide tools to minimize risk and increase computer system security by proposing the establishment of a third agent or entity that will store reputation records about other entities (Abdul-Rahman and Hailes 1997). In some way it resembles the situation of impersonal trust, where the third agent (an institution: for instance, an insurance company) regulates relationships between two partners. The difference, however, is that organizations and people involved in such relationships – as for example, between stockbrokers, their clients and insurance companies – know their rights, regulations and all are aware that legal norms are available to punish the untrustworthy. Although online one's reputation record can be established and exposed, it does not mean that on the Net there are clear norms to guide activity or methods to control or punish unwanted conduct. This accentuates the need to rethink the notion of civility online. As the combined effects of information technology and globalization become more pronounced, the search for such a balance between the informality and formality of online interaction which could ensure the civility of 'cybersociety' will expand. Turning now to an examination of the nature and qualities of virtual communities, we will discuss sociability online as an expression of the balanced relationships between informality and formality.

VIRTUAL COMMUNITY: SOCIABILITY ON THE NET

> There is an intimate connection between informal conversation, the kind that takes place in communities and virtual communities, in the coffee shops and computer conferences, and the ability of large social groups to govern themselves without monarchs or dictators (Rheingold 1993:281).

The WELL story paints a very enthusiastic picture of virtual community, which emerges when 'enough people carry on those public discussions long enough with sufficient human feelings, to form webs of personal relationships in cyberspace' (Rheingold 1993:6). This example of electronic networks of interactive communication organized around a shared interest or purpose has been encouraging many writers to equate, or at least to compare, virtual community with the real world community. However, it is still unclear what the exact nature of relationships and communications taking place in such electronic networks actually is, as well as what the cultural effects of such networking really are. There are many contradictory evaluations of the nature of these bonds, the characteristics of sociability and the features of electronic discourse. At the core of this controversy is the difference in the perceived balance between the informality and formality of exchange on this new medium. Writers who view computer mediated communication as offering new potential for the recreation of communities, improvement of democracy, construction of a less conventional and a more egalitarian society – these writers tend to stress not only the reality of technologically generated communities but also the informality of this type of communication. New forms of interaction are seen as stimulated by 'the informality, spontaneity, anonymity of the medium' (Castells 1996:363). According to this perspective, moreover, the essence of the informality of communication online manifests itself in emergent cultures that unify once disperse social actors into electronic communities. In this way, virtual communities' characteristics are the main evidence of the informality of computer mediated communication. In contrast, for other writers, computer mediated communication represents a return to the constructed, rational and written discourse, which results in purposive, relatively formalized communities (Doheny-Farina 1996). Nonetheless, regardless of all these differences, there is a general sense that some new forms of community are created technologically.

The most interesting and very frequently used notion to describe the nature of virtual community is the concept of 'a third place'. Cafes, coffee shops, community centres, bars and 'hangouts' or 'third places', as Oldenburg calls them in his book *The Great Good Places* (1989), are informal meeting places where communities come into being and which sustain the life of neighbourhoods. Arguing that all great cultures have had a vital informal public life, Oldenburg defines them as places that 'host regular, voluntary, informal, and happily anticipated gatherings of individuals beyond the realm of home and work' (1989:16). They differ from both large, highly structured organizations and from families and other small groups as their main activity is conversation. The main attraction of these 'homes away from homes' is that on their neutral grounds people can talk without constraints and in a 'playful mood' (1989:39, 42). These places of good talk serve to level their guests to a condition of social equality and 'whatever hint of a hierarchy exists is predicated upon human decency'; therefore the decline of informal public life can, argues Oldenburg, make 'a jungle of what had been a garden while, at the same time, diminishing the ability of people to cultivate it' (1989:78). Third places 'thrive best in locales where community life is casual, where walking takes people to more destinations than does automobile, and where the interesting diversity of neighbourhood reduces one's reliance on television' (Oldenburg 1989:210), hence, 'great good places' require the attachment to area, the sense of place and familiarity with the place. This raises questions: do virtual communities meet these conditions and what are the main differences between virtual communities and 'third places'?

Following Oldenburg's characterization of the third place as the place we gather for conviviality, Rheingold (1993:25) describes the WELL as a community of people who develop emotional attachment by communicating electronically with each other.

He argues that the 'third place' concept describes what 'every virtual communitarian knows instinctively, the power of informal public life' (*ibid*). In a similar mood, William Mitchell says '[t]he keyboard is my cafe' (1995:7). Both types of community are presented in this type of writing as ways of meeting people, both are seen as having their regulars and as allowing for 'peeking' or logging on for just a minute. In a similar way, the main value of virtual community reflects the main attraction of public informal places, that is, the fact that they are both viewed as neutral meeting grounds where social conventions are democratic and where the dominant mood of exchange is reciprocity. Virtual community, therefore, is a kind of gift economy in which people do things for one another 'out of a spirit of building something between them, rather than as spreadsheet-calculated *quid pro quo*' (Rheingold 1993:59). Consequently, the dominant egalitarian and open conversations which are found there are the perfect union of egoism and altruism, just the same as in cohesive communities in the real world.

Despite Rheingold's encouraging picture of virtual communities, many features of virtual communities differ from those of real world communities. In the case of virtual communities physical location is irrelevant and physical distance has no influence on the size or shape of networks (Sproull and Faraj 1997:35–52). It is not an accident of proximity, a common place or locality, but a shared interest that brings people together online. Time is also obliterated since in the new communication system past, present and future can be programmed to interact with each other in the same message. Furthermore, the structure of the Net encourages specialized relationships because it permits shopping for social relationships in the safety of our homes or offices. Not only are participants in computer mediated communications better educated and generally enjoy a higher socio-economic status, but also they are selected by the commonality of their leisure or professional interest. Consequently, electronically linked groups are more specialized and their scope of common interest is narrower, while at the same time more participants can be included, and these participants, moreover, do not share a common mental model of the sense of place. 'Different people in cyberspace look at their virtual communities through differently shaped keyholes ... In virtual communities, the sense of place requires an individual act of imagination' (Rheingold 1993:63). Hence, due to lack of physical presence, Net members tend to base their feelings of closeness on shared narrow interests rather than on shared social characteristics such as gender, race or age. They also have control over the timing and the content of self-disclosure, therefore it can be said that the Net encourages membership in multiple and partial communities. As people can extend the diversity of their contacts, the multiplicity of groups and the varieties of belonging become the main features of participation online. Moreover, most participants are relatively invisible because only the presence of people who post messages, not those who only read them, are registered. Taking into account the enormous percentage of people who only read messages (the so-called lurkers: readers who never post) and are therefore invisible, suggests that this kind of group thinks together differently from face-to-face groups, where physical presence matters even if people are silent. For example, on the WELL, the lurkers out-number the posters by about nine to one (Seabrook 1997:151). In other words, about 80 per cent of its 66 000 members posted no message during a one-month study period (Sproull and Faraj 1997:35). Similarly, on the Usenet, which houses more than 3500 newsgroups, the most postings were made by 2–4 per cent of the population (Seabrook 1997:151). This silent participation of lurkers adds to the difficulties in identifying a virtual group membership, which is always unstable and fuzzy (McLaughlin, Osborne and Smith 1995:102).

Furthermore, it should not escape our attention that the majority of elec-tronic groups are not autonomous but linked to commercial markets. Although online there is no central authority that monitors access or con-tent, many writers on cyberspace point out that the increasing amount of control over the traffic is exercised by some owners of conferencing net-works or individual site administrators (who can determine whether to pro-vide access to users or whether to provide connections to other sites). This can lead to the expansion of the gap between the managers/owners' inter-ests and community interests, and subsequently could threaten the relatively democratic and egalitarian nature of networks. While virtual communities pay little attention to the power structures off the Net, some legal regulation will sooner or later affect their governance; the issue is only 'what group will determine which laws or operating rules shall apply' (Branscomb 1993:99). Moreover, in practice, the intensivity of some interaction means that per-sonal differences can also be communicated and felt, consequently generat-ing power dynamics (and frequent 'flaming', that is, sending aggressive and nasty messages) within these relationships. The intensity with which personal differences are felt also undermines the egalitarianism of the relationships. While online many personal characteristics are non-visible, it is nonetheless 'a monumental task to develop close relationships while keeping the particu-lars of the body anonymous' (Doheny-Farina 1996:65). This, together with the fact that the Net is not free from cultural biases that exist offline, means that online groups frequently reproduce inequalities and power structures from real life.

Furthermore, the Net tends to reward knowledge and literary skills, thus those who can manipulate attention and emotion with the written word and who can present their knowledge in an attractive way enjoy higher status and recognition (MacKinnon 1995). Even more importantly, the egalitarian idea of the Net is undermined by the fact that participation in communication requires both technical skill and social expertise. In order to learn how to manipulate this new medium, we need to forget about the distinction between social and technical skills, because both of them need to be applied simultaneously. Nonetheless, at least at this initial stage, computer mediated communication as a new medium tends to benefit previously salient or marginalized groups or people. 'It works as though the symbolism of power embedded in face-to-face communication has not yet found its language in the new CMC' (Castells 1996:360). Search for evidence of an authoritarian control in Usenet (one of the most popular conferencing network that links an estimated three million users) also testifies to a relative lack of coercion to obey a common power; 81 per cent of a selected sample of 200 Usenet articles showed no signs of control or censorship. Consequently, MacKinnon (1995:133) concludes that newsgroup postings, by virtue of their spontaneity and uncensored state, are more representative of true dialogue, being an essential aspect of community.

With physical distance no longer a barrier for effective participation, with timeless time, with the opportunity to 'construct' identities, with partial and multiple involvement, and with the technology shaping, at least to some degree, the content of exchange, is the nature of sociability online the same as in 'third places'? Even the best example available, the WELL, which 'was the closest thing to a functional utopia of free speech' and personalized relationships (Seabrook 1997:1) suggests the need to acknowledge differences between these two types of communities. However, maybe we should not exaggerate the importance of face-to-face relationships or their lack and ask how close does an act of voluntary subscription to a discussion group online come to be a synonym for joining a cohesive community, which is able to offer warmth and fulfilment? Could computer mediated communication reproduce real social relations in cyberspace?

Many writers argue that rich and intense interpersonal relationships, emotionally rewarding and strong enough to sustain intimacy, can be developed via computer-mediated communication, even though only no face-to-face or nonverbal communication takes place there. The WELL's story is often quoted in support of this type of claim. However, while not denying the unusual quality of the WELL community, we need to see that the WELL virtual community is a result of several specific factors, such as the timing of its expansion (the early era of CMC, which was relatively free of commercial pressure) and the positive selection of its participants and its conferencing software, which all made it impossible for users to be anonymous (which gave a measure of personal accountability to the discussions that was missing from some of the newsgroups). Moreover, probably the most distinctive feature of the early WELL was the fact that nearly all the participants shared a geographical place. Because they all live relatively closely, in the Bay Area around San Francisco, they not only contacted each other by phone but also they organized real meetings. 'It is out of the face-to-face WELL picnics at a public park that simple text on a screen begins to develop into something more than just the image community' (Doheny-Farina 1996:27). Other studies likewise confirm that out of virtual relationships personal, more intimate contacts can evolve. For example, more than half of participants in the electronic support groups also contact each other by phone or in person (Wellman *et al* 1996:221). It prompts some writers to argue that 'the virtual community demands a real one prior to it in order to function successfully' (Stallabrass 1995:14). In a similar vein, others talk about technologically generated communities as only being a pseudo-*gemeinschaft* experience and warn, quoting much evidence, that the level of commitment between people communicating online cannot be assumed to be the same as in real world relationships (Beniger 1987). This perspective argues that computer networks can only sustain weak ties because of the lack of physical and social cues within the exchange process. Interacting by digital means is seen as only expanding the size and diversity of our networks, without, however, increasing the strength of these ties, while at the same time lowering our sense of responsibilities for others because '[a]ccountability is diminishing with every added length in the lines of communication' (Brown 1997:243). This mood seems to be well expressed by Turkle's remark pointing out that: 'Our communities grow more fragile, airy, and ephemeral, even as our connections multiply' (1996:265).

Are electronic communities, like real life communities, able to develop informal forms of social control? While the dominant rhetoric on the Net is that there are no rules at all, in practice there is pressure to conform and there are some informal rules; for instance, both participants and hosts perform custodian functions in respect to 'netiquette' (abbreviation of 'net etiquette'). Apart from the constraints imposed by the technology, the need to control cost and some external factors, there are both discursive and sociostructural factors that encourage following conventions and rules of conduct online (McLaughlin, Osborne and Smith 1995). Consensus on informal, unwritten rules and ways of acceptable behaviour are seen as the only alternative to imposing formalized restrictions on freedom of expression. Because the honouring of netiquette begins with the individual users of the network, a breach of norms that attracts many complaints will therefore be see as unacceptable conduct. For example, an enormous protest against a member of one of the virtual collectivities, the lawyer who advertised his services over the Internet, resulted in his expulsion from the network and led in turn to the establishment of a set of guidelines or a standard of behaviour specific to this virtual community (Carnevale and Probst 1997). By exercising informal control, members tend to reinforce many unwritten norms, and – by the same token – they also promote divisions between insiders and outsiders (Seabrook 1997:197). Thus, informal Net conventions, which are honoured and taught rules about what members can and cannot do with the medium, are essential to the process of creating community. In this way, the nature of electronic communities resembles – at least to some degree – some features of cohesive real-life communities.

For many observers, however, the question about the nature or 'the reality' of virtual communities is not important because what counts, according to them, is the fact that the emergence of new electronic communities is a response to people's need and desire for community that has followed the disintegration of traditional communities (Rheingold 1993). With the loss of real communities or third places, many writers tend to agree with Stephen M. Case (the founder of America OnLine) that now we can build a strong sense of community only through the Net. These researchers hope that maybe 'cyberspace is one of the normal public places where people can rebuild the aspects of community that were lost when malt shop became a mall' (Rheingold 1993:26). Others raise the question 'is it really sensible to suggest that the way to revitalize community is to sit alone in our rooms, typing at our networked computers and filling our lives with virtual friends?' (Turkle 1996:235). Doheny-Farina (1996), who values real communities more than electronic ones, thinks that the Net should be committed to the rebuilding of communities in real places.

There are still many unanswered questions about the reality of the impact of electronic communities and about their characteristics. Much evidence that CMC can play an important role in the provision of social and emotional support systems allows us to say that electronic communities can provide some 'collective goods', such as social capital, knowledge capital and communication or emotional support (Rheingold 1993:13). The WELL, the Young Scientists Networks or the Systers are all good examples of networks of informal support, companionship and friendship based on sharing common interests, problems and mutual understanding (Wellman *et al* 1996:220). However, we still do not know exactly whether the Net enhances community by enabling a new kind of local space or whether it undermines communities by disconnecting us from localities. Inconclusive evidence from a study of interactions in electronic groups and social support suggests that while the Internet is a social setting in which strangers can exchange useful support, it could also enhance the rejection of traditional social networks, therefore increasing the isolation from the locality (Mickelson 1997:157–79). Furthermore, abandoning the old assumption, which uncritically assigns community to territorially based face-to-face relations, does not mean that computer mediated communication is a sufficient factor in itself to re-construct and sustain new communities. The French experiment with the Minitel networks of electronic chat lines in two different types of communities, one rural, another urban, suggests that electronic communication does not necessarily reduce isolation caused by physical distance. One surprising outcome of this study was that although dwellers in both areas had free and anonymous access to chat groups, the service was not a success in the rural community, while being extremely popular with the centrally located actors in the city, for whom this new means of communication was an additional tool to their regular exchanges. Thus, seen in this way, the new technologies do not substitute but reinforce and complement spatially bound relations (Marinotti 1994). Therefore, taking into account that electronic communities can provide some 'collective goods' and that CMC is not a sufficient factor in itself to re-vitalize community life, we need to acknowledge the differences between real-world and virtual communities, while at the same time recognizing the reality of electronic communities and their importance in our lives.

The fact that electronic groups do more than provide information does not mean that the nature of their ties is the same as those developed in co-presence circumstances. Even though computer mediated communication can develop into emotional, strong and supportive relationships, it seems that electronic networks are particularly suited to fostering weak, diverse, voluntary, multiplex and specialized relationships. 'The spare, unbounded nature of the Internet means that people unhappy with the one interaction can manoeuvre between different computerized conferences and private e-relationships' (Wellman 1997:195). The usefulness of weak ties established through computer networks, as Constant, Sproull and Kiesler's (1997) research shows, is a result of their bridging capacities. The same study also discovered that while weak ties offer information, help and advice, they are often limited to more specialized type of assistance. Quite surprisingly, reciprocity proved to be a relatively common phenomenon online, even between people with weak ties. When somebody online asks for information or help, it is very likely that help will be provided. This willingness to help and generally to engage with strangers online is explained by the fact that messages for help are read by people alone at their screens, and this situational context of being alone rather than 'one in a big crowd' enhances motivation to act. Furthermore, the fact that 'on-line intervention will be observed by entire groups and will be positively rewarded by them' also perpetrates a norm of mutual aid (Wellman *et al* 1996:223). Moreover, although online conversation tends to facilitate 'the ephemeral and informal feeling of a telephone', it has a different impact because of 'the reach and permanence of a publication' (Rheingold 1993:37). In a large electronic context, a small number of small acts, because of their visibility and relative durability, can sustain a large community and foster kindness to strangers (Sproull and Faraj 1997; Wellman *et al* 1996).

Summarizing our argument that virtual communities are real but different to real-life communities, we can say that electronic gatherings have the potential to offer a new kind of informal public space, which – although weak ties tend to be its most pronounced kind of bonds – can still be an important source of information, support and even emotions. This electronic community seems to resemble more 'lifestyle enclaves', which are defined by Bellah *et al* (1985) as segmental because they describe only parts of their members' private lives, usually the activities connected with their after work interests. While normal communities, as collectivities dependent on bringing together private and public lives, are complex and integrated, interpersonal relationships on the Net, where several levels of abstraction separate people and where 'the representation of the representation of affection replaces affection' constitute communities that 'provide only the *sense* of community' (Dohney-Farina 1996:65, 50). In some way, computer mediated communication tends to free electronic exchange from any reality and erect its airy realm according to the technological requirement of the operating system. This 'superficial' character of communication online allows us to compare it with sociability in real life, the nature of which is also superficial and artificially constructed according to its own intrinsic laws, so well described by Simmel (1950:40–57).

The nature of sociability online resembles the characteristics of exchange at the cocktail party rather than exchange in cohesive communities. 'Unlike face-to-face interaction, computer mediated interaction can turn on a dime as we instantaneously move from one conversation to the next. An apt metaphor is the cocktail party' (Jones 1995:vii). Exchange in cyberspace is in many ways like cocktail party conversation also because of its equally transitory nature; in both types of conversation what really counts is the impression one can make on others. 'The most you can hope for is that it will make an impression before it disappears into air', says Jack Mingo about computer mediated communication (quoted in Moore 1995:99). The cocktail party and various different online social structures (for instance, computer bulletin-board systems, hosted conferences or some interactive computer games), share many common characteristics. In both situations, in electronic exchange and at the cocktail party, participants and hosts are expected to play according to the rules of etiquette or netiquette. In both contexts, participants' conduct is shaped by some formal factors, although people still enjoy a diversity of contacts, freedom to select between different conversations and the opportunity to shape their own presentations. Additionally, the Internet Chat area can be seen as a core group, which dominates at any cocktail party. In principle, sociability 'creates an ideal sociological world in which the pleasure of the individual is closely tied up with the pleasure of the others' (Simmel 1950:48). In both cases, relatively widespread reciprocity illustrates that one's satisfaction cannot be totally disconnected from the cost of this conduct for others. Both types of sociability, online and at the cocktail party, favour inhibited communication, while excluding some personal elements from exchange. Formal rules of conduct, tact, self-discipline and discretion are the main conditions of sociability at the cocktail party (Simmel 1950:48–67), while in the case of computer networks, infrastructures and netiquette shape interaction. Hence, as a consequence of this specific balance between formality and informality, a relatively egalitarian participation all 'present' becomes the feature of both types of sociability.

Sociability of computer mediated communication and sociability at the cocktail party are distinguished by relatively egalitarian relations, which result from the elimination of many personal characteristics from the frontstage (Simmel 1950:46). This exclusion of the most personal elements happens because their exhibition would be seen as tactlessness or because the CMC technology does not allow for it. 'Yet the democracy of sociability even among social equals is only something *played*' (Simmel 1950:48). Similarly, sociability in cyberspace is a game and its enjoyment does not necessarily have much to do with the 'we-feeling', as optimistic believers in virtual community declare. Its attraction lies rather, as in the case of sociability in real life, in the dynamics and hazards of these forms of activities themselves. 'The more profound, double sense of "social game" is that not only the game is played in a society (as its external medium) but that, with its help, people actually "play" society' (Simmel 1950:50). In the case of sociability online, computer operating systems are an additional external medium helping people to 'play' the game of sociability, therefore in order to grasp the sense of it, we also need to understand not only society but also technology. Now much software and hardware – by enhancing the richness of information, simulation and conversation structures – try to provide the most 'lifelike' interaction possible, hence allowing for intimacy in cyberspace.

ELECTRONIC PROXIMITY: INTIMACY IN CYBERSPACE

> Whatever the impact, e-mail manages to combine four vital elements of modern communication – intimacy, immediacy, informality and lawlessness (Golds 1996:1).

The development of computer mediated communication poses many urgent questions about privacy, intimacy and identity. New connections between privacy, identity and intimacy generate new queries about the relationships between public and private, privacy and intimacy and about the nature of fidelity (Rheingold 1993; Turkle 1996). The best example of these new relations between privacy, intimacy and identity is the case of a woman who broadcasts her daily life over the Internet. Although at the beginning the JenniCam was not a public address, soon the 21-year-old middle-class girl from Washington converted her site into a pay-per-view operation. Now thousands of people visit her site monthly and have a chance to see what she is doing twenty-four hours of the day (the computer camera in Jennifer's bedroom records about 20 millions hits every day). Living without any privacy and sharing with outlookers all her intimate moments (even lovemaking is recorded since 'it's nothing extreme, its all normal stuff – just part of life') has brought her celebrity status. Not only has she been interviewed for various magazines, radio and television stations, Jennifer's living in 'a fishbowl' has attracted many followers, also trying to achieve her 'notoriety'. Despite her commitment to recording every moment of her life, Jennifer considers herself a private person. 'The only privacy that really matters is the privacy of having your own thoughts and in that respect I haven't lost anything' (Wilson 1997:9). This disconnection of privacy and intimacy and the reduction of privacy to control over conduct and freedom of thoughts, also illustrates the total disappearance of boundaries between backstage and frontstage behaviour. Sharing with an unknown public all intimate, usually unseen, backstage behaviour (the title of the article about Jennifer is very characteristic here: *What the butler saw*), also opens up debate about what the nature of intimacy is and about the consequences of the spread of electronic intimacy: will it result in the radicalization of relationships or in their impoverishment? It also raises the question of the nature of electronic partners' knowledge about each other. While our knowledge of others is always fragmentary and imperfect, when entering electronic relations we cannot take for granted a 'reciprocity of perspectives' as in face-to-face interaction. Online, our knowledge of others is incompletely formulated, unclear and indeterminate because we do not have the opportunity to test, revise, reenact or modify our experiences of others. Thus, in cyberspace our 'typification' of others will be 'a shot in the dark compared to the knowledge one has of one's consociate in the face-to-face interaction' (Schutz 1967:181). According to Schutz, in indirect social experience, the more anonymous my partner is, the more 'objective' signs must be used and greater the need for questioning about meanings. Experience on the Net, where there is not the integrity of the situation and where the meaning of what goes on in the interaction is open to partners' interpretation, implies an absence of contextual determination of social events and does not provide partners with much information about actual impersonal characteristics of each other. An electronic partner is only indirectly accessible and her or his subjective experiences can only be known via his or her e-mail messages or screen statements, which do not necessarily enlarge our knowledge of each other, since we rely on our partner's interpretation and self-presentation, not on 'objective signs'. Thus, since many statements in virtual conversation can be generated by invoking what is known as feature object – which means that 'the power to shape discourse belongs, in part, to the programmers' (Doheny-Farina 1996:65) or that communication is partly formalized – in order to discuss the quality of intimacy online we look at the dominant opinions about the nature of electronic communication.

The explosion of e-mail popularity is a result of its many liberating qualities, in which electronic exchange resembles the telephone. Although, unlike the phone, e-mail is both an asynchronous and a computer-readable medium, it shares with the telephone 'the lack of formality', which is 'definitely liberating' (Dunbar 1996:1). Because of it, e-mail is compared with 'a vastly improved version of an answering machine' (Seabrook 1997:48). However, the case of electronic exchange is more complex and the peculiarity of this form of communication is that it is neither writing nor speech, and therefore can permit both the feeling of intimacy and the demonstration of formality or indifference.

'The informality of e-mail is widely noted and often celebrated' (Lawrence 1996:81) and it is attributed to by several factors. For some writers, the informality of electronic mail is a consequence in part of the speed of the medium or its immediacy and the fact that it is so easy to send a reply, and both factors encourage the sender's impulsiveness. Consequently, e-mail language is more dynamic, less carefully constructed and less inhibited. For other analysts, e-mail's informality is a result of the absence of any constraints and conventions: 'Don't worry about grammar, spelling, form ... just say what you want to say' (Dunbar 1996:1). This lack of concern about style and form comes from the feeling that in electronic communication things can be said 'more freely' because of the ephemeral nature of this type of communication. Hence, writing e-mail is like making sandcastles since you are aware that 'no matter how much care you put into the process, it will all be washed away after a while' (Moore 1995:99).

Not only do people perceive an e-mail message as being transitory in its nature or disappearing into the air of the Net, but they also feel free because there are no censors nor editors. E-mail writing is shorter, quicker, denser, usually fitting on one screen and is done without thinking about its form; as one of the users says: 'I am not a very good letter writer, but I am a good e-mail writer. I think it's editing' (Moore 1995:44). E-mail is also perceived as being more informal, intimate and more comforting than writing a regular letter or using the phone because it 'takes the confrontation out of contact and the panic out of replying' (Golds 1996:1). Seeing e-mail as a medium for the intimate exchange of thoughts, which moves between the permanence of print and the transience of talk, leads, moreover, to another assumption, which says that 'e-mail favours the imaginative, the lowly, the polite and the introverted' (Golds 1996:1).

However, not everybody agrees with such a vision of e-mail and its users. According to Moore (1995), e-mail is less intimate than a phone call or even a regular letter. 'There is no voice to convey meaning, and on e-mail everyone's handwriting looks the same. Most of the electronic mail I receive, in fact, even when it comes from good friends, seems chilly, too blunt, more like a memo than anything else' (Moore 1995:44). Moore attributes this 'formality' of e-mail to the same factors that other authors use to explain the informality of e-mail, that is, to its speed and ephemerality. The fact that seconds after we push a button the e-mail arrives at its destination and the fact that you avoid the risks that you might encounter in face-to-face contact or in a phone call (such as the expression of the recipient's face or her disappointed voice) make e-mail less intimate and an illusionary safe (Moore 1996).

Both of these contradictory views, the first one arguing that people writing e-mail are more intimate and informal and the other stressing that e-mail exchange is formal and not intimate, are based on the observation that when people perceive communication to be ephemeral, the stake of communication seems smaller. However, each perspective draws a different conclusion from this statement. The more optimistic approach argues that the transitory nature of e-mail makes people more 'confessional', informal, open and wanting spontaneously to share with others. The second position states that because of the brisk nature of e-mail, people feel less responsible for what they say, therefore with the dominant rhetoric that 'you have the courage, you can get away with writing almost anything to almost anyone' (Golds 1996:1), incidences of flaming are so frequent.

Empirical research proves that the latter assumption is correct, that e-mail users 'feel less committed to what they say, less concerned about it, less worried about the social reception they will get' (Sproull and Kiesler 1991:42). It does not mean, however, that everybody online behaves in the same way and that everybody is conditioned to become less friendly or simply rude. Although some healthy scepticism is required towards claims that using e-mail greatly affects our sense of standards and changes our personalities, we also need to watch carefully how electronic communication shapes the form and style of exchange. The realization that e-mail reproduces some of the features of face-to-face communication (since it can be quick and dialogical), together with the awareness of the differences between these two types of exchange (e.g. only in co-present situations do we share common contexts), allow us to see that electronic communication, like all mediated interactions, narrows the range of clues. For example, many users of e-mail complain that it has a 'narrow emotional bandwidth, which means that people 'find it difficult to express inflexions of the voice by the mere use of words on a screen, so all their criticisms tend to come across as rude' (*The Economist*, 11 May, 1996:16). Moreover, e-mail is not a direct type of conversation since it is 'a great way of not answering your correspondent's questions, and instead delivering some monologue of your own' (Seabrook 1997:50).

Although, as in the case of the phone, e-mail exchange is not going to replace the importance of face-to-face interaction and it will not become the main ground for developing intimate relationships, it has enormous potential for sustaining existing intimate relationships (almost all authors of books on cyberspace proudly stress that now, for the first time in years, after they have managed to convince their mothers to join the Net, their relationships with their parents are blossoming, at least online). Furthermore, because e-mail is so often used for professional, recreational and other specific reasons, one communicates not only with people from one's city, culture, region or country, but also with people of different nationalities, race, ethnic background, age or religion. This can have important consequences because, as research on the relationship between electronic connections and feelings of affiliations shows, it can help people to overcome some barriers and prejudices. Sproull and Kiesler (1991:84) prove that: 'if you have a choice of face-to-face contact with people exactly like you or meeting via electronic communication, then you would like each other more if you meet in person. The situation is different for meeting people you would otherwise not see in person, whom you might avoid, who are different'.

While there are some dangers and pleasures in electronic mail exchange, various commercial services providing chats online, combining real time interaction, anonymity and the possibility to assume different roles, reproduce them in extreme forms. These various chat groups, conversational forums and MUDs – by allowing the sharing of the temporal reference system, while preserving anonymity – enhance users' self-promotion, while at the same time protecting their privacy. On Internet Real Chat, as on MUDs, users can also open a channel and attract guests to it, all of whom speak to each other as if in the same room and where one has the ability to assume any identity one desires. All these online services are interesting examples of how computer mediated communication can serve as a place for the construction and reconstruction of identity. On the Net people are able to 'build a self by cycling through many selves', they become 'addicted to flux', they learn to take things at interface value and to think about 'identity as multiplicity' (Turkle 1996:178, 23). Online, people experience the sense of freedom that comes from being able to behave differently as the medium encourages them to think of themselves 'as fluid, emergent, decentralized, multiplicitous, flexible and ever in process' (Turkle 1996:263–4). They invent themselves as they go along, exploring, constructing and reconstructing their identities; many change their genders, sexual orientations and personalities.

The Internet brings new fluidity to human relationships and breeds 'a kind of easy intimacy' (Turkle 1996:206). In electronic meeting places, because of their isolation and remoteness from real and familiar life, intense, deep and intimate relationships develop very quickly. However, after this first phase of the excitement of a rapidly deepening intimacy, usually comes disappointment. Turkle illustrates this with Peter's story. Peter (or Dante, his online character), a young academic, developed online an intimate love relationship with Beatrice. 'Their relationship was intellectual, emotionally supportive, and erotic. Their virtual sex life was rich and fulfilling' (Turkle 1996:207). However, meeting the woman behind Beatrice left Peter very disappointed. He realized that online one sees what one wants to see and it became clear to him that he unconsciously constructed this relationship and created a love object according to his desire and dreams. Moreover, to his own surprise, while reading the record of his interaction with Beatrice, he could not find warmth or a sense of empathy there. This case shows how people come to invest technology with a magical aura and how their need for the feeling of emotional intimacy leads them to the idealization of virtual partners. More importantly, we not only project our desires on our cyberpartner, we also create our own desirable cyberselves because – even if we do not lie online – we are different there since we are less inhibited (Turkle 1996:178–206).

Turkle believes that our awareness of what stands behind our screen personae is the way to self-improvement. While virtual reality and our experience there should be treated seriously, using virtual experience for personal transformation seems to be more questionable. This scepticism is supported by three observations about the ways in which the Net is popularly used. Firstly, on the Net, thoughtful, productive discussions are not so frequent because no one is accountable for what is being communicated and because the Net is 'a forum for individuals who care little about authenticity' (Rutenbeck 1996:12). Secondly, cyberspace increasingly provides a means for individual expression that would not be appropriate or acceptable in real life (Doheny-Farina 1996). Thirdly, arguing that MUD intimate relationships can have a positive effect on self-understanding is rather too optimistic, especially when we realize that not self-improvement but a search for pleasure and entertainment drives people to chat in electronic rooms (Kramarae 1995; Moore 1995; Callaghan 1997; Seabrook 1997). While we still do not have answers to so many questions (such as how can we be multiple and coherent at the same time? What are the social implications of the multiplicity of selves? What is at the heart of sex: bodies or minds?), we are already overpowered by the reality of communication online, which is 'a fairly representative illustration what people want to do with their lives; talk about sex, go to the movies, and if there is any time left over, find a good paying job' (Moore 1995:151).

This focus on sex in cyberspace discussions and games prompts some writers to thinks that 'lust motivates technology' (Sanez, quoted in Kramarae 1995:48). The proliferation of sex discussion groups on the Net and their enormous popularity (the top forty of the most visited newsgroups are all consistently sex discussion groups; Moore 1995:157) should be seen, however, as a more natural phenomenon or as one of the ways of enjoying the expanded personal freedom that computer mediated communication permits. The disproportionate amount of sex chats can be attributed to the fact that 'sex was merely the easiest and most obvious form of discourse for two people who knew nothing about each other, and perhaps had nothing to say to each other, to borrow in order to have a half-interesting conversation' (Seabrook 1997:139). Cybersex is an ideal medium for sexual fantasy because, by removing fear of rejection, it promotes risk taking. Furthermore, the popularity of sex online is also a result of the fact that this type of sex suits busy and single yuppies who are accustomed to using computers all day long. Finally, Net sex is popular because it is safe from fears of pregnancy, HIV, and – since we can always just switch off – it is also safe from 'commitment, from entanglement, from having others witness our embarrassment ... . The perfect answer in a society that is increasingly busy, and increasingly unsafe' (Moore 1995:172). Cybersex, as the dominant way of expressing intimacy online, comes without any responsibility, 'without any necessity or even desirability of giving to another' (Kramarae 1995:48). Cybersex is intrinsically fragmentary and episodic, allowing one to move quickly from flirtation to cross-dressing, from one partner to another. This lack of commitment to sharing and the freedom from the demands of reciprocity as well as the fluidity of identities generate many ethical questions. Are real intimate relationships possible under such conditions? Can electronic types of easy intimacy undermine or impoverise real-life relationships?

It is easy to find much anecdotal evidence to support totally different or conflictual answers to the above questions. On one hand, we have heard the countless stories of true love being found online and, on the other hand, there is evidence that giving away everything for a fantasy generated online often means paying a high cost. The first argument is supported by reports of numerous happy weddings of transatlantic couples who met on the Net (*Guardian Weekly*, 1 September, 1996:25). Warning signals come from different kinds of stories, such as, for example, the history of an American girl's traumatic life with the boy whom she met on the Net. In order to live with him in a different part of the USA, she 'compromised her values, pushed away her family', and she now reflects: 'How can something so simple as IRC (Internet Relay Chat) be so dangerous? I do know that the wounds from this experience are deep, and will take a long time to heal. I still frequent the IRC scene; however, I am more cautious about who I talk to and who I get to know' (*The Australian*, 30 August, 1997:3).

Electronic communication can also indirectly affect our intimate relationships by pulling people away from their loved ones or from making any attempt to search for and to invest in real relationships. 'The Internet is wrecking marriages' according to Ann Landers, America's best-known advice columnist, who prints many letters from spouses being left by their partner for people met on the Net (*The Australian*, 9 July, 1996:10). While not blaming the technology, she argues that the Internet is a toy for lonely people because it makes them feel that they are a part of the living world and that on the Net 'they can get romantic overtures from somebody and it appeals to them'. Also Young (1998) reports that many long-lasting marriages are being destroyed by one of the partners moving away to live with a man or woman that they just met on the Net.

Net relationships also generate a new set of questions about the meaning of fidelity. A young Sydney taxi-driver, Ben, who late at night, when his partner sleeps peacefully, meets online a 'very sexy' blonde from the USA, is totally convinced that he is not being unfaithful – but is only indulging in some 'harmless' sex on line (Callaghan 1997:1). Not everybody accepts, of course, Ben's evaluation of his conduct, as examples of women deserting cybersex-devoted husbands illustrate. Electronic communication also affects friendship bonds – which, when moved online, seem to be more 'artificial' – as a teenager girl complains when her friends, instead of calling her on the phone, which she regards as natural and intimate, send her electronic messages (Turkle 1996:237). According to a new study (Young 1998), eight million people are Internet addicts and psychologists warn that Net addiction is a real danger. It can lead to loss of jobs, money and partners (*The Australian*, 18 June, 1996:13). Addicts, people who spend more than forty hours a week online, have a lot in common. They are mainly people with low self esteem, often depressed, lonely, insecure and anxious, for whom the Net is some kind of escape from a less promising and much too demanding reality (Young 1998). Thus, it is not surprising that the pace and scale with which electronic networks are allowed to become the dominant conduits for human interaction worry many people. 'Already, it begins to seem as if the more we "interact" by digital means, the more we are disconnected from each other, the more we are distanced from the social codes which lend meaning to our lives, the more we are deprived the richness of direct, face-to-face, exchange with our fellows and friends' (Brown 1997:242).

However, on the other hand, for many people the Net offers many comforting moments. People with serious and fatal illnesses could turn to virtual support groups as a way of coping with stress and finding understanding and a common interest. For many isolated or immobile people electronic exchange is the essential way of sustaining their sociability. Also the argument that easy intimacy online means that people are free from the demands of reciprocity and responsibility is sometimes contradicted by evidence of reciprocity, as we showed when discussing virtual communities. There are also examples of people's responsibility for their electronic, otherwise unknown, friends (*The Australian*, 18 February, 1998:7). Furthermore, electronic communication does not need to be such a lonely experience. Enthusiasts of computers like to tell us that computing, instead of being a solitary pleasure, should and can be the gathering point for family activities. Families should congregate around a large monitor attached to a PC, they should have their own sites on the Net, which will permit them to develop and preserve their family history and cultivate relationships with all members of the family, regardless of their physical locations. The PC should be the centrepiece of the home entertainment system, so consequently, the family role and function will become even more important.

To summarize, the Internet allows people to explore and experience today's fragmented culture and, because of it, the Net can be seen as 'a significant social laboratory for experimenting with the constructions and reconstructions of self that characterize postmodern life' (Turkle 1996:180). The new experience of identity as a set of fragmented, self-created constructs generates a sense of freedom and expectations for more informal, intimate and creative relationships with others. While we should not give up hope for new dialogues between liberated people, free of constraints of race, gender or age, we also need to recognize the dangers connected with the new kind of multiplicity of self and the new kind of fluidity of human relationships. Since there is no way back to the solidity of 'inner directed' man, and nobody would welcome back any strict control over her or his conduct and the nature of relationships, the only way to cope with the emergence of a new type of intimacy is to search for a new balance between the informality and formality of interaction online, which would allow us to enjoy relationships via this medium without giving up on our obligations to each other.

Since it cannot be assumed that 'cybersociety' will generate its own morality, the network society in order to be successful needs to be held together by a strong sense of mutual obligation, responsibility and respect. Civility, sociability and intimacy require the socio-political preconditions securing the optimal balance between the informality and formality of each style of interaction. Online, that is, in these situations where there is no mutual embeddedness in social relations, there is a need for some regulations or agencies (for example, for educational ones) that can govern social relationships. At the same time, in order to take advantage of the new opportunities provided by the Net, namely, the possibility for a more creative, open, flexible, free, innovative, less hierarchical and more democratic order, the informality of this type of communication should also be valued.

8 Political change and informality

If realizing our freedom partly depends on the society and culture in which
we live, then we exercise a fuller freedom if we can help determine the shape
of this society and culture. And this we can do only through instruments of
common decision. This means that the political institutions in which we live
may themselves be a crucial part of what is necessary to realize our identity as
free beings (Taylor 1985:208)

FROM COMMUNISM TO POSTCOMMUNISM: THE
LIBERATION OF THE PRIVATE SPHERE

Following the above quotation's argument, that in the absence of free community we cannot speak meaningfully of any awareness of oneself as a free
and moral being, it can be claimed that the type of political order, by prescribing a space free of official rules and limitations, shapes the norms ruling
interpersonal relationships. The nature of the political system is reflected in
the crucial part of our identities as free beings since our self-respect and dignity depend upon the possession of human rights and are aided by democratic forms of social and political institutions. Furthermore, since
responsibility requires the freedom to be the author of one's world, the
nature of the political system can be seen as influencing an individual's
capacity to define and make independent choices, including relationships
with others. Hence, if autonomous selves are impossible without the experiences of freedom, the nature of the political system, which determines the
scope of an open space on which people can act in collectively responsible
ways, underpins the levels of civility, sociability and intimacy.

As we have already discussed in Chapter 3, a totalitarian system is the obvious example of a society characterized by the deficit of civility, and thus – in
turn – also by the erosion of sociability and by the degeneration of intimacy.
Such a system undermines civility because it violates people's privacy by
reducing their control over their lives and because it delegalizes the social
division of labour, which, in turn, results in societal perception of the existing social differences as not fair, thus leading to societal rejection of the

norm of generalized respect (Elias 1978; Margalit 1996). Here our main focus will not be on a totalitarian system but on societies of 'really existing socialism' (the so-called communist societies), whose political form evolved from a totalitarian to a more authoritarian one, and on postcommunist societies, where the threat to the private sphere has been removed. Nonetheless, communist and postcommunist societies, due to their unique relationships between public and private, provide a good illustration of the fate of civility, sociability and intimacy in undemocratic systems and in systems that are not yet fully democratic. The differences between these two types of societies and traditional liberal democratic societies – in terms of the conception of human autonomy, liberty, the negative freedom from oppression and the positive freedom of rational control of one's life – are real and essential in shaping the formal and informal norms ruling interpersonal relations.

Communist societies provide a good example of political systems where the scope left out of the authorities' control is rather limited. These societies were characterized by the authorities' attempts to suppress from the public sphere spontaneous, unplanned and informal conduct, and that not approved of in advance. With the help of various methods, starting with terror and moving later to economic sanctions, the system was trying to make sure that the public adopted only one possible, that is, 'official' line of arguing and seeing reality. This had several consequences. Firstly, in communist societies there was a high level of discrepancy between the official, that is, the public or the frontstage, and the private, that is, backstage behaviour and opinion. Various types of backstage, unofficial, informal strategies and games were, consequently, developed in the innovative process of adjustment to this division. Secondly, with the continuous expansion of the scope for 'informal' conduct, (e.g., hidden lobbies functioning within the industrial system, 'reciprocal services', informal bargaining), these various forms of informal adaptive behaviour exercised increasing pressure on the official political rules. Subsequently, formal control became too expensive and inefficient, while the deficiencies of the economy were forcing people to rely on personalized networks to secure necessary goods and services. This resulted in the further expansion of clientelism, the second economy and corruption. In the context of the continuous problem of shortages and difficulties in the coordination of the economy as well as the increased wastefulness of the economy, the emerging informal exchange, manifesting itself in the informalization of the economy, contributed to, rather than subverted, the system's formal tasks and general interest. Nonetheless, the informalization of the economy reversed the legal principle according to which 'everything is prohibited that is not explicitly allowed' to a new principle in which 'everything is allowed that is not explicitly prohibited' (Stark 1989). Subsequently, in the long run these informal practices undermined the system's organizational integrity (Jowitt 1992:121–32).

Communist societies' inability to react in innovative ways to these emerging problems and their inability to cope with the following crisis, both failures being the result of the fact that in these societies formal rules were not complementary to and not supported by informal norms, forced people to develop mechanisms of informal adjustment. Since 'the mechanisms generating this informal adaptive behaviour were the government and the formal structure' (Rychard 1993:34), these formal characteristics of state socialism can also be seen as responsible for the deficit of civility. By enlarging the gap between private and public spheres of life, the structural features of communist societies, such as the absence of the principle that protects privacy and the division of labour unjustified by rational and technological requirements, contributed to a widespread deficit of civility. Furthermore, in the context of the shortages and the narrow margin for change, correction and alteration to formal rules, people were forced to rely on family, kin, friends and co-workers for meeting their needs. This process of the instrumentalization of sociability was accompanied by the crystallization of people's identity consisting of 'declaring oneself' rather than constructing one's identity through discourse or 'negotiating meanings'. People's open-mindedness and self-understanding were not supported or enhanced by communist society's institutions. Hence, the importance of a mechanical and emotional identification was growing. This resulted in the increased significance of intimate groups, whose isolation from the wider social context contributed in turn to the further reduction of people's capacities to enter into reciprocal, non-instrumental relations with non-members of their small circles.

All the main characteristics of the communist type of society did not disappear automatically with the collapse of the Berlin Wall. Although postcommunist societies provide a larger scope for autonomy, a greater opportunity for the expression of personal preferences, opinions and feelings and more opportunities for people to change, correct or alter the formal rules than do communist societies, their reality, and especially the existence of confusing and overlapping relations between the public and private spheres, still differs from western democracies. Hence, postcommunist societies can be seen as societies undergoing structural changes aimed at redefining the relationship between the public and private realms. Although attempts to reduce the power of the political centre and increase democratic freedoms can contribute to the lowering of the deficit of civility and constructing better conditions for less instrumental sociability and for less exclusionary intimacy, the scope of these achievements is still an empirical question. Furthermore, the process of new institutional changes has not yet blocked the role and functioning of the old informal norms and networks, the legacies of the past. Taking into consideration the lack of clarity and coherence of the new formal rules, chaos characteristic to the process of institutional change and the fact that some mechanisms of control, monitoring and sanctioning are still not well institutionalized, it can be said that informal connections and informalities of adaptive behaviour continue to play a significant role in postcommunist societies. This in turn contributes to the establishment of social interaction based on confused and unclear rules. The coexistence of conflicting institutional arrangements, unclear social attitudes and vague guidelines for action (Wesolowski 1994:41) means that one of the main characteristics of the postcommunist situation is the overlapping of the 'backstage', that is, private, informal, unofficial or semi-official games, with the public, formal, and legal rules of social interaction. Thus, it can be said that the process of political change in postcommunist societies will not be finished until the nature of relationships between the public and private spheres becomes clearly defined in such a way that they enjoy the effective protection of their respective independence, while their overlapping is well-proportioned. This will find an expression in societal acceptance and the practice of civility, sociability and intimacy as the dominant styles of interaction.

While in different countries the severity of the threat of reform being blocked varies, none of them seems to avoid it totally. The Czech Republic and Hungary are often seen as models of transformation, while Russia's confusing 'muddling through' worries many external observers. I will pay particular attention to the Polish case not only because I am familiar with it, but also because Poland, an achiever in some aspects and clearly lagging behind in others, is an interesting example of a country persistently searching for an appropriate balance between formality and informality of interactional practices.

COMMUNIST SOCIETIES: THE DISTINCTION BETWEEN THE PUBLIC AND PRIVATE REALMS

Not much new can be added to the numerous descriptions of 'really existing socialism' or communist societies, therefore we look here at only some chosen phenomena that are indicative of the deficit of civility, the instrumentalization of sociability and the expansion and privileging of particularistic personalized relationships. Because of our rather specific interest in communist societies, the evolution of this system will be only partially reflected in our discussion. Furthermore, our discussion of differences between liberal democratic societies and communist societies will be narrowed to their contrasting views on the freedom of the public sphere and their different patterns and scope of bureaucratization.

Although with the evolution of state socialism, state intervention in public life had been slowly reduced, the threat to the private sphere, due to the absence of effective protection and the conditions necessary for the existence of an independent and separate public realm, always remained a real one (Krol 1996:183). The aspiration of the early communist state to overstep the conventional border of the 'private' led the party-state to interfere in the most private matters of citizens' lives. At the early stage of the existence of communist rule, the party activists 'may convoke the work collective to discuss publicly the marital infidelity of an employee or the persistent quarrels between two families and in the case of the "public interest" being endangered, the public procurator may enter any case that is related to those issues' (Kurczewski 1993:97). Thus, because there was no independent public realm, distinction between public and private was conditional upon the discretion of authorities. However, as people learned to cope with the centralized control and totalitarian aspirations of the state, their strategies contributed, consequently, to narrowing the state-party project aimed at forcing the public to surround the private. With the passing years, it became clear that the world of official institutions, designed to inculcate a sense of loyalty, faithfulness and obligation towards the new regime, proved itself incapable of 'generating congruent motivations among their strategic actors' (Offe 1996b:27). The final result of the failure of communist institutions to shape 'socialist preferences', therefore, was a widespread cynicism and a total withdrawal into private life. Consequently, this low level of social trust and support for the system, being indicative of the system's cooperation problem, could not compensate for its economic failures. The hierarchical and undemocratic state and the centralized and inefficient planned economy resulted in the strong opposition between the public and the private sphere.

While in capitalist systems the differentiation between public and private spheres generates civil privatism and increases people's concern with their families, careers and status (Habermas 1973:75–8), in state socialism this division facilitated the deficit of civility and the extension of horizontal links and personal relationships that grew into social networks of the second society and which offset the shortages of the centralized economy. Due to an absence of voluntary associations, suspicion towards the state-party and under the condition of economic difficulties, intimate relationships, such as friendship and family ties, became substitutes for other forms of social organization. The privatization of society through the expansion of webs of social ties was accompanied by the growing process of informalization of the economy, which served as channels for semi-legal or even illegal exchanges, which were important resources to overcome the deficiency of the official system. In what follows I will present some evidence of how the above processes affected the nature of interactional practices.

In the context of the authorities' control over public communication, an open exchange of values and opinions was limited to one's own small informal circles. Communication in the public sphere was dominated by 'newspeak', which in Orwell's vision of totalitarianism was seen as a part of the system that attempted to coerce people through control of their thoughts and feelings. In Orwell's novels (*1984* and *Animal Farm*) newspeak is presented not as a language of description, exchange of information or debate but as an evaluative and arbitrary monologue of the unlimited and unaccountable central power. This monopolistic public speech claimed the exclusive right to the truth and universalism. Its pragmatical, ritual and magic nature served to impose values and opinions on a speechless and silenced society. In accordance with it, what was not named did not have the right to exist (Glowinski 1990). Since open societal communication was limited to one's own intimate circles, people from outside the chosen circles were treated with suspicion and denied the right to any identity other than 'being the enemy'. This created a 'ghetto' political culture, which viewed 'the governmental and political realm suspiciously, as a source hoarding information, goods, even danger' and which was based on rumours 'as a mode of discourse that works against sober public discussion of issues' (Jowitt 1992:310). Both functions of the official language of the public realm not only managed to postpone for a long time the process of the emergence of a vertical voice, which expresses itself via collective action (Hirschman 1986), but also to undermine the norms of civility.

In social consciousness the truth was defined as everything that should not have been expressed in public (Marody 1981:120), while newspeak was perceived as neither telling the truth nor naming social reality in a direct way. Newspeak was a symbol of the ruling elite's identity, whereas the circulation of gossip and rumour marked the borders of the informal 'us' groups. The acute perception of the existence of two 'truths' made people very suspicious and not very open towards others. The lack of coherence between the official version of reality and people's own experiences created an atmosphere of threat and fear, resulting in the tendency to hide, enclose and to protect oneself. Consequently, encounters with strangers were always evaluated negatively and people's attitudes to strangers were not open and forthcoming. This is reflected in much empirical research in which the low level of civility is reported as the main source of dissatisfaction in public encounters. According to 90.5 per cent of Poles surveyed in 1985, a low culture of interpersonal relationships was the main problem of their daily life (Giza-Poleszczuk 1991:74). Moreover, the respondents thought that civility was the most eroded aspect of life under state socialism and the most difficult to correct. A common awareness of the 'crisis of good behaviour', 'a lack of manners', 'an unfriendliness' or 'an absence of civility' was accompanied by a shared negative evaluation of widespread social indifference, unkindness and unfriendliness. Society was seen as ruled by an ethical dualism in which moral principles were binding among primary groups but not towards strangers, who were treated with a lack of sensitivity, hostility and aggression (Nowak 1986; Giza-Poleszczuk 1991; Tarkowski 1994a). This public assessment and worries about the lack of civility in public encounters were enhanced by the lack of a commonly shared recognition of the exiting division of labour as legitimate and just. The official distribution of material rewards and respect was not coherent with society's feeling on this issue as people's contribution, skills, education and courage were not evaluated according to the recognized standards. This resulted in widespread social frustration, which led to a perception of the existing distribution of rewards as illegitimate or even illegal. Delegitimization or even delegalization in the public eye of the basis of social differentiation resulted in a restriction on the granting of respect only to people whom one knew and who proved themselves to be worthy of respect (Giza-Poleszczuk 1991:78–86). Hence, a norm of generalized respect was rejected as nobody was seen as deserving respect for simply being another human being.

Under the condition of economic difficulties and in the absence of a formal–legal framework, this deficit of civility, together with the absence of intermediary structures – such as voluntary organizations which can be a significant terrain for overcoming social alienation, atomization and for teaching social cooperation – contributed to the development of familial-particularistic ethics (Tarkowski 1994a; Ray 1996). These familial-particularistic ethics, being in total contrast to universal civic ethics but resembling Banfield's notion of 'amoral familism', refer to the dualism of norms in dealing with members of one's group and in dealing with strangers. Communist societies' culture of privatism manifested itself in horizontal integration based on the particularism of family and friendship and through the development of a 'de-bureaucratized social space' of the second economy, characterized by relationships of mutual obligation and patronage (Ray 1996:125–8). Particularistic and clientelistic order, the second economy and corruption, accompanied by reciprocal labour exchanges, mutual assistance and barter of scarce commodities, can be seen as these societies' distinctive mechanisms of social integration.

Any description of the culture of privatism and the role of informal networks in the daily life of communist societies needs to start with an exposition of the specific role of the workplace in this system because all members of informal networks used their positions in state organizations for channelling public resources for personal use. It was possible because in a socialist shortage economy impersonal relations at work were replaced by personal ones. The socialized workplaces 'privatized' the individual, which meant that employees failed to see the general interest and instead perceived a series of 'individual interest' that could be exploited in a socialized workplace, turning it into a 'private farm', which was to be 'milked' as much as possible (Poleszczuk 1991:119–23). This total lack of perception of any link between one's own interest and the interest of a broader community, together with the feeling that the exchange is unequal (that their, that is the employees', contribution is not adequately rewarded due to low wages, empty shop shelves and so on), resulted in the development of various informal ways of coping with the permanent shortages. The existence of parallel structures and the widespread functioning of relationships of reciprocity based on informal networks meant that, instead of an institutional vacuum, the public sphere was covered with webs of social ties and bonds that provided bases for credible commitment, exchange and the coordination of resources to overcome the deficiency of the official system. These relations of reciprocity were common inside all public institutions. 'At the shop-floor level, shortage and supply bottlenecks led to bargaining between supervisors and informal groups; at the managerial level, the task of meeting plan targets required a dense network of informal ties that cut across enterprises and local organizations' (Stark 1992:79). The existence of a zone of things to be arranged in an informal way between people acting in private, though making use of their formal roles, was taken for granted as a fact of life in every state firm, cooperative or office and further lowered individual responsibility or feelings of guilt (Pawlik 1988).

The company was transformed by the existence of these informal ties and networks into an informal welfare institution, which informally was a source of many services and goods. This transformation and the subsequent nature of the company were accepted by all since, despite the lack of good wages, people valued it as a place of social encounters and a place where so many things could be 'arranged' (Zukowski 1988:153–92). While in any type of formal institution, informal relationships are important, what was unique to the socialist institutions was their scale, their importance for meeting employees' needs, the fact that they were spread within all hierarchical levels and that they split up the society into an 'archipelago of networks' (Lonkila 1997) whose members were primarily loyal to their fellow network members. Since everybody was dependent on these networks for the provision of goods, services, information, jobs and access to education, hospital care and so on, the role of this instrumental sociability was of the utmost importance.

The second aspect of the uniqueness of the informal sphere in the public arena of state socialism was connected to the fact that informal ties, games and exchanges were not only dysfunctional, they were also functional for the preservation of the socialist economy throughout almost the entire time the system existed. In a communist company informal networks – by being 'pathology of pathology' (Rychard 1980) – were indispensable to the functioning of the production system. Only because people trusted each other and were ready to enter into all the necessary deals and semi-legal or illegal arrangements was the plan performed (Crozier 1967:229). However, in the long run the system's integrity was threatened by these widespread informal practices. Particularly dangerous to the organizational identity of the system proved to be the informalization of mechanisms of exchange on the macro level, which brought the economic relations between enterprises in the socialist economy very close to a barter type of economy 'based upon the reciprocity principle' (Kurczewski 1993:367). In the long-term perspective, these informal games and exchanges, while securing daily operations, contributed to the deepening of dysfunctions of the centralized economy.

The prevalence of corrupt patron–client relationships also constituted a structural element of these societies because in hierarchical and centralized systems it was 'extremely important to have friendly persons strategically located at the higher rungs of the hierarchical ladder who can directly provide the desired goods, deliver information, secure connections to other influential people or mediate between client and upper levels' (Tarkowski 1989:53). The lack of accountability of the elite in a one-party bureaucratized state, coupled with its administrative responsibility for non-market investment and supply policy, facilitated and provoked the arbitrary use of state property to enhance private interests via vertical and horizontal informal links among officials. A corrupt routinization developed that 'entails the subordination of office charisma to the incumbents' particular interest' (Jowitt 1992:284). This process intensified with the growing central-ization of power and the declining ability of the state to meet public demands.

Consequently, despite the growing bureaucratization of state socialism, the system did not acquire an ethos of bureaucratic impersonalism, but rather increased the demand for endless personalized tributes and privileges to confirm the party-state officials' supreme status (Los 1990:204). Further-more, in state socialism, unlike in formal-rational bureaucracies, rules were not procedurally formalized and the *nomenklatura* was always accustomed to operating within a political space that was very loosely defined in political terms (the slogan of the 'leading role of the political party' had never received operational expression in institutional categories; Staniszkis 1995:22). These unofficial, often very personalized patron–client relation-ships played a very important role not only as the way to a new alternative redistribution of goods and services but also as important alternative chan-nels of communication between various levels of the hierarchy of power. Moreover, informal exchange and patronage within an organization played – at least to some degree – the role of substitute for channels of democratic articulation of various internal differences and conflicts. Internal battles between various factions within the communist party over the monopoliza-tion of resources were for many years the only mechanism of change avail-able in state socialist countries. Finally, in this system built on distrust, personalized relationships, frequently rooted in old-boy networks or family ties, were significant sources of constructing networks of trust and coopera-tion (Tarkowski 1994b:86).

These informal relationships, where members' particularistic interests and mutual obligations were the bases of closed and trustful exchange, facili-tated a new economic reality in Soviet-bloc countries. Taking the shape of patronage relationships between party-state functionaries and private busi-nessmen, these networks contributed to the early processes of liberalization, which took place in Poland and Hungary in the 1970s and other countries in the 1980s. In Poland in the 1950s and 1960s any kind of friendly relations between party-state functionaries and private businessmen were highly unlikely; however, gradually a number of informal ties grew (Tarkowski 1989). Assuming a patron–client character, where a member of the establish-ment used influence, authority and connections to protect and/or support friendly businessmen in exchange for cash payment or mutual exchange of gifts and favours, these types of relationship were enhanced by the growth of the second economy and its vulnerable political situation. The functioning of the second economy, which included all areas of economic activity that were officially viewed as being inconsistent with the ideologically sanctioned dominant mode of economic organization (Los 1990:2), by creating a growing interconnection and overlaps between the official and unofficial elites, provided many members of the political class with economic power. 'At the top of the unofficial economy are the large-scale underground businessmen' whose 'survival depends on their ties to members of the official elite' (Shelley 1990:23). In some cases these ties assumed a close personal character, with public officials becoming regular, albeit silent partners in private business (Tarkowski 1989:59). These new types of informal, personalized relationships between the party and state officials and the private sector, being often nothing more than 'legalized corruption' and abuse of power by the power elite, prepared the way for the transformation of the system.

Corruption, however, was not only indicative of the behaviour of the power elite. It was widespread throughout the entire communist society, in which difficulties in distinguishing between universalistic and particularistic interests were continually increasing and where people used their social relations to circumvent official regulations. Corruption 'at the bottom' was surrounded by ambiguity because, although it included illegal action, people frequently tended to consider it as altruistic help or to justify it as necessity. It became judged in less straightforwardly negative terms and was seen as a sign of societal life and energy since, under the conditions of the opposition between 'them' and 'us', between the party-state and civil society, corruption was one of the few options left to society to oppose 'them'. Arguing that 'sickness is better than death' (Bensancon quoted in Smolar 1994:26), led to a view of corruption 'at the bottom' as the sign of the rebirth of civil society, as one of the ways of protesting against the state's arbitrary and unjust distribution and as a method for overcoming the absurdity of the centralized economy by the spontaneous and informal organization of society. This increase in informal provisions, ensuring the softness of the enforcement of rigid formal rules, transformed the last period of state socialism into a softer 'winking oppressive' variant of state socialism (Borocz 1993:104). The informalization of the social relations of production and distribution, being the main characteristic of the last stage of evolution of state socialism (Stark 1989) meant that 'informality constituted not a separate "sphere" or sector of the economy but something of a "systematic principle". It saturated the most important processes of control, production and distribution of all levels of society, including the "first" as well as the second economy, the workings of the ruling party apparatus, the state organs, and all major institutions' (Borocz 1993:103).

Another important aspect of the culture of privatism, which manifested itself in the expansion of the gap or void between the state and primary groups (that is, the family and close personalized networks), intensified and continued to be the dominant characteristic of the social organization of these societies. Being part of an informal circle was seen as the main way of achieving some level of social, financial and psychological security.

Particularly important was, as Nowak (1989) stresses, the role of friendship as a means of attaining social approval and social acceptance because of the social discreditation of the official sources of social recognition. Since the 1970s Polish sociologists have described the increased opposition between the private and the public using the term 'social void'. This sharp dualism between the private world and the public realm was illustrated by much Polish empirical research (Nowak 1989; Wnuk-Lipinski 1990; Kurczewski 1993; Tarkowski 1994a) showing the domain of institutions and the world of people as two different and conflictual realities and pointing out that people retreated into informal, primary groups and narrowed their involvement and interest in what happens in the public arena. People identified themselves first with family, whereas 'friends constituted a second type of "important object"; both single friends, ties with whom involved people in a network of interpersonal connections, and whole – as a rule – small groups of friends, if such groups became formed from a network of interpersonal contacts' (Nowak 1989:136). In the 1980s the importance of informal particularistic relationships was further enhanced by the increased inefficiency and inability of the state to meet social demands and provide security and stability (Wnuk-Lipinski 1990:95). This process of growing opposition between the private and public reinforced people's ties and identities with primary groups. These identifications, shaped by the emotional and rather mechanical belonging to the primary group, were clear cut and rigid, not open to any negotiation and confrontation but amounting to manifestations of faithfulness to values and interests of one's informal circle. This degeneration of the role of informal groups as the main source of emotional support, and the increase of their function of helping to cope with everyday economic problems 'had a negative impact on social morality and even decomposed societal life' (Lukasiewicz and Sicinski 1989:119), leading to 'amoral familism'. Consequently, a highly privatized society emerged in which the ethic of 'defend your own and take what you can' dominated its social interaction (Marody 1981).

This example illustrates that intimate bonds as the basic form of social organization cannot always be seen as playing only a positive role in increasing social integration by mitigating some of the societal tensions (Eisenstadt and Roniger 1984:12). In communist societies the expansion of monopolizing and exclusionary primary groups was a cause of many problems. In a situation of total distrust of the state and distrust towards unfamiliar others, relying solely on the intimate ties of families and other primary groups enhanced escapism into privacy rather than in general social solidarity. The role of the family, kin and friends in providing elements of reciprocity and trust in a situation where there is no freedom and security is well illustrated by the evolution of the importance of these groups in Poland. The role of intimate relationships declined significantly during the rise of Solidarity (1980–1) due to the enormous increase in participation in a relatively free and independent public life, while after the declaration of martial law the significance of the role of primary groups grew again (Lukasiewicz and Sicinski 1989:126–7). Moreover, in the situation of a social vacuum or lack of institutions at the intermediary level, there was nothing to protect these informal networks from an inevitable transformation into more 'clique' types of relationships. In communist societies, when the dynamics of a situation pushed members of informal networks to increasingly rely on each other's help, the nature of pure or intimate relationships was eroded since their task was not only to provide affection and companionship but also to provide instrumental support. Consequently, in really existing socialism informal networks often grew full of distrust of outsiders and evolved into egoistic and closed groups, oriented towards the reciprocal provision of scarce goods and services exclusively to their own members. Many social relationships, while on the surface still preserving a language of intimacy and warmth, tended to acquire more instrumental features, with the exchange of goods and services as their main function (Nowak 1989).

To sum up, the state socialism system reinforced many traditional characteristics of Eastern European societies, particularly 'the exclusive distinction and dichotomic antagonism between the official and private' (Jowitt 1992:71 and 287), which contributed to a widespread deficit of civility. Communist societies also enhanced the culture of privatism by not allowing citizens to forge generalized cooperative ties among themselves. At the same time, it facilitated the perception of the official sphere as the locus of demands and sanctions rather than of political support and recognition, leading to the domination of calculative and instrumental attitudes to the public sphere of life and the particularism of informal networks, which negatively affected general social solidarity. Thus, the inability of the official system to foster loyalty and support for the formal rules and its facilitation of 'amoral familism', as illustrated by the deficit of civility, the instrumentalization of sociability and the particularism of primary groups, contributed to its collapse and pointed the way out of the old economic and political structures. Consequently, 'the exit route from communism, the symbolic "turning point" boiled down to the formal recognition of informal structures and rules that had previously been used to stabilize the system, while simultaneously – in a way imperceptible to the protagonists themselves – laying the basis for the new order' (Staniszkis 1995:21–2).

POSTCOMMUNIST SOCIETIES: THE OVERLAPPING OF PUBLIC AND PRIVATE

The postcommunist stage has opened new opportunities for the democratization and liberalization of Eastern Europe. The nature of legacies of the past and the character of the main processes of transformation have influenced postcommunist societies' capacity to further reform themselves. Both issues, namely, the character of the way out of state socialism and the specificity of the postcommunist process of accusation of property, have been negatively reflecting on state legitimacy and its ability to carry out the process of democratization as well as on civil society's ability to collaborate. Instead of being a period of learning how to cooperate and build consensus, the first several postcommunist years have reinforced the culture of distrust, the habit of informal dealings and the strengthening of particularistic visions and demands (Krzeminski 1993; Misztal 1996; Sztompka 1996). Consequently, postcommunist societies consist of 'only a partially understandable conglomerate of groups' (Weslowski 1994:41), the informal ties in which have very often already been forged under the conditions of the centralized, hierarchical and planned economy of the communist period. At the same time the 'moralistic and highly ideological orientation of elites and informality of ties connecting their members deprived them of an ability to understand the importance of institutional order for the functioning of the society' (Kaminski and Kurczewska 1994:150). The weak postcommunist state and the fragmented civil society, acting within a loosely defined and rather chaotic environment, have been unable to challenge the old bases of identities and networking.

Despite many Western observers' tendency to see the postcommunist transformation as 'capitalism by democratic design' (Offe 1991), in reality the effect of a critical mass of informal networks has been equally important. The absence of legal norms and procedures has left an enormous sphere of ambiguity and unsolved problems, which facilitates the use of informal methods of coping with many issues and which allows many informal networks, often the legacies of the past, to take advantage of information and contacts accumulated under the previous regime. Since these groups try to shape a new institutional order to suit their interests and since the institutional choices of the transition stage are of the greatest significance for the future distribution of power and wealth, 'hardly anyone can be expected or trusted to make these choices in a fair, non-partisan and disinterested way' (Offe 1996b:20). Consequently, difficulties with formalization and battles over institutionalization have contributed to the emergence of a culture of distrust, which manifests itself in people's distrust of the political system and its reforms (56 per cent of surveyed Poles declared distrust towards the systematic reforms' future prospects) and in a general dissatisfaction with institutions (only 29 per cent of the respondents unconditionally approve reforms) (*Central and Eastern European Eurobarometer*, February, 1993). The culture of distrust, introduced by an inefficient 'capitalism by design' and its unclear rules and laws, which are often left unenforced, has enhanced attitudes of particularism and reinforced the deficit of civility.

Although the low level of institutionalization of postcommunist societies has been accompanied by a very high level of distrust and general uncertainty, it has not, however, resulted in a total paralysis of people's initiatives or their disorientation. Instead, some actors, those already accustomed to negotiating the ambiguity of contradictory forms, have challenged these new uncertainties by improvising on practised routines (Stark 1992). These types of activism have not only challenged the processes of social integration by contributing to growing social fragmentation and polarization but have also blurred the boundaries between the frontstage and the backstage regions. The overlapping of these two spheres: the frontstage, that is, the official and public arena, and the backstage space, where informal and private encounters occur, lowers the chance of radical, structural and novel solutions to postcommunist societies' problems. The combined effect of a lack of structural solutions and the reliance on semi-formal or informal and fragmented solutions, produces a civil society that consists of informal groups devoted to their own particularistic interests and where people hide their identities from each other, consequently blocking societal communication and therefore cooperation. Hence, postcommunist societies' activism, while contributing to the expansion of the market economy, has not empowered civil society. In today's Eastern European countries, where the centralized strong power of the communist state has been abolished, both co-partners, the state and civil society, are relatively weak. The declining credibility and legitimacy of the state and the expansion of particularism in civil society further increase the apathy and weaknesses of postcommunist society.

The widespread belief in postcommunist societies that public life is dominated by sets of contradictory but camouflaged interests and therefore that it is safer not to acknowledge one's true identity and to treat with suspicion others' identities and the credibility of institutions, has reinforced the old habit of seeing 'the other' as the enemy and the social world as divided between 'them' and 'us' (Krzeminski 1993). Such a dualism promotes a short-termism and quick, risky and particularistic arrangements and deals, which resemble more backstage or 'behind the scenes' remedies than structural and lasting solutions. People, without being able to rely on state regulation and institutions, try to fulfil their particular needs and aspirations through their own contacts, access and wit. The result is the adoption of a calculative and instrumental approach to the official or public sphere of life, while the virtue of solidarity is transformed into informal groupings to protect their particularistic interests. By the same token, unable to trust others and the state, people resign from any attempt to regulate or change the frontstage according to long-term structural interests because it requires societal cooperation and the credible political actor as an executor of change. The final stage of this type of development results in a very conducive environment for the hiding of real interests and real identities, where people's informal adaptive strategies co-exist alongside the official ineffective and unworkable remedies. Hence, when people are taught to rely on informal adaptive responses, which reinforce personalism and suspicion (Jowitt 1992:288), any possibility for honest discourse and cooperation is lost. The fragmentation of postcommunist societies into different 'demanding groups' results in the absence of a shared public identity as citizens, which does not allow for truthful discussion or mutual respect. When the main function of public communication is not to facilitate compromise, cooperation and debate but rather to hide one's interest and to uncover one's enemies' interests, the escape to privacy of the primary groups follows.

These processes of the declining legitimacy of the state and the growing feeling of powerlessness and distrust of politics are well illustrated by the data about the dynamic of the Polish state legitimacy rates and the nature of Polish civil society. Although there was enormous euphoria surrounding the rebirth of civil society in Eastern Europe after 1989, and although the first Polish postcommunist government scored very highly on the scale of legitimacy, since 1992 a negative dynamic has started, with social support for the government dropping below 30 per cent. In 1990 only 25 per cent of surveyed Poles agreed that the majority of politicians are interested solely in their own careers, in 1993 already 41 per cent of those asked shared this opinion, while two years later 54 per cent of respondents had a negative view of politicians. With the majority of people being distrustful of the government, seeing political parties only as vehicles for politicians' careers and with only 20 per cent of those asked believing that new laws are passed in the common interest, the postcommunist state faces the real problem of the erosion of its credibility and legitimacy (Zakowski 1995:8–9). The level of people's involvement in politics has been continuously declining; fewer Poles participate in each new election, fewer declare any interest in politics (75 per cent in 1993; in 1997 only 59 per cent) and only 18 per cent of those surveyed in 1997 felt that they had a voice in shaping the country's fate (Bobinska-Kolarska 1998:31–2). It can be concluded that Poles, left with many morally ambiguous attitudes from the communist era and in the context of the growing importance of market forces, together with the lack of a democratic tradition, have started looking at politics and politicians with an increasing distrust and cynicism and have withdrawn from participation in public life and escaping into the closed, private world of family and friendship circles (Zakowski 1994:8–11). This process of the growing feeling of the loss of trust in and control over politics, does not contribute positively to the development of democratic habits or respect for law. Hence, the movement towards the reduction of the deficit of civility, the legacy of the communist era, is not very advanced, as witnessed by the fact that 62 per cent of Poles surveyed declared weakened mutual sympathy and less readiness to help one another (Sztompka 1996:51). Further proof comes from a dramatic increase in the sale of guns, gas pistols and personal alarms as well as the installation of reinforced doors, all of which can be seen as indicators of the growing feeling of insecurity. With 67 per cent of those asked declaring that Poland is not internally safe and with only 26 per cent feeling secure (Sztompka 1996:52), it is not surprising that one of the fastest growing new services in postcommunist societies is the private security business. Russia, for instance, already has 483 000 private security guards (*Guardian Weekly*, 22 March, 1998:4). The majority of the new generation in former Soviet bloc countries does not think much about public virtues; they believe that money is the most important thing in life. Not only do 57 per cent of young Russians, for whom 'crony capitalism' is the only known reality, want money, almost half of those surveyed said that 'they believed it was acceptable to take what you want by force' (*Guardian Weekly*, 22 March, 1998:4).

The low level of civility in the fragmented and polarized society has not been assisted by the nature of public speech, which demonstrates an absence of a language enabling people to express their identities and interests and, hence, helping them to reduce mutual distrust. To some degree the main thinking schemes of the communist 'newspeak' are still present (Glowinski 1997:2) as social communication is still dominated by the political elites' monopoly over the presentation and naming of social reality. Social communication is still neither covert, clear nor direct. The readability of intentions and sent signals is also rather low. All main political camps try to use public speech to present social reality in such a way as to squeeze others from the public sphere. Polish political discourse is monopolized by two ways of talking about public matters; the first employs cynical language and the second uses an integralist language (Spiewak 1997:3). The main characteristic of the first language, the cynical one, is that its users, showing a total lack of a stable identity or an understanding of their responsibilities, treat public discourse – by switching from one to another type of ideological argumentation as it suits their political interests – as the instrument for the manipulation of the social reality. The users of the integralist language, the politicians of the opposite extreme of the political spectrum, offer an organic and very broad vision of the world, in which all terms and notions have rather one-dimensional and stereotypical meanings, which only reinforce the various types of extremist views. Consequently, in both of these languages the question of the political location of the speaker (whether the speakers are one of 'us' or one of 'them') becomes more important than the content or merit of their message. This means that the main function of public communication is not to facilitate compromise, cooperation and debate but rather to mask one's interests and un-mask one's enemies' interests. Such a situation is far away from Habermas' ideal discourse, which assumes that political decision-making reflects rational argument, the *sine qua non* of which is the disinterested pursuit of truth and where what matters is the content of what is said.

The deficit of civility in postcommunist societies has also not been helped by the nature of the process of acquisition of public property. Three characteristics attributed to this trend have undermined, in the public eye, the legitimacy of the emerging division of labour and have contributed to the lowering of generalized social respect. Firstly, the acquisition of property rights is frequently seen as a continuation of the trend of transforming the position of power into economic wealth. Secondly, it has often taken place in a rather 'informal way', that is, without clear rules or formal procedures, often 'among friends' and making use of 'anarchy as a quasi-solution' (Staniszkis 1991:28). Thirdly, the financial accumulation of private capital, by not always clearly defined and legally prescribed channels, and methods of the transfer of public resources into private hands of members of the former elite have resulted in many forms of hybrid ownership (Staniszkis 1995).

There is no clear agreement among scholars on the nature of the process of acquisition of public property in postcommunist societies. Researchers arguing that what we have witnessed in the former Soviet bloc countries is not the replacement of the elite but rather its reproduction, point out that the main characteristic of the process of acquisition of property in postcommunist societies has been the utilization of one's position achieved under the old system and that this has resulted in the specific nature of 'political capitalism' (Staniszkis 1995). This belief, that in postcommunist society the process of conversion rather than replacement of elites takes place, is also voiced by Hankiss (1991) who argues that the former party, state and economic *nomenklatura* has transformed itself into the ruling economic class and that in this process informal contacts, family relations and the informal alliance with the former strata of small owners were essential. Consequently, despite the collapse of communism and despite the loss of formal political power, the old elite preserves its economic influence due to its informal coalitions and alliances (Hankiss 1991:27–39).

More empirically oriented studies (e.g., Szelenyi, Treiman, Wnuk-Lipinski 1995) do not provide final and total support for the radical version of the 'political capitalism' thesis, although they admit that their data strongly point out that the former political power of the old *nomenklatura* has been converted into economic power. For example, according to the results of Polish empirical studies, the majority of the Polish *nomenklatura* members preserved their elitist positions or found alternative ways to high status, with private business being the main channel of social and occupational mobility for *nomenklatura* (Wasilewski 1995:417). Comparative studies also demonstrate differences between countries, with Russia being the case of the most visible conversion, followed by the less clear cases of Hungary and Poland (Eyal and Wasilewski 1995:126). This type of research also illustrates the difference between the new political and economic elites, with the former's socio-professional background being considerably different to the occupational breakup of the party *nomenklatura* before 1989. In can be generalized that while in the case of the political elite we have witnessed a process of replacement of elites rather than their direct continuation, in the case of the economic elite the reproduction of the elites has been equal to their replacement.

Turning now to the second characteristic of the way in which capitalism has been built in Eastern and Central Europe, it can be said that the process of acquisition of property rights has often taken place in a rather 'informal way' with people taking advantage of their access to power, information and credit. Members of the *nomenklatura* not only had greater access to all these goods but they 'were also involved in informal relationships which must have improved their chances of success in the market situation' (Wnuk-Lipinski and Wasilewski 1995:43) and they were accustomed to operating within a political space that was very loosely defined in political terms and was accustomed to not-so-open ways of providing for their needs. Consequently, they have been 'better' prepared and 'better' equipped to create various companies or take over public property. Their skilful way of externalizing their cost in all possible manners as well as taking advantage of personal connections within the former structures of political power as a substitute for as yet undeveloped markets, have secured their control over the postcommunist economy (Staniszkis 1995:22). The absence of adequate, clear and formalized procedural rules as well as the lack of execution of such rules has also increased the political and economic elite's freedom of movement by further blurring distinctions between the public and private realms. This has contributed to the growth of social ambiguity and confusion as the overlapping of the public and private has ensured that many semi-illegal types of behaviour, clientelism, speculations and varieties of scandals have been tolerated for a relatively long time. This kind of behaviour was, moreover, sanctioned – at least to some degree – by the media and elites' claims that at the first stage of the capitalist development some criminality was inevitable, thus normal, and that even in the West the first stage of capitalist development was full of speculations, fast money and corruption. The history of so many scandals in postcommunist societies and the 'untouchability' of many people involved in them has reinforced people's feelings that the new wealth has not been achieved in a respectable and legitimate way (Kryshtanovskaya 1994). The majority of surveyed Poles feel that fairness and justice is absent in public institutions, with 93 per cent of them indicating the growth of crime and 87 per cent pointing out the existence of economic rackets (Sztompka 1996:51). Taking into account that postcommunist societies are not only poorer (40% of Poles, 31 per cent of Russians and 60 per cent of Bulgarians live below the poverty line (*Guardian Weekly*, 7 May, 1995:6) but also that they have become even less egalitarian than their Western partners and that the primary accumulation of capital takes place there at a very rapid rate (the 'fast money' of the new economic elite was acquired just in a year or two) ostentatious displays of wealth by a new elite (in which, for example, can be included 4.3 per cent of Moscovites but only 0.6 per cent of the Russian population as a whole; Kryshtanovskaya 1994:10) leads to resentment, social distrust and dissatisfaction. Hence, because the emergence of new economic power is seen as an evolutionary phenomenon of 'survival of the first, not simply the fittest' (Jowitt 1992:296), the deficit of social respect and civility has become a normal occurrence in postcommunist societies.

The third characteristic of the process of acquisition of property, that is, the hybrid nature of ownership, has also contributed to a decline of trust in institutions and to an increase of orientation toward short-term advantages, consequently, spreading privatism and instrumental attitudes towards others. In the context of the hybrid forms of ownership and uncertainties about its legal regulations and where formal property rights cannot fully be executed, economic success and the actual functioning of property rights 'depend to a high degree on the actors' location in the network of informal personal relations, that run across the formal functional differentiation of political, administrative and economic spheres' (Tatur 1994:112). Therefore, since informal networks can be seen as responsible for the development of diverse variants of hybrid ownership, one of the main problems for postcommunist societies is a question: will these informal networks 'get the job done' or will they inhibit the further process of democratization and marketization? (Stark 1992:83).

This brings us to the issue of sociability in postcommunist societies. Despite changing forms and functions, the networks of personal relations are still the most significant part of social life in postcommunist societies. Comparative studies of informal exchange in Russia and in Finland between 1993 and 1994 and in 1996 discovered differences in the scope and nature of these practices in postcommunist society and in liberal democracy (Lonkila 1997). Russians exchanged more favours, goods and important information; they used their relatives, friends, colleagues or acquaintances in order to obtain products and services informally. In Russia this informal exchange took place mainly in the workplace or through work-mediated relations and more exchange was mediated by a third person than in Finland. 'The resulting forms of social life can be characterized as personalized and mediated' (Lonkila 1997:1). Notes taken by Russian teachers, who kept diaries on informal exchange for the purpose of the research, are very illustrative of this process of informal exchange, which consists of people using their work-related opportunities to help each other with small repairs, loans, finding jobs and services or arranging access to hospitals, school and other institutions. These exchanges are necessary to protect oneself from the main problems of daily life, namely a lack of an adequate level of services and the deficit of civility. According to one Russian woman: 'If one respects oneself, one has to have one's own dentist, gynaecologist, hairdresser, masseuse, tailor. If these are friends, it's the best. It is much more pleasant to socialize than just to get rude service' (quoted in Lonkila 1997:20). All these mutual favours are presented as if the instrumental and altruistic aspects of social relations were intertwined to the extent that they seem impossible to separate. Nonetheless, the majority of informal exchange carried out by Russians implied the use of social relations in order to obtain materials, goods or services, 'whereas such cases and the corresponding vocabulary were absent in the Finnish diaries' (Lonkila 1997:6). It is clear that the informal exchange of goods and services has not been abolished in the process of transformation to the market economy. The significant social life of people in postcommunist countries is intertwined with instrumental exchange relationships and the nature of this exchange confirms the special nature of the workplace. The domination of personalized forms of social life manifests itself in turning replaceable relations into personal and unique ones (Lonkila 1997:1). Exchange of goods and services in personalized relations has also solidified distrust to official institutions, therefore it has a negative impact on state legitimacy.

The existence in postcommunist societies of a multiplicity of networks, ranging from 'old *nomenklatura* networks' – through small producers' networks – to ordinary people's daily exchanges, has not helped the process of democratization and marketization because they are 'too clan-like' and they are unable to promote dynamism in the long run since when times get difficult, they are used to defend the perception of 'interest' shaped by 'long-standing habits and routines inimitable to marketization' (Stark 1992:82). For example, the dominating Eastern European economies' networks of small producers do not provide a basis for long-term dynamism because they are too restrictive, based mainly on the nuclear family, lacking more generalized trust and cooperation (Stark 1992:82). Because producers, due to a lack of extensive networks of cooperation and exchange, tend to turn for help to the state, clientelism and patronage are normal occurrences in postcommunist societies. The petrification of the networks of protectionism further blocks reforms by interfering with the social and economic efficacy of the system. Connections between politics and the business world can also lead to the actual privatization of the state, which undermines state legitimacy because informal groups 'taking the state into their possession' do not promote universal societal interests but their own particularistic interests. For instance, in Poland, where 'every second top manager in the private sector used to be the director of a socialist enterprise' (Unger 1994:6), massive industrial lobbies and agricultural groups secure enormous subsidies and privileges from the state. Clientelism has also not been beneficial for the development of social solidarity as informal networks have contributed to the preservation of societal fragmentation and to the reduction of clarity and openness in social communication.

The domination of clientelistic ties and informal networks of exchange has contributed to the instrumentalization of sociability and the confusion between private interest and public duties. This ambiguity has been further deepened by the fact that in former Soviet bloc countries a household's social position is determined by a multitude of factors and its members often combine the duties of their official, semi-official and private roles and participate in overlapping networks. In postcommunist countries there is a growing number not only of households whose members are working in the private sector but also households that are combining different forms of employment: for instance, in Russia only 61 per cent of average household incomes came from wages (*The Economist*, 29 April, 1994:42), which reflects a relatively high level of employment in a shadow/second economy. The functioning of the relatively expanded sphere of the second economy creates a conducive environment for the promotion of particularistic interests and for blurring divisions between types of ownership and types of responsibility. The second economy, which in Russia may be as big as the official one (according to government sources, it accounts for around one-fifth of GDP;

The Economist, 3 May, 1997:75), shapes the culture of semi-legality or illegality. While it is difficult to draw a clear line between normal business practices and illegality, it is even harder to see a clear line between the second economy and criminality. Although the majority of Poles declare that they see both positive and negative aspects of the 'grey sphere' for the whole society (Smejdy 1996), the fact that around 2.5 million of them are employed in the second economy (*Polityka*, 10 May, 1997:68), suggests that informal adaptive responses are accepted ways of searching for additional sources of income.

The domination of personalized forms of life means the continuation of the importance of intimate circles or primary groups. Family, kin and friends still continue to play a significant role in postcommunist societies. The 'exit' option, namely withdrawal from participation in public life and escape into the closed private world of family and friends, is also enhanced by the general uncertainty of the transitional period and by the negative public opinion of postcommunist politics and political elites (Sztompka 1996). Postcommunist societies, due to the high level of uncertainties concerning their future can be described as 'waiting societies' (Tarkowska 1994). People's anxiety about their long-term future manifests itself in their attitudes and behaviour in both public and private realms. Not only do people show an increasing reluctance to tie marriage knots (in the 1980s in Poland there were 9 new marriages per 1000 inhabitants, in the late 1990s there are only 5), they also postpone or reduce their desire to have children, which is reflected in the decline of birth rates in all former Soviet countries (*Polityka*, 14 February, 1998:1–6). Although Poland is still one of the countries with the most stable families (the divorce rate even declined in the second part of the 1980s), in 1993, for the first time the number of new marriages was lower than the number of dissolved marriages. This trend, despite the introduction of legal changes that made divorce procedures more difficult, still continues, with 1500 more divorces in 1996 than in 1995 (*ibid*:6). All the above changes, together with the growing popularity of cohabitation (the rate of which doubled in the 1990s in Poland), bring postcommunist societies into Western patterns of demographic trends (*Polityka*, 14 February, 1998:1–6).

The transitional character of Eastern European societies means that people are confronted with a new situation in which there is no single, given normative order, and where there is a need for choice, which involves taking risks, demands confronting uncertainties and accepting new responsibilities. For many people the necessity of an individual search for criteria of decisions and for solutions to new problems is too demanding a task. It results in widespread nostalgia for the past order (a large proportion of Poles still feel that they were better off under state socialism, *Gazeta Wyborcza*, 28 June, 1994:2), which is, however, accompanied by the belief that democracy is the best possible political set up (Bobinska-Kolarska 1998:30). This 'confused consciousness' (Krzeminski 1993), characteristic of mainly older generations, expresses itself in extreme evaluations, in a language full of contradictions, identities built on declarations and in affiliations with others based on

emotional bonds. Hence, participation in intimate circles and strong emotional ties with members of primary groups are still important aspects of
social life in postcommunist countries because these relations and strategies,
by reducing the complexity and uncertainty of the new order, help people to
mask the ambivalence of their attitudes (Jawlowska 1995:23). Family, kin and
friends continue to be significant sources of identity and trust because they
are seen as the only groups able to compensate for the lack of a clear normative order as well as for an absence of coherence and predictability of the
external world. A strong loyalty towards intimate groups, expressing itself in
the closing in and construction of boundaries around limited and intimate
relationships, increases the danger of the 'ghettotization' of postcommunist
societies (Sztompka 1996:45–8). Evidence of lower levels of social tolerance
in former Soviet bloc countries than in Western democracies seems to match
this picture (Misztal 1996:230–4). Other worrying attitudes are adopted by a
young generation that grew up in the first stage of implementation of market
reforms and who witnessed many of their disturbing consequences. For
example, 65 per cent of surveyed young Russians said that they would marry
for money and 28 per cent declared that they would consent to paid sex
(*Guardian Weekly*, 22 March, 1996:4). These disturbing views seem to reflect a
high level of acceptance of an environment that is perceived as both threatening and demanding a total acceptance of market rules. Another option
open to young people in newly democratized societies is the escape into subcultures and alternative groups. This and the growing participation in intermediary, voluntary institutions (various associations, movements and
institutions) can be seen as forms of 'norms-creating activity', undertaken in
order to reconstruct a normative order. However, solutions offered by this
multiplicity of 'ethos groups' seem to be too specific, too particularistic,
localized, changing and accidental to be able to ensure the creation of a new
universal normative order (Jawlowska 1995). This lack of an assurance or
guarantee that a stable, universal normative order will be found makes
postcommunist societies very postmodern, before they really had a chance to
enjoy being modern.

Postcommunist Eastern and Central Europe still faces the task of creating
credible frameworks for communication within society and between society
and the state. The successful completion of this task requires, first of all,
formal democratic procedural structures that are able to support and facilitate the legitimation of authority and the integration of society. Seeing the
processes of democratization and legitimation as essential for the reduction
of the deficit of civility, for the lowering of the instrumentalization of sociability and for the undermining of the culture of privatism, is based on an
assumption that formal rules are elementary incentives for those willing to
undertake change. Next steps after attempts to 'supersede the existing informal consists with new formal rules' (North 1993:47) should be focused on
the construction of a system of norms facilitating changes in people's
interactional practices. Because state socialism has not left codes of

behaviour that could help to construct a democratic and collaborative civil society and because informal norms and conventions, particularly those ones contributing to cognitive dissonance and resulting in incoherent and polarized loyalties and identities, change very slowly, many difficulties of postcommunist societies may only be overcome by the passage of time and the arrival of new generations better adapted to a new social world. Furthermore, since we live in an interconnected world, our culture is more than ever determined by others nations' political practices. The spectrum of contemporary European culture and political practice is wide enough for postcommunist societies to be included, if generalized respect, reciprocity and mutual responsibility become the main features of their styles of interactional practices. Being part of a democratic order does not guarantee the certainty and stability of social order but it can provide the framework for predictability, while at the same time leaving more space than in undemocratic systems for the self-organization of society.

Conclusion: Informality and democracy

The 'reciprocal informality' of our time has two sides. It could be said that people are now allowed to drop formal communication, or it could be said that we are now forced to drop it (Meyrowitz 1985:321).

The book shows that although the process of formalization is the dominant trend in modern social life, informality is the essential element in constructing trust relationships and, thus, in any cooperative arrangement aimed at improving the quality of life. Its main assumption holds that only a society that achieves an optimal balance between the informality and formality of interactional practices is in a position to create the conditions for cooperation and innovation.

We started our discussion by pointing to a new breed of global managers who, in order to enhance informal contacts seen as way of ensuring trust and creativity, live more or less on planes. Paradoxically, for these 'overtravelled bosses' new means of communications are more help as a way of keeping them in touch with home rather than as ways of carrying out business contacts. Since, as one of those managers says, technology depends on trust ('a bossy e-mail from somebody you had never met could put you off them'), it is important to meet people first; 'it is important to gesticulate' (*The Economist* 9 January, 1999:64).

To develop a theoretical framework for understanding people's creative and flexible responses to situational complexity and ambiguity requires, however, more than the appreciation of people's informal conduct. It also demands the recognition of the importance and the necessity of formal rules as well as the awareness of the potential negative consequences of informality, both of which lead to the conclusion that the positive dimensions of informality can only be sustained by a simultaneous process of formalization. The argument that the fine tuning of formality and informality is central to the creation of social trust has been introduced with the help of the concept of 'the formality–informality span' (Elias 1996), which assumes that a moderate type of self-constraint, co-existing with neither too weak nor too excessive external constraints, will contribute to the improved quality of social life.

The shape of 'the formality–informality span' has changed alongside 'the advance of civilization' (Elias 1978:190). The historical transformation of Western societies has sharpened the polarization of social life between increasingly impersonal realms of market, state and bureaucratic organization, on one side, and an informal realm of increasingly intense intimacy within the modern family on the other. In modern societies 'this split is taken so much for granted, becomes so compulsive a habit, that it is hardly perceived in consciousness' (Elias 1978:190). As the evolution of 'the formality–informality span' illustrates, the formal–informal distinction is interlinked with other concepts used to demarcate boundaries between private and public, between emotion and reason, between spontaneity and calculability, between community and bureaucracy and between universalism and particularism. Although the formal–informal dichotomy compromises a complex usage, it brings us closer to the essential problem of our times, namely, the freedom available to an actor.

While the formality is characterized by the centrality of explicit external constraints, rules, contracts, instrumental calculation and impersonality, the most common and underlying element of all definitions of informality is the scope of relative freedom of conduct. To avoid the question to 'which degree twentieth-century informalization has been accompanied by an increasing internalization of restraint rather than a conformity to external rules' (Newton 1998:73), Goffman's focus on role distance has been adopted and this has led to defining informality as a style of interaction among partners enjoying relative freedom in interpretation of their roles' requirements.

Goffman, by assuming that 'one can never expect complete freedom between individual and role and never complete constraint' (1974:269), equates the notion of informality with role distance and argues that when a performer shows his or her distanciation to the role, s/he puts brackets around the central task activity and enjoys more freedom in selecting the style or form of interaction (1961:123–5). Informality, therefore, refers to situations with a wider scope of choices of behaviour where, in order to make the most out of the possibilities in given circumstances, that is, to reach 'a working understanding' (Goffman 1983:9), people employ various not pre-made forms of action. The space for informality, or the opportunity to shift frames, is indicative of actors' social sophistication, which reflects actors' social standing and their ability to construct an unproblematic type of interpersonal relationship.

However, while our capacities for interpersonal concordance and our socially, culturally and economically determined opportunities to distance ourself from the role allow us to shift frames, the expansion of informality cannot be unlimited because society requires predictability and orderliness for its long-term functioning. Furthermore, 'a human passion for clarity and order' and 'passion for generalising, simplifying, and subordinating' (William James [1909], quoted in Barbalet 1998:54), also direct our attention into attempts to increase the predictability of our lives. People's desire for order and for control over the future can be realized in two different ways. Firstly, it can be attained through the expansion of the process of formalization, conventionalization and rationalization, with all these trends introducing 'calculation as rationality', seen as 'the basis of everything' (Weber 1991:22). Secondly, it can be secured through reliance on trust since to show trust is 'to behave as though the future were certain' (Luhmann 1979:10). So, both trust, which relies on informality of personalized relationships, and calculability, which contributes to 'the importance of formal rules in rational law and administration' (Weber 1991:25), are useful and mutually dependent strategies for increasing control over the social world. The scope of both processes and their relationship need to be assessed empirically by looking at the actual shape and expansion of formalization and informalization.

In Goffman's stable view of social life with its fixed rules, roles and institutions, role distance is seen as referring to role as fashion is to custom. The problem is, however, that today we do not only 'revolt against custom' to embrace fashion, which can give us 'a feeling of adventurous safety' (because others do the same), but we feel free to adopt increasingly more individual styles, which often means mixing up various performances and breaking old barriers between the front and back regions. Of course, even the most indvidualized styles are not totally free-floating inventions. However, the erosion of the distinction between high and low culture, what Mannheim (1992) called the 'de-distanciation' of culture, the separation of politics and culture (Bauman 1987), as well as the process of fragmentation and pluralization of culture have made 'the cultural field more fluid and uncertain' (Turner 1992:xxviii). All these factors together with the spread of electronic media and new means of communication, which have eroded the traditional boundaries between the backstage and frontstage regions (Meyrowitz 1985) and the growing role differentiation, lead to 'a greater role distance and looser "fit" between any particular role and the social actor' (Seligman 1997:166).

Furthermore, there are still important differences between countries in terms of the culturally prescribed relations between informal and formal. Different cultures provide their members with different scope for informal behaviour as they tend to classify differently which performance is relevant for the backstage and which for the frontstage. For example, in Germany, where the span between formality and informality is relatively wide, formal behaviour is more ostentatious than in Britain (Elias 1996:30). Some studies argue that informal exchange of information is more culturally accepted in the USA than in Germany (Flap and De Graff 1988), while other works point to the Netherlands as an 'informalized' country due to the dramatic social transformations that took place there in the 1960s and 1970s (Mennell 1989:241). Generally, it is assumed that those countries that have undergone the social revolution of the 1960s, subsequently 'informalized' their public manners (Hopper 1996:24). In contrast, the 1980s are presented as characterized by an increase in the formalization of emotional and social codes and as the period in which the informalization process, especially in countries with greater economic inequality, 'seems to have a halt, and a process of formalization has once again come into effect' (Wouters 1986:1). However, 'there has been little clear evidence of increases in formalization' (Newton 1998:73) and, moreover, the following decade has again brought new claims of deconventionalization, lessening of external regulations and increases in informality and flexibility.

As many empirical studies suggest, recent change can be seen as the process of deconventionalization, the erosion of boundaries, hierarchies, breaking up the established rules, disorganization, instability and fragmentation (Wagner 1996:107). Consequently, it is often argued that the previous image of modernity, seen as the triumph of rationalization, formalization, standardization and conventionalization, stands in a clear contrast to today's society. Touraine, while proclaiming the disappearance of 'what we formerly called society', calls for 'the courage to admit that social life is modern only to the extent that it is no longer regulated by norms, and even less by common cultural values' (1998:175). The collapse of formal organizations, the decline of hierarchical order, the weakening of the social and political order, the growing autonomy of technology and economy, accelerated by the process of globalization, which – by removing economic exchange out of political and social control – creates perception that 'things are getting out of hand' and that 'no one seems to be now in control' (Bauman 1998:57–9), all have been increasing the diversity of cultural scripts, strategies and expectations upon which people draw as they devise their performances.

With ambivalence, shifting boundaries and unpredictability becoming the main characteristics of contemporary societies, the 'age of contingency' is proclaimed (Bauman 1996:50). Since fears of the uncertainty, unpredictability and provisionality of all arrangements may threaten the integrity of people's lives, the reconstruction of the coherence and orderliness of widely divergent worlds is a battle for the quality of life. Devising ways of tuning formality and informality should be done in such a way that will allow us to take full advantage of the expanded opportunities to shift frames, without, however, undermining the basic structures of society. So, the essential issue is how to synchronize the processes of informalization and formalization so they will contribute to the improved quality of social life. The reformulation of this issue as the question about styles of interaction to which we should be socialized in order to achieve a better quality of individual and social life, has been followed by an observation that the optimal style or, in other words, how people manage to treat others as a matter of 'having the right touch' or tact, depends upon particularities of a given type of interaction. Since a different tactful behaviour is essential for different types of interaction, it has been assumed that civility, sociability and intimacy, as the manifestations of the optimal balance between informality and formality in different social settings, are central to the creation of social trust.

Despite the fact that modern societies can free us 'from dependence on particular others for a host of practical needs' and therefore create 'the possibility of personal relations valued as expressions of inner intention and commitment apart from practical agendas and formal obligations' (Silver 1997:48), they often suffered from the decline of civility and sociability as well as from the 'tyranny of intimacy'. The weakening of standards of conduct and the dominance of privatism are attributed, on one hand, to a general relaxation of the regulations and, on the other hand, to contemporary societies' unprecedented depersonalization of economy, polity and administration and their degree of impersonality. All these features increase people's feelings of the loss of control and lead 'individuals to become aware of their emotions as objects of self-regulations' (Barbalet 1998:174). The emancipation of emotions manifests itself in the primacy of private life and the decline of the importance of the public realm and 'all things considered as bad' (Wolfe 1997:185) because, as the home becomes isolated from the wider society, private life takes on the form of narcissism and neurosis, while political apathy dominates the public sphere. Furthermore, when 'the public realm of sociability contracted, the family became increasingly defenceless' (Kumar 1997:231). The decline of sociability, as illustrated by the shrinking of the so-called 'third place' (Oldenburg 1989), and the growing number of reports about uncivil conduct, prompt calls for revitalization of codes of conduct, 'the acknowledgment of the degree to which private and public are inevitably intertwined' (Wolfe 1997:201) and the balancing of formality and informality.

Three styles of interaction, namely, civility, sociability and intimacy, are described as rooted in a balance between formality and informality. They are seen as kinds of context specific tact, which help to preserve distance, to avoid offensive, intrusive violations of the private sphere of the person and to suppress socially unacceptable levels of spontaneity and particularism within their respective realms. On the other hand, these styles of interaction mitigate the unnecessary formalism and abstractness of universalism and help to train receptivity and sensitivity towards others. The argument that civility, sociability and intimacy represent the essential basis for any meaningful reinvention of an individualized and deconventionalized modern society is based in the assertion about the importance of the essential elements of those three styles of interaction, that is, respect, reciprocity and responsibility, for the quality of social life.

Since the quality of social life depends upon our ability to cooperate, to 'make music together' and to be creative, a closer look at the leading sociological explanations of these phenomena is required. In order to reveal the role attached to the significance of informality in the processes of cooperation, innovation and integration, the critical evaluation of the main approaches to the question of collective action, creativity and solidarity has been undertaken. Lessons from this attempt allow us to construct a more convincing argument about the significance of understanding the changing relationships between formality and informality in any project aiming at enhancing the quality of social life.

On the assumption that the reduction of uncertainty and the establishment of reciprocal expectations is essential for cooperation, I have argued that the relationships of formal and informal elements are dynamic ones and shaped by the system's orientation towards predictability. The answer to the question of how public goods are produced, as provided by both rational choice theory and the normative approach, is rooted, more or less explicitly, in the assumption that it is the informality of the process of interaction and co-presence that creates mutual obligations and relations of cooperation, because only informal face-to-face interaction allows us to overcome reputational uncertainty. Therefore, the informality of co-present interaction, denoted as granting partners with the needed information about their mutual trustworthiness, is implicitly assumed to be solving the free-rider dilemma and facilitating cooperation.

The concepts of proximity and informality in sociological studies seem to overlap. Statements about the informal nature of co-present interaction often take the form of a more theoretical presumption about links between informality and proximity. This supposition is based on the incorrect assumption that informality is the direct result of, and can be reduced to, the time-space proximity of agents. In reality, the relationships between informality and proximity are complicated. By looking at 'making music together' (Schutz 1964), which refers to the relationships which are established by the reciprocal sharing of others' experiences and experiencing togetherness, it is argued that such relationships depend upon the balancing of proximity and individual autonomy, the essence of which is best expressed by the creation of the condition for negotiating everybody's acceptance of restrictions on their autonomy. It is further suggested that a more promising way of living in modern societies requires dealing successfully with the shifting of boundaries between visible, private, emotional and informal, on one hand, and formal, public, distant and inaccessible, on the other. Assuming that an absence of any sharp and consistent way of drawing distinctions between formalities of the frontstage and informalities of the backstage is the main factor explaining a given group's achievements 'in making music together', moves us away from a dichotomous vision rooted in a preference for either co-presence and intimacy of backstage regions or for formalities of frontstage regions. In this proposed perspective, social networks, or sociability, should be seen as appealing not solely to the sense of emotional bonds but as being sustained on the basis of self-interest, mutual understanding and consensus attained on the basis of convincing others. By bringing interest and solidarity together, we can conceptualize sociability as contributing to socio-cultural constraints on self-interested behaviour and as playing an important part in open, widespread networks connecting people in their formal as well as informal roles.

The evaluation of the extent to which anecdotal evidence about the relationships between creativity and informality are supported by theory reveals that these connections can be enhanced by the provision of the opportunity for the development of networks, which allow participants to join forces with others in the collective process of learning. The networks are seen as the essential condition to maintain the flow of tacit knowledge and creativity because, while providing the opportunity to enlarge the chance of communication and commitment, they function, at the same time, within the formal patterns of regulation. In this view, the innovation process can be successful only when people involved in it are, on one hand, relatively free from rules and regulations, while on the other hand, they function within wider formalized structures able to provide them with some codes of behaviour.

The analyses of sociological theories reveals that an opportunity of the open-ended negotiation of trust depends upon free negotiations of the boundaries of interaction and free-of-rules interaction, while their practical results are connected with the existence of limits to openness and with the introduction of coherent rules and formalized procedures. Therefore, both informality and formality should be seen as the crucial and dynamic aspects of the processes of innovation, cooperation and solidarity. The constituting of a new balance between formal and informal styles of behaviour is a process that depends upon the piecing-together of new modes of social control, new institutions and new means of communication. With the complexity of relationships between informal and formal being increased by new means of communication, it is necessary to rethink ways of combining formal and informal rules that go into social order and look how various interactional practices may become useful tactics to alleviate the growing ambiguity of the world and to facilitate cooperation and creativity.

The examination of informality online and its role in enhancing the Internet's function provides evidence of the significance of the issue of informality in modern life. The effects of electronic computerized communication on the nature of interaction has been studied by looking at civility, sociability and intimacy online through analysis of the network society, virtual communities and the main features of the relationships resulting from electronic proximity. The Internet allows people to explore and experience today's fragmented culture and to 'play' the game of sociability; it also provides the most 'lifelike' interaction possible, thus permitting intimacy in cyberspace. Online, that is, in these situations where there is no mutual embeddedness in social relations, there is a need for some regulation or agencies that can govern social relationships. At the same time, in order to take advantage of the new opportunities provided by the Net, namely, the possibility for a more creative, open, flexible, free, innovative, less hierarchical and more democratic order, the informality of this type of communication should also be valued.

The significance of informality has also been illustrated with the help of the discussion of the nature of the dichotomy between public and private in both communist and postcommunist societies. On the basis of the assumptions that autonomous selves are impossible without the experiences of freedom and that the scope of an open space on which people can act in collectively responsible ways is determined by the nature of the political system, it has been argued that the broader political context underpins the levels of civility, sociability and intimacy. A totalitarian system, because it violates people's privacy by reducing their control over their lives and because it delegalizes the social division of labour, is an obvious example of a society characterized by the deficit of civility. These features of the political regime, in turn, contribute to the erosion of sociability and the degeneration of intimacy, hence leading to societal rejection of the norm of generalized respect (Elias 1978; Margalit 1996). Consequences of the communist authorities' unlimited control, such as an increasing expansion of the process of informalization of the economy, the instrumentalization of sociability and the importance of a mechanical and emotional identification, resulted in the expansion of clientelism, the second economy, the increased significance of intimate groups and the reduction of people's capacities to enter into reciprocal and non-instrumental relations with non-members of their small circles. Subsequently, those processes, in the context of the economic shortages and the narrow margin for political change, correction and alteration to formal rules, eroded the structural coherence of the system.

In postcommunist societies the process of new institutional changes has not yet blocked the role and functioning of the old informal norms and networks and it has not yet removed confusing and overlapping relations between the public and private spheres. The coexistence of conflicting institutional arrangements, unclear social attitudes and vague guidelines for action means that one of the main tasks faced by postcommunist societies is the creation of credible frameworks for communication within society and between society and the state. The successful completion of this task requires formal democratic structures that are able to support and facilitate the legitimation of authority and the integration of society. The processes of democratization and legitimation, by constructing the public sphere with clearly formulated rights and obligations of citizens, are the first steps in the reconstruction of the universalized trust and promotion of solidarity, which can, consequently, undermine the culture of privatism and facilitate civility and sociability.

The nature of the political system, by shaping the extent of the overlap between the public and private spheres as well as the size of each sphere, provides the context for comparing the relationship of informal and formal styles of interaction in communist and postcommunist systems. It can be argued that the same characteristics – overlap and size – also produce 'a framework for comparing civil society' in different political regimes (Janoski 1998:15). This brings us to an important point connecting the informal–formal dichotomy with the private–public distinction and with the concept of civil society. Since it is suggested that civil society helps 'to bring that delicate balance of private interests and public concern vital for a vibrant democracy' (Hefner 1998:17), it can be assumed that weak civil society, which is dominated by the state or market sphere, will be controlled by administrative and bureaucratic formal rules and it will be characterized by a limited scope for the public realm of sociability and by an expanded scope for 'amoral familism'. Strong civil society, which constructs much of the citizen–society discourse, will be dominated by a more balanced relationship between formal and informal as well as between public and private, therefore bolstering sociability and civility and connections between household and their wider networks of relations. As the tensions between public and private are constitutive of civil society (Seligman 1992), the conceptualization of the relationship between formal and informal style of interaction provides an essential step in developing our understanding of civil society and solidarity that holds it together.

The concept of civil society is overloaded with meanings and expectations. It is commonly hoped that vital civil society ensures a manageable scale of social life and will 'make democracy work'. Civil society is also expected to reassert a sense of shared public interest and integration of the individual and society as well as to offer participation and confirm particularistic identities of diverse groups. Since democratic civil society also promises to secure the universalization of citizenship rights, it faces the ambitious task of the reconciliation of many, often conflicting, tendencies. Today, its role of creating spaces that open the way for public participation and action, while preserving individual difference and diversity, is perceived as being especially important and urgent. However, an attempt at both preservation of universal rights and broadening of inclusion brings into the light the limitations of both formal procedural democracy, which reduces participation to universalistic, formal rules and institutions, and the communitarian perspective, which is in favour of particularistic arrangements connected with those 'aspects of social life that refer to the informal, the local and the intimate' and which can be 'a recipe for parochialism and privilege' (Wolfe 1992:311).

Avoidance of both impersonality of formal democracy and the reduction of individual freedoms and diversity into homogenized community, as both limitations can result in the reduction of social solidarity and trust, demands that we come to terms with complex actualities of contemporary pluralist societies by means of combining inclusion and exclusion or democratic incorporation and pluralistic particularism (Wolfe 1992). This can be realized when civil society, as a progressive force for deepening democracy in a substantive sense, becomes 'a sphere of solidarity in which abstract universalism and particularistic versions of community are tensely intertwined' (Alexander 1998:97). In order to know conditions for the existence of civil society, we need to apprehend how inclusive citizenship rights actually are and how widespread is social acceptance of a normative framework of shared purposes and consensus, within which diversity can be both cultivated and contained. Understanding of civil society as an 'informal, non-state, and non-economic realm of public and personal life' (Alexander 1995:34) allows us to examine the relation between universal individual rights and particularistic restrictions on these rights and to look at how the shared space of interaction and interpersonal trust is formed. The following argument that vital civil society would manifest itself by high levels of civility, sociability and intimacy, understood as balanced styles of interactional practices, does not assume that there is an linear path from intimate, private and particularistic identities to civic and universal solidarities but it rather asserts that 'civic solidarity can decrease or increase as economic and ideological factors change' (Reis 1998:37). By implying balance between individual participation and social obligation, private interest and those of society, this approach emphasizes that 'democracy depends on the self-control the individual initiates' (Alexander 1998:99), while at the same time stressing the role of the macrostructural factors in ensuring people's opportunities for autonomy and participation.

Here lies the importance and usefulness of the formal–informal distinction. This dichotomy can illuminate the relationships between inclusion and exclusion, individual and society, public and private, autonomy and community. It can demonstrate a way to mitigate the universalizing tendencies of large bureaucracies, while expanding freedom and diversity and small group participation and creativity. The value of informality is connected with its ability to enhance our move away from formal accountability and unreflective obedience to regulation to the ethics of responsibility and obligation, while the importance of formality is connected with the aspiration of modernity to universalistic inclusion. Understanding that a proper balance between informal, which lays basis for more formal citizenship, and formal aspects of civil society is essential for further enhancement of the process of democratization is, for example, indirectly promoted by Janoski (1998), when he describes the role of rituals in enriching civil society.

Today's 'societies must develop more positive sanctions through renewed emphasis on rituals', such as recognition of exemplary citizens with rewards (Janoski 1998:235). Rituals and rites, as Connerton (1989:44) notes, 'are not merely formal', they are mixtures of formal and informal, public and private, internal and external. They are not empty forms since they 'are felt by those who observe them to be obligatory' and since 'people resist being forced to pay lip-service to an alien set of rites, incompatible with their own vision of the "truth", because to enact a rite is always, in some sense, to assent to its meaning' (Connerton 1989:44).

To sum up, by arguing that the fine tuning of informality and formality is central to the creation of social trust, which is constitutive of civil society, this perspective offers not only a potentially more imaginative approach to the problems of cooperation, integration and innovation, but also a more comprehensive perspective on civil society and the process of democratization. Nonetheless, seeing the balanced relationships between informality and formality as the main factor responsible for the quality of social life should not be equated with believing in the power of informality to reinforce the emotional energy of society and to bind society together. The danger of idealizing the potential of informality is illustrated by a post-Diana cartoon of the Queen standing unhappily in front of a mirror in a magnificently furnished reception room, hopelessly repeating to herself: 'One must be less formal, one must be less formal ...' (*The Australian*, 10 September, 1997:12). One can feel equal pity for employees of the company that proudly and everywhere exhibits its motto: 'Informality is a rule' (*The Australian*, 12 March, 1998:34). Such 'a tyranny of informality' may constitute a new strategy of 'subjugation' and it can be felt as the forced imposition of an artificial equality, which undermines individual uniqueness.

Although the lack of formality is liberating because it means a lack of constraints, it can also, however, change the roles we play, undermine universal rights, bring new difficulties, remove many certainties, lead to the unnecessary 'sentimentalization' of relations and cause much confusion. Furthermore, it can also be a barrier to the development of communication since the lack of formal codes or formal conventions on how to address others may result in silence. A total freedom from conventions and formal regulation, by removing mystique, secrecy and challenge from social relations, can make life rather uninteresting and dull. While the relaxation of regulations and forms can result in emancipation of emotion, it can also make our lives less creative and degenerate our conversation to 'plain talk', which becomes 'the equivalent of fast food' (Zeldin 1998:12). When everything is subjugated to 'informality', social arrangements are weakened, the boundaries between private and public are blurred and the satisfactory experience connected with performance of roles is also gone. Furthermore, with the disappearance of formalized codes of behaviour many people experience the feeling of insecurity. Moreover, the elimination of formal rules, conventions and rituals can contribute to the emergence of a value crisis as people endure agonies of self-examination before taking on any behaviour in public. Without formality, which induces rules and standards, the preservation of privacy is also endangered. Five decades ago, writes Bayley, 'life was more constricted and formal, but at the same time more comfortable and relaxed [...]. We maintained public standards and conventions almost without being conscious of them, while leading our private lives' (1998:12). Hence, while realizing the significance and benefits of informality, we should also remember that the pressure to be 'informal' can be equally dysfunctional as a more rigid formal regulation and that unless we 'recapture a sense of forms we are doomed to boredom' (Bethke Elshtain 1996:13).

Yet the value of informality in today's complex and global world and the ability of informal strategies to create the opportunity to achieve a more responsible and creative society should not be ignored. Recent changes demand openness, flexibility and a capacity to manage multiple encounters with strangers, together with the new communication technologies' impact on the timing and spacing of interaction. This means that the conditions of 'nearness and contemporaneity no longer hold, and the ethical universe must be enlarged to comprise distant others who, while remote in space and time, may nevertheless be part of an interconnected sequence of actions and their consequences' (Thompson 1995:262). Although the process of global-ization problematizes the concept of society and the notion of state, it does not mean a return of stateless societies where informal mechanisms of government and customary arrangements were the main ways of organization. It requires, however, rethinking the bases of obligations and responsibilities in such a way as to increase awareness of mutual interdependence, which, in turn, demands a new institutional design able to enhance links between people and societies on the global scale.

Such universalization of trust can endanger the mutuality of group inter-action upon which trust ultimately depends and it can lead to the restoration of a set of beliefs embodied in the life of smaller groups, which subsequently means an increased risk that they put 'trust in persons rather than in argu-ments' (MacIntyre 1988:5). As geographical mobility expands, as exchange of information becomes unlimited by national boundaries, resources for exploration and rethinking our mutual obligations and responsibilities are increasingly provided by communities of shared beliefs. Inasmuch as the values, conventions and rituals of larger collectives, such as nation-states, are replaced by values and attachments to smaller communities, which are seen as providing more authentic and emotional bonds, there is a threat that such groups can reshape the assumption of liberal politics. Thus, in order to avoid it and for fundamental disagreements to be systematically explored in such a way that does not undermine democratic principles yet is relevant for people, there is a need for forums where people can engage in debate, which – although subject to universalistic rules – is protected from formal control and sanctions. It is necessary to invent such a balance between formality and informality, which will assist, supplement and expand the inventiveness, flex-ibility and creativity of democratic process of the collective decisions for the common good.

Bibliography

Abdul-Rahman, A. and Hailes, S. (1997) 'A distributed trust model', paper presented at the DIMACS Workshop on Trust Management, New Jersey, September.

Ajzner, J. C. (1994) 'Some problems of rationality, understanding, and universalistic Ethics in the context of Habermas's theory of communicative action', *Philosophy of the Social Science* 24, 4:466–84.

Akerlof, G. A. (1984) *An Economic Theorist's Book of Tales*, Cambridge: Cambridge University Press.

Alexander, J. (1998) 'Citizens and Enemy as Symbolic Classification', in J. Alexander (ed.) *Real Civil Societies*, London: Sage:96–114.

—— (1997) 'The paradoxes of civil society', *International Sociology* 12, 2:115–33.

—— (1995) *Fin de Siècle Social Theory*, London: Verso.

—— (1992) 'Shaky foundation', *Theory and Society* 21:203–217.

—— (1991) 'Bringing democracy back', in C. C. Lemert (ed.) *Intellectuals and Politics*, London: Sage.

—— (1985) 'Habermas's new critical theory: Its promise and problems', *American Journal of Sociology* 91, 2:400–24.

Allen, T. *et al* (1983) *Managing the Flow of Technology; Technology Transfer and the Dissemination of Technological Information with the R&D Organisation*, Cambridge, MA: MIT Press.

Allum, P. (1995) *State and Society in Western Europe*, Cambridge: Polity Press.

Amin, A. (1994) 'Post-Fordism: models, fantasies and phantoms of transition', in A. Amin (ed.) *Post-Fordism*, Oxford: Blackwell.

Arendt, H. (1963) *On Revolution*, New York: Viking.

—— (1958) *Human Condition*, Chicago: Chicago University Press.

Aries, P. (1977) 'The Family and the City', in A. S. Rossi *et al* (eds.) *The Family*, New York: Norton.

—— (1973) *Century of Childhood: A Social History of Family Life*, Harmondsworth: Penguin.

Ascott, R. (1991) 'Connectivity: Art and interactive communication', *Leonardo* 24, 2:111–17.

Atkinson, J. M. (1985) 'Etnomethodology: a critical review', *American Review of Sociology* 14:441–65.

—— (1982) 'Understanding formality: the categorisation and production of "formal" interaction', *British Journal of Sociology* 33, 1:86–117.

Baldwin, J. D. (1988) 'Mead's solution to the problem of agency', *Sociological Inquiry* 58, 2:139–62.

Banfield, E. C. (1958) *The Moral Basis of a Backward Society*, New York: Free Press.

Barbalet, J. M. (1998) *Emotion, Social Theory, and Social Structure*, Cambridge: Cambridge University Press.

Barnes, B. (1995) *The Elements of Social Theory*, London: UCL Press.

—— (1992) 'Status group and collective action', *Sociology* 26, 2:259–70.

Barnes, B. and Edge, D. (eds) (1982) *Science in Context*, Milton Keynes: The Open University Press.

Bartlett, C. A. and Ghoshal, S. (1995) 'Changing the role of top management: beyond systems to people', *Harvard Business Review*, May–June: 132–142.

Bauman, Z. (1998) *Globalization*, New York: Columbia University Press.

—— (1996) 'Morality in the Age of Contingency', in P. Heelas *et al* (eds) *Detraditionalization*, Cambridge: Polity Press.

—— (1995) *Life in Fragments*, Oxford: Blackwell.

—— (1989) *Modernity and the Holocaust*, Ithaca, NY: Cornell University Press.

—— (1987) *Legislators and Interpreters*, Cambridge: Polity Press.

Bayley, J. (1998) *Iris: A Memoir of Iris Murdoch*, London: Duckworth.

Beck, U. (1992) *Risk Society*, London: Sage.

Beck, U. and Beck-Gernsheim, E. (1995) *The Normal Chaos of Love*, Cambridge: Polity Press.

Beckert, J. (1996) 'What is sociological about economic sociology?', *Theory and Society* 25, 6:803–40.

Bell, D. (1973) *The Coming of Post-industrial Society*, New York: Basic Books.

Bellah, R. N. *et al* (1985) *Habits of the Heart*, Berkeley: University of California.

Beniger, J. (1987) 'Personalization of mass media and the growth of pseudo-community', *Communication Research* 14, 3:352–371.

Benn, S. I. (1988) 'Privacy, freedom, and respect for person', in F. D. Schoeman (ed.) *Philosophical Dimensions of Privacy: An Anthology*, Cambridge: Cambridge University Press.

Benz, A. (1993) 'Commentary on O'Toole and Scharpf', in F. W. Scharpf (ed.) *Games in Hierarchies and Networks*, Westview:Campus Verlag.

Berlin, I. (1992) 'Philosophy and Life: An Interview with Ramin Jahanebegloo', *The New York Review of Books*, May 28:46–54.

Bethke Elshtain, J. (1996) 'A life of texture and depth requires a culture of distance', *The Australian*, 10 August: 13.

Bewes, T. (1997) *Cynicism and Postmodernity*, London: Verso.

Bikson, T. K. and Panis, C. W. A. (1997) 'Computers and connectivity: current trends', in S. Kiesler (ed.) *Culture of the Internet*, Mahwah, NJ: Lawrence Erlbaum Associates.

Bittner, E. (1967) 'The police on skid-row: a Study of peace keeping', *American Sociological Review* 32, 5:699–715.

Blau, P. M. (1964) *Exchange and Power in Social Life*, New York: John Wiley.

Blumer, H. (1962) 'Society as symbolic interaction', in A. Rose (ed.) *Human Behaviour and Social Processes*, London: Routledge and Kegan Paul.

—— (1954) 'What is wrong with social theory', *American Sociological Review* 19, August: 146–58.

Bobinska-Kolarska, L. (1998) 'Nowa mala stabilizacja', *Polityka* 8, 21 February: 30–2.

Boden, D. (1994) *The Business of Talk*, Cambridge: Polity Press.

— (1990) 'The world as it happens: ethnomethodology and conversation analysis', in G. Ritzer (ed.) *Frontiers of Social Theory: The New Syntheses*, New York: Columbia University Press.

Boden, D. and Molotch, H. L. (1994) 'The compulsion of proximity' in R. Friedland and Boden, D. (eds) *Now, Here: Space, Time and Modernity*, Berkeley: University of California Press.

Boden, D. and Zimmerman, D. H. (1991) *Talk and Social Structure*, Cambridge: Polity Press.

Boland, R. J. and Schultze, U. (1996) 'Narrating accountability', in R. Munro and Mouritsen, J. (eds) *Accountability. Power, Ethos and The Technologies of Managing*, London: International Thompson Press.

Born, G. (1996) '(Im)matriality and sociality: the dynamics of the intellectual property in a computer software research culture', *Social Anthropology* 4, 2:101–16.

Borocz, J. (1993) 'Simulating the great transformation: property change under prolonged informality in Hungary', *Archive Européennes de Sociologie* 34,1:81–107.

Boswell, D. M. (1969) 'Personal Crises and the Mobilization of the Social Network', in J. C. Mitchell (ed.) *Social Networks in Urban Situations*, Manchester: Institute for African Studies.

Bourdieu, P. and Wacquant, L. J. D. (1992) *An Invitation to Reflexive Sociology*, Cambridge: Polity Press.

Bovone, L. (1989) 'The Theories of Everyday Life', in H. Maffesoli (ed.) *The Sociology of Everyday Life*, New York, Sage.

Boyne, R. and Rattansi, A. (1990) *Postmodernism and Society*, London: Macmillan.

Branscomb, A. W. (1993) 'Jurisdictional quandaries for global networks', in L. M. Harasim (ed.) *Global Networks*, Cambridge, MA: MIT Press.

Brass, D. J and Burkhardt, M. E. (1992) 'Centrality and power in organizations', in N. Nohria and R. G. Eccles (eds) *Networks and Organizations*, Boston: Harvard Business School Press.

Brookner, A. (1997) *Visitors*, London: Jonathan Cape.

Brown, D. (1997) *Cybertrends: Chaos, Power, and Accountability in the Information Age*, London: Viking.

Brown, D. W. (1995) *When Strangers Cooperate: Using Social Conventions to Govern Ourselves*, New York: Free Press.

Buchan, J. (1997) *Frozen Desire: An Inquiry into the Meaning of Money*, London: Picador.

Bull, M. and Rhodes, M. (1997) 'Between crisis and transition: Italian politics in the 1990s', *West European Politics* 20, 1:2–13.

Burns, T. R. (1992) *Erving Goffman*, London: Routledge.

Burns, T. R. and Flam, H. (1987) *The Shaping of Social Organization*, London: Sage.

Burns, T. R. and Stalker, G. (1961) *The Management of Innovation*, London: Tavistock.

Burt, R. S. (1992) 'The Social Structure of Competition', in N. Nohria and R. G. Eccles (eds) *Networks and Organizations*, Boston: Harvard Business School Press.

Burt, R. S. (1987) 'Social contagion and innovation: cohesion versus structural experience', *American Journal of Sociology* 92, 6:1287–335.

Cairncross, F. (1997) *The Death of Distance*, London: Orion Business Books.

Calhoun, C. (1997) 'Nationalism and the Public Sphere', in J. Weintraub and Kumar, K. (eds) *Public and Private in Thought and Practice*, Chicago: University of Chicago Press.

Callaghan, G. (1997) 'Chat me up', *The Australian*, 30 August; Syte:1.

Campbell, C. (1996) *The Myth of Social Action*, Cambridge: Cambridge University Press.

Campell, K. E., Marsden, P. V., Hurbert, Y. S. (1986) 'Social resources and economic status', *Social Networks* 8:97–117.

Carnevale, P. J. and Probst, T. M. (1997) 'Conflict on the Internet', in S. Kiesler (ed.) *Culture of the Internet*, Mahawah, NJ: Lawrence Erbaum Associates.

Cash, W. (1998) 'Sex, lies and e-mail', *The Australian Magazine*, February 28–March 1:25–6.

Castells, M. (1997) *The Power of Identity*, Cambridge: Polity Press.

—— (1996) *The Rise of the Network Society*, Oxford: Blackwell.

Cerulo, K. A. (1997) 'Identity construction', *Annual Review of Sociology* 23:85–409.

Cherry, C. (1977) 'The telephone system', in I. de Sola Pool (ed.) *The Social Impact of the Telephone*, Cambridge, MA: MIT Press.

Chesnais, F. (1996) 'Technological agreements, networks and selected issues in economic theory', in R. Coombs *et al* (eds) *Technological Collaboration*, Cheltenham: Elgar.

Christie, N. (1993) *Crime, Control as Industry: towards Gulags, Western Styles*, London: Routledge.

Cohen, I. J. (1989) *Structuration Theory. Anthony Giddens and the Constitution of Social Life*, London: Macmillan.

Cohen, J. K. (1997) 'Rethinking privacy: autonomy, identity, and the abortion controversy', in J. Weintraub and Kumar, K. (eds) *Public and Private in Thought and Practice*, Chicago: University of Chicago Press.

Coleman, J. S (1993) 'The rational reconstruction of society', *American Sociological Review* 58, February: 1–15.

—— (1990) *Foundations of Social Theory*, Cambridge, MA: The Belknap Press.

Coleman, J. S. *et al* (1966) *Medical Innovation*, New York: Bobbs Merril.

Collins, H. (1982) 'Tacit knowledge and scientific networks', in B. Barnes and Edge, D. (eds) *Science in Context*, Milton Keynes: Open University.

Collins, R. (1995) 'Featured essay: Review of the Handbook of Economic Sociology', *Contemporary Sociology* 24, 3:300–4.

—— (1994) *Four Sociological Traditions*, New York: Oxford University Press.

—— (1988) 'Theoretical continuities in Goffman's work', in: P. Drew and Wooton, A. (eds) *Erving Goffman: Exploring the Interaction Order*, Cambridge: Polity Press.

Connerton, P. (1989) *How Societies Remember*, Cambridge: Cambridge University Press.

Constant, D., Sproull, L. and Kiesler, S. (1997) 'The kindness of strangers: on the usefulness of electronic weak ties for technical advice', in S. Kiesler (ed.) *Culture of the Internet*, Mahawah, NJ: Lawrence Erbaum Associates.

Cooley, C. H. (1962) S*ocial Organization*, New York: Schocken.

—— (1902) *Human Nature and Social Order*, New York: Scribner.

Coombs, R. *et al* (eds) (1996) *Technological Collaboration*, Cheltenham: Elgar.

Coser, L. A. (1978) 'American trends', in T. Bottomore and Nisbet, R. (eds) *A History of Social Analysis*, London: Heinemann.

—— (1977) *Matters of Sociological Thought,* Atlanta: Harcourt Brace Jovanovich.

Crane, D. (1972) *Invisible Colleges*, Chicago: Chicago University Press.

Cringely, R. X. (1992) *Accidental Empires*, London: Penguin Books.

Crozier, M. (1967) *The Bureaucratic Phenomenon*, Chigaco: University of Chicago Press.

Dasgupta, P. (1988) 'Trust as a Commodity', in D. G. Gambetta (ed.) *Trust: Making and Breaking Cooperative Relations*, Oxford: Blackwell.

Davidow, W. H. and Malone, S. M. (1992) *The Virtual Corporation*, New York: Edward Burlingame.

Davidson, J. D. and Rees-Mogg, W. (1997) *The Sovereign Individual: The Coming Economic Revolution: How to Survive and Prosper in It*, London: Macmillan.

Delamont, S. (1995) *Appetites and Identities*, London: Routledge.

della Porta, D. and Meny, Y. (1997) *Democracy and Corruption in Europe*, London: Pinter.

Dery, M. (1996) *Escape Velocity*, London: Hodder and Stoughton.

de Sola Pool, I. (ed.) (1977) *The Social Impact of the Telephone*, Cambridge, MA: MIT Press.

Dodd, N. (1994) *The Sociology of Money*, Cambridge: Polity Press.

Dogson, M. (1996) 'Leering, trust and inter-firm technological linkages', in R. Coombs *et al* (eds) *Technological Collaboration*, Cheltenham: Elgar.

Doheny-Farina, S. (1996) *The Wired Neighborhood*, New Haven: Yale University Press.

Dorris, M. F., Gentry, G. G. and Kelly, H. H. (1971) *The Effects on Bargaining of Problems: Difficulty, Mode of Interaction and Initial Orientations*, Amherst: University of Massachusetts Press.

Dosi, G. (1988) 'Sources, procedures and microeconomic effects of innovation', *Journal of Economic Literature*, 26:1120–71.

Dunbar, J. (1996) 'Postcards from cyberspace', *The Australian*, 28 June: 1.

Dunn, J. (1993) 'Trust', in R. E.Goodin and P. Pettit (eds) *A Companion to Contemporary Political Philosophy*, Oxford: Blackwell.

Durkheim, E. (1984) *The Division of Labour in Society*, London: Macmillan.

Edwards, B. and Foley, M. W. (1998) 'Conclusion: beyond Tocqueville: civil society and social capital in comparative perspective', *American Behavioural Scientist* 41, 6, Special Issue ed. by Bob Edwards and M. W. Foley.

Eisenstadt, S. N. and Roniger, L. (1984) *Patrons, Clients and Friends*, Cambridge: Cambridge University Press.

Elam, M. (1994) 'Puzzling out the post-Fordism debate', in A. Amin (ed.) *Post-Fordism: A Reader*, Oxford: Blackwell.

—— (1993) 'Markets, morals and power of innovation', *Economy and Society* 22, 1:1–41.

Elias, N. (1996) *The Germans: Power Struggles and the Development of Habitus in the Nineteenth and Twentieth Century*, Cambridge: Polity Press.

—— (1982) *State Formation and Civilization*, Oxford: Basil Blackwell.

—— (1978) *The Civilising Process*, Oxford: Blackwell.

Elster, J. (1989) *The Cement of Society*, Cambridge: Cambridge University Press.

Emirbayer, M. and Mische, A. (1998) 'What is Agency?', *American Journal of Sociology* 103, 4:962–1023.

Epaminondas, G. (1996) 'Unsuitability', *The Australian*, 13 April: 1.

Ester, P. *et al* (1993) *The Individualizing Society*, Tilburg: Tilburg University Press.

Etzioni, A. (1996) *The New Golden Rule*, New York: Basic Books.

Eyal, G. and Wasilewski, J. (1995) 'Pochodzenie spoleczne I postkommunityczne losy nomeklatury', in I. Szelenyi, Treiman, D. and Wnuk-Lipinski, E. (eds) *Elity Polsce, Rosji i na Wegrzech*, Warszawa: Instytut Studiow Politycznych PAN.

Fallows, J. (1995) 'Positions of trust', *Times Literary Supplement*, 27 October: 7–8.

Favell, A. (1998) 'A politics that is shared, bounded, and rooted', *Theory and Society* 27, 2:208–25

Fineman, S. (1993) 'Introduction', in S. Fineman (ed.) *Emotion in Organization,* London: Sage.

Fischer, C. S. (1984) *The Urban Experience,* Orlando: Harcout Brace Jovanovich.

—— (1982) *To Dwell among Friends,* Berkeley: University of California Press.

Flap, H. D. and De Graaf, N. D. (1988) 'With a little help from my friends', *Social Forces* 67, 2: 452–72.

Freeman, C. (1991) 'Networks of inventors: a synthesis of research issues', *Research Policy* 20, 5:499– 514.

Freeman, C. and Perez, C. (1988) 'Structural crises of adjustment, business cycles and investment behaviour', in G. Dosi *et al* (eds) *Technical Change and Economic Theory,* London: Pinter.

Friedman, R. A. (1994) *Front Stage, Backstage: The Dramatic Structure of Labor Negotiations,* Cambridge, MA: The MIT Press

Fuchs, S. (1988) 'The constitution of emergent interaction orders', *Sociological Theory* 6:122–4.

Fukuyama, F. (1995) *Trust: The Social Virtues and the Creation of Prosperity,* New York: Free Press.

Furedi, F. (1997) *The Culture of Fear,* London: Cassell.

Gadamer, H. G. (1975) *Truth and Method,* London: Sheed and Ward.

Galt, A. H. (1974) 'Rethinking patron-client relationship', *Anthropological Quarterly* 47:182–202.

Gamardella, A. (1992) 'Competitive advantages from in-house scientific research. The US pharmaceutical industry in the 1980s', *Research Policy* 21:391–407.

Gambetta, D. (1988a): 'Can we trust trust?', in D. G. Gambetta (ed.) *Trust: Making and Breaking Cooperative Relations,* Oxford: Blackwell.

—— (1988b) 'Mafia: the price of distrust', in D. G. Gambetta (ed.) *Trust: Making and Breaking Cooperative Relations,* Oxford: Blackwell.

Garfinkel, H. (1967) *Studies in Ethnomethodology,* Englewood Cliffs, NJ: Prentice-Hall.

— (1963) 'A conception of, and experiments with "trust" as a condition of stable, concerted actions', in O. J. Harvey (ed.) *Motivation and Social Interaction,* New York: The Ronald Press Company.

Garfinkel, H. and Sacks, H. (1970) 'On formal structures of practical actions', in J. C. McKinney and Tiryakian, E. A. (eds) *Theoretical Sociology,* New York: Appleton Century Crofts.

Giddens, A. (1993) *New Rules of Sociological Method,* Cambridge: Polity Press.

—— (1992) *The Transformation of Intimacy,* Cambridge: Polity Press.

—— (1991) *Modernity and Self-Identity,* Cambridge: Polity Press.

—— (1990) *The Consequence of Modernity,* Cambridge: Polity Press.

—— (1989) *Sociology,* Cambridge: Polity Press.

—— (1987) *Social Theory and Modern Sociology,* Cambridge: Polity Press.

—— (1984) *The Constitution of Society,* Cambridge: Polity Press.

—— (1981) *A Contemporary Critique of Historical Materialism, Volume 1: Power, Property, and the State,* London: Macmillan.

Giza-Poleszczuk, A. (1991) 'Stosunki miedzyludzkie I zycie zbiorowe', in M. Marody (ed.) *Co nam zostalo z tych lat,* London: Aneks.

Glazer, N. (1997) *We Are All Multiculturalists Now,* Cambridge, MA: Harvard University Press.

Glowinski, M. (1997) 'Miedzy nowym totalitaryzmem a nihilizmem aksjologicznym', *Gazeta Wyborcza*, 7 February: 2.

—— (1990) *Nowomowa po Polsku*, Warszawa: Wydawnictwo PEN.

Goffman, E. (1997) *Goffman Reader*, edited and introduction C. Lemert and A. Branaman, Oxford: Blackwell.

—— (1983) 'The Interaction Order', *American Sociological Review* 48, February: 1–17.

—— (1974) *Frame Analysis: An Essays on Face-to-Face Behaviour*, New York: Anchor.

—— (1969) *Strategic Interaction*, Philadelphia: University of Pennsylvania Press.

—— (1963) *Behavior in Public Places*, New York: The Free Press.

—— (1961) *Encounters: Two Studies in the Sociology of Interaction*, Indianapolis: Bobbs Merill.

—— (1959) *The Presentation of Self in Everyday Life*, Harmondsworth: Penguin.

Goldgar, A. (1995) *Impolite Learning*, New Haven, NJ: Yale University Press.

Golds, R. (1996) 'Syte: the power of e-mail', *The Australian* , December 7–8, Syte:1.

Goleman, D. (1996) *Emotional Intelligence*, London: Bloomsbury.

Gonos, G. (1977) 'Situation versus "frame": the interactionist and the structuralist analyses of everyday life', *American Sociological Review* 42, 6:854–67.

Gornick, V. (1997) 'Closing the book of love', *The Australian*, 8 October: 30.

Gouldner, A. W. (1960) 'The norm of reciprocity. A preliminary statement', *American Sociological Review* 25:161–79.

Granovetter, M. (1985) 'Economic action and social structure', *American Journal of Sociology* 91:481–510.

—— (1973) 'The strength of weak ties', *American Journal of Sociology* 78:1360–80.

Gruber, H. E. (1989) 'The evolving systems approach to creative works', in D. B. Wallace and Gruber, H. E. (eds) *Creative People at Work*, Oxford: Oxford University Press.

Gundelach, P. (1992) 'Recent Value Changes in Western Europe', *Future*, May: 301–19.

Gunes-Ayata, A. (1994) 'Clientelism: premodern, modern, postmodern democracy', in L. Roniger and Gunes-Ayata, A. (eds) *Democracy, Clientelism, and Civil Society*, Boulder: Lynne Rienner.

Habermas, J. (1996) *Between Facts and Norms: Contributions to a Discourse Theory of Law and Democracy*, trans. William Rehg, Cambridge: Polity Press.

—— (1993) *Justification and Application: Remarks on Discourse Ethics*, Cambridge, MA: MIT Press.

—— (1992) *Autonomy and Solidarity. Interview with J. Habermas*, edited and introduced by Peter Dews, London: Verso.

—— (1987) *The Theory of Communicative Action, vol. 2*, Cambridge: Polity Press.

—— (1984) *The Theory of Communicative Action, vol. 1*, London: Heinemann.

—— (1973) *Legitimation Crisis*, Boston: Beacon Press.

Hage, J. and Powers, C. H. (1992) *Post-Industrial Lives*, London: Sage.

Hankiss, E. (1991) 'Reforms and the conversion of power', in P. R. Weilmenn, Brunner, G. and Tokes, R. L. (eds) *Upheaval against the Plan*, Oxford: Berg.

Hansen, K. V. (1997) 'Rediscovering the social', in J. Weintraub and Kumar, K. (eds) *Public and Private in Thought and Practice*, Chicago: University of Chicago Press.

Hardin, R. (1982) *Collective Action*, Baltimore: Johns Hopkins University Press.

Hart, K. (1988) 'Kinship, contract as trust: the economic organisation of migrants in an African city slum', in D. G. Gambetta (ed.) *Trust. Making and Breaking Cooperative Relations*, Oxford: Blackwell.

Hechter, M. (1987) *Principles of Groups Solidarity*, Berkeley: University of California.

Hefner, R. W. (1998) 'Civil Society: Cutural Possibility of a Modern Ideal', *Society* 35, 3:15–27.

Heimer, C. A. (1992) 'Doing your job and helping your friends', in N. Nohria and Eccles, R. G. (eds) *Networks and Organizations*, Boston: Harvard Business School Press.

Heritage, J. (1987) 'Ethnomethodology', in A. Giddens and Turner, J. H. (eds) *Social Theory Today*, Stanford: Stanford University Press.

—— (1984) *Garfinkel and Ethnomethodology*, Cambridge: Polity Press.

Heydebrand, W. (1990) 'The technocratic organization of academic work', in C. Calhoun, Meyer, M. W. and Scott, W. R. (eds) *Structure of power and constraint. Papers in honor of P. M. Blau*, Cambridge: Cambridge University Press.

Hirschman, A. O. (1986) *Rival Views of Market Society*, New York: Viking.

Hochschild, A. R. (1997) *The Time Bind: When work becomes Home and Home Becomes Work*, New York: Metropolitan Books.

Hochschild, A. (1979) *The Managed Heart*, Berkeley: University of California Press.

Homans, G. (1962) *Sentiments and Activities*, New York: The Free Press

—— (1961) *Social Behavior: Its Elementary Forms*, New York: Harcourt Brace Jovanovich.

Honneth, A. (1995) *The Struggle for Recognition*, Oxford: Polity Press.

Hopper, J. (1996) 'Italians believe in showing respect', *Guardian Weekly*, 20 October: 24.

Husted, B. (1996) 'Decision in isolation can endanger the human touch', *The Australian*, 2 December: 33.

Jamieson, L. (1997) *Intimacy. Personal Relationships in Modern Societies*, Cambridge: Polity Press.

Janoski, T. (1998) *Citizenship and Civil Society*, Cambridge: Cambridge University Press.

Jawlowska, A. (1995) 'Lad czy rozpad? Zmiany w sferze aksjologicznej', in A. Sulek and Styk, J. (eds) *Ludzie i Instytucje*, Lublin: UMCS.

Jones, S. G. (1995) 'Preface', in S. G. Jones (ed.) *Cybersociety. Computer-mediated Communication and Community*, London: Sage.

Jowitt, K. (1992) *New World Disorder. The Leninist Extinction*, Berkeley: University of California Press.

Kadushin, C. (1995) 'Friendship among the French finanical elite', *American Sociological Review* 60, April: 202–21.

Kaminski, A. Z. and Kurczewska, J. (1994) 'Institutional transformations in Poland: the rise of nomadic political elites', in M. Alestalo *et al* (eds) *The Transformation of Europe. Social Conditions and Consequences*, Warszawa: IFiS

Katz, E. and Lazarsfeld, P. L. (1955) *Personal Influence*, New York: The Free Press.

Keane, J. (1988) 'Despotism and Democracy', in J. Keane (ed.) *Civil Society and the State*, London: Verso.

Kelley, R. and Caplan, J. (1993) 'How Bell Labs creates star performers', *Harvard Business Review*, July–August: 128–9.

Kermode, F. (1997) *Not Entitled*, Flamingo: London.

Kiesler, S. (1997) 'Preface', in S. Kiesler (ed.) *Culture of the Internet*, Mahawah, NJ: Lawrence Erbaum Associates.

Klima, I. (1997) *The Ultimate Intimacy*, London: Granta Books.

Kohn, M. (1997) 'The chosen collage and the global village', *Times Literary Supplement*, 4 July: 45.

Kostler, A. (1964) *The Act of Creation*, New York: Dell.

Krackhardt, D. and Hanson, J. R. (1993) 'Informal networks: the company behind the chart', *Harvard Business Review*, July–August: 104–11.

Kramarae, C. (1995) 'A backstage critique of virtual reality', in S. G. Jones (ed.) *Cybersociety. Computer-mediated Communication and Community*, London: Sage.

Kraut, R. E. and Attwell, P. (1997) 'Media use in a global corporation', in S. Kiesler, (ed.) *Culture of the Internet*, Mahwah, NJ: Lawrence Erlbaum Associates.

Krol, M. (1996) *Liberalizm Strachu czy Liberalizm Odwagi*, Krakow: Znak.

Kryshtanovskaya, O. (1994) 'Rich and poor in post-communist Russia', *The Journal of Communist Studies*, 10 ,1:3–24.

Krzeminski, I. (1993) 'Idealy i interesy: swiadomosc spoleczna zaklopotana', in M. Grabowska and Sulek, A. (eds) *Polska 1989–1992*, Warszawa: UW Instytut Socjologii.

Kumar, K. (1997) 'Home: The Promise and Predicament', in J. Weintraub and Kumar, K. (eds) *Public and Private in Thought and Practice*, Chicago: University of Chicago Press.

Kurczewski, J. (1993) *The Resurrection of Rights in Poland*, Oxford: Clarendon Press.

Kurke, L. B. and Aldrich, H. E. (1983) 'Mintzberg was right: a replication and extension of the nature of managerial work', *Managerial Science* 2, 8 August: 975–84.

Kuzmics, H. (1988) 'The Civilizing Process', in J. Keane (ed.) *Civil Society and the State*, London: Verso.

Lamont, M. (1992) *Money, Morals, and Manners*, Chicago: Chicago University Press.

Lasch, C. (1997) *Women and the Common Life*, New York: Norton.

—— (1995) *The Revolt of the Elites and the Betrayal of Democracy*, New York: Norton.

—— (1977) *Haven in a Heartless World*, New York: Norton.

Lash, S. and Urry, J. (1987) *The End of Organized Capitalism*, Cambridge: Polity Press.

Layder, D. (1994) *Understanding of Social Theory*, London: Sage.

Lawrence, J. (1996) 'Intellectual property funds', in C. Ess (ed.) *Philosophical Perspectives on Computer-Mediated Communication*, Albany: State University of New York.

Lawrence, P. R. and Lorsch, J. (1967) ' New management job: the integration', *Harvard Business Review*, 45, 6:142–51.

Leavitt, H. J. and Lipman-Blumen, J. (1995) 'Hot groups', *Harvard Business Review*, July–August: 110–7.

Lechner, F. J. (1990) 'The new utilitarianism', *Current Perspectives in Social Theory*, 10: 93–110.

Levi, M. (1996) 'Social and Unsocial Capital: A Review Essay of Robert Putnam's Making Democracy Work', *Politics and Society* 24,1:45–55.

Lewis, D. (1969) *Convention*, Cambridge, MA: Harvard University Press.

Lewis, J. D. and Weigert, A. (1985) 'Trust as a social reality', *Social Forces* 63:967–85.

Lonkila, M. (1997) 'Informal exchange relations in post-Soviet Russia: a comparative perspective', *Sociological Research Online* 2, 2:http://www.socresonline.org.uk/socresonline/2/2/2.html

Lockwood, D. (1992) *Solidarity and Schism*, Oxford: Clarendon Press.

Los, M. (1990) 'Introduction', in M. Los (ed.) *The Second Economy in Marxist States*, London: Macmillan.

—— (ed.) (1990) *The Second Economy in Marxist States*, London: Macmillan.

Luckmann, T. (1996) 'The privatization of religion and morality', in P. Heelas *et al* (eds) *Detraditionalization*, Oxford: Blackwell.

Luhmann, N. (1988) 'Familiarity, confidence and trust', in D. G. Gambetta (ed.) *Trust. Making and Breaking Cooperative Relations*, Oxford: Blackwell.

—— (1986) *Love as Passion*, Cambridge, MA: Harvard University Press.

—— (1982) *The Differentiation of Society*, New York: Columbia University Press.

—— (1979) *Trust and Power*, Chichester: Wiley.

Lukasiewicz, P. and Sicinski, A. (1989) 'Stabilization, crisis, normalization and life-styles', in W. Adamski and Wnuk-Lipinski, E. (eds) *Poland in the 1980s*, Warsaw: Polish Scientific Publishers.

Lundvall, B. A. (1992) 'User-producer relationships, national systems of innovation and internationalisation', in B. A. Lundvall (ed.) *National Systems of Innovation*, London: Pinter.

MacIntyre, A. (1988) *Whose Justice? Which Rationality?*, Notre Dame: University of Notre Dame Press.

—— (1981) *After Virtue. A Study of Moral Theory*, London: Duckworth.

MacKinnon, R. C. (1995) 'Searching for the Leviathan in Usenet', in S. G. Jones (ed.) *Cybersociety. Computer-mediated Communication and Community*, London: Sage.

Madrick, J. (1998) 'Computers: waiting for the Revolution', *New York Review of Books*, 26 March: 29–33.

Maffesoli, M. (1996) *The Time of the Tribes. The Decline of Individualism in Mass Society*, London: Sage.

Maier, C. S. (1992) 'Democracy since the French revolution' in J. Dunn (ed.) *Democracy, the Unfinished Journey*, Oxford: Oxford Univerity Press.

Mandeville, B. (1729) (1970) *The Fable of the Bees, vol. II*, Introduction and edited by P. Harth, Harmondsworth: Penguin.

Mannheim, K. (1992) *Essays on the Sociology of Culture*, London: Routledge.

Manning, P. (1992) *Erving Goffman and Modern Sociology*, Cambridge: Polity Press.

Marcuse, H. (1969) *Eros and Civilization*, Boston: Beacon Press.

Margalit, A. (1996) *The Decent Society*, Cambridge, MA: Harvard University Press.

Marinotti, G. (1994) 'The new social morphology of cities', UNESCO/MOST, Vienna, 10–12 February, unpublished paper.

Marody, M. (1981) *Polacy 1980*, Warszawa: ISUW.

Marwell, G. and Oliver, P. E. (1988) 'Social networks and collective action: a theory of critical mass', *American Journal of Sociology* 94:502–34.

Mayer, C. *et al* (1995) 'An integrative model of organizational trust', *Academy of Management Review* 20, 3:709–34.

McLaughlin, M. L., Osborne, K. K. and Smith, C. B. (1995) 'Standards of conduct on Usenet', in S. G. Jones (ed.) *Cybersociety. Computer-mediated Communication and Community*, London: Sage.

McKenney, J. L., Zack, M. H. and Doherty, V. S. (1992) 'Complementary communication media', in N. Nohria and Eccles, R. G. (eds) *Networks and Organizations*, Boston: Harvard Business School Press.

Mead, G. H. (1934) *Mind, Self and Society from the Standpoint of a Social Behavior*, Chicago: University of Chicago.

Melucci, A. (1996) *The Playing Self*, Cambridge: Cambridge University Press.

—— (1989) *Nomads of the Present: Social Movements and Individual Needs in Contemporary Society*, Philadelphia: Temple University Press.

Mennell, S. (1989) *Norbert Elias*, Oxford: Blackwell.

Meny, Y. (1996) 'Politics, corruption and democracy', *European Journal of Political Research* 30 September: 111–23.

Merton, R. K. (1952) 'Bureaucratic structure and personality', in R. K. Merton *et al* (eds) *Reader in Bureaucracy*, New York: The Free Press.

Meyerson, E. M. (1994) 'Human capital, social capital and compensation', *Acta Sociologica* 37:383–99.

Meyrowitz, J. (1985) *No Sense of Place*, Oxford: Oxford University Press.

Mickelson, K. D. (1997) 'Seeking social support', in S. Kiesler (ed.) *Culture of the Internet*, Mahawah, NJ: Lawrence Erbaum Associates.

Milgram, S. (1974) *Obedience to Authority: An Experimental View*, London: Tavistock.

Miller, A. I. (1989). 'Imagery and intuition in creative scientific thinking', in D. B. Wallace and Gruber, H. E. (eds) *Creative People at Work*, Oxford: Oxford University Press.

Minzberg, H. (1973) *The Nature of Managerial Work*, New York: Harper and Row.

Misztal, B. A. (1996) *Trust In Modern Societies*, Cambridge: Polity Press.

Mitchell, J. N. (1978) *Social Exchnge, Dramaturgy and Ethnomethodology*, New York: Elsevier.

Mitchell, W. (1995) *The City of Bits: Space, Time and the Infobahn*, Cambridge, MA: MIT Press.

Moore, D. W. (1995) *The Emperor's Virtual Clothes*, Chapell Hill: Algonquin Books.

Morley, I. E. and Stephenson,G. M. (1970) 'Interpersonal and interparty exchange', *British Journal of Psychology* 60:543–5.

Mouzelis, N. (1997) 'Social and system integration: Lockwood, Habermas, Giddens', *Sociology* 31, 1:11–19.

—— (1995) *Sociological Theory: What Went Wrong?*, London: Routledge.

—— (1993) 'The Poverty of Sociological Theory', *Sociology* 27, 4:675–96.

—— (1991) *Back to Sociological Theory: The Construction of Social Order*, London: Macmillian.

Moyal, A. (1989) 'The feminist culture of the telephone', *Prometheus* 17, 1:5–31.

Mozlowski, A. (1995) 'Zmowa milczenia', *Polityka* 27 May: 14–5.

Mulgan, G. J. (1997) *Connexity. How to Live in a Connected World*, London: Chatto & Windus.

Murray, Les (1997), *Subhuman Redneck Poems*, Sydney: Farrar, Straus, and Gorroux.

Negroponte, N. (1995) *Being Digital*, Rydalmere: Hodder and Stoughton.

Newton, T. (1998) 'Sociogenesis of emotion', in G. Bendelow and S. J.Williams (eds) *Emotions in Social Life*, London: Routledge.

Niosi, J. (1996) 'Strategic technological collaboration in Canadian industry', in R. Coombs *et al* (eds) *Technological Collaboration*, Cheltenham: Elgar.

Nisbet, R.A. (1970) *The Sociological Tradition*, London: Heinemann.

Nohria, N. and Eccles, R. G. (1992) 'Face-to-face', in N. Nohria and Eccles, R. G. (eds) *Networks and Organizations*, Boston: Harvard Business School Press.

North, D. C. (1990) *Institutions, Institutional Change and Economic Performance*, Cambridge: Cambridge University Press.

Nowak, S. (1989) 'The attitudes, values, and aspirations of Polish society', in W. Adamski and Wnuk-Lipinski, E. (eds) *Poland in the 1980s*, Warsaw: Polish Scientific Publishers.

Offe, C. (1996a) *Modernity and the State*, Cambridge: Polity Press.

—— (1996b) *Designing Institutions for East European Transistions*, Budapest Institute for Advanced Study, Public Lecture.

—— (1991) 'Capitalism by design' *Social Research* 58, 4:856–92.

Oldenburg, R. (1989) *The Great Good Places: Cafes, Coffee Shops, Community Centers, Beauty Parlors, General stores, Bars, Hangouts and How They Get You through the Day*, New York: Paragon House.

Olson, M. (1982) *The Rise and Decline of Nations*, New Haven: Yale University Press.

Oommen, T. K. (1995) 'Contested boundaries and emerging pluralism', *International Sociology* 10, 3:251–68.

Osowski, J. V. (1989) 'Ensembles of metaphor in the psychology of William James', in D. B. Wallace and Gruber, H. E. (eds) *Creative People at Work*, Oxford: Oxford University Press.

Ostrom, E. (1990) *Governing Commons: The Evolution of Institutions for Collective Action*, Cambridge: Cambridge University Press.

Parsons, T. (1951) *The Social System*, New York: Free Press.

Passmore, J. (1979) *The Perfectibility of Man*, Duckworth: London.

Pawlik, W. (1988) *Prawo, Moralnosc, Gospodarka Alternatywna*, Warszawa: Instytut Profilaktyki Spolecznej i Resocjalizacji, Universytet Warszawski.

Perkins, D. N. (1981) *The Mind's Best Work*, Cambridge: Cambridge University Press.

Piattoni, S. (1995) 'Review of Putnam's Making Democracy Work', *Journal of Modern Italian Studies* 1, 1, Fall: 160–5.

Pliskin, N. and Romm, C. T. (1994) 'Empowerment effect of electronic group communication: a case study' *Working Paper*. Department of Management, University of Woollongong.

Polanyi, M. (1969) *Knowing and Being*, London: Routledge.

—— (1967) *The Tacit Dimension*, New York: Doubleday.

—— (1958) *The Study of Man*, Chicago: University of Chicago.

—— (1948) *Full Employment and Free Trade*, Cambridge: Cambridge University Press

Poleszczuk, J. (1991) 'Praca w systemie gospodarki planowej', in M. Marody (ed.) *Co Nam Zostalo z tych Lat 1991*, London: Aneks.

Porter, M. (1990) *Competitive Advantages of Nations*, New York: The Free Press.

Porter, T. M. (1995) *Trust in Numbers*, Princeton: Princeton University Press.

Porters, A. and Sensenbrenner, J. (1993) 'Embeddedness and immigration', *American Journal of Sociology* 98:1332–50.

Poster, M. (1990) *The Mode of Information*, Cambridge: Polity Press.

Price, D. L. De Solla (1963) *Little Science, Big Science*, New York: Columbia University Press.

Putnam, R. (1995) 'A generation of loners?' in *The World in 1996*, The Economist Publications.

—— (1993) *Making Democracy Work: Civic Tradition in Modern Italy*, Princeton: Princeton University Press.

Radosovic, S. (1991) 'Techno-economic networking and social intelligence as useful concepts in technology policy making', in B. Cronin and Tudor-Silovoc, N. (eds) *From Information Management to Social Intelligence*, London: Tavistock.

Rawls, J. (1993) *Political Liberalism*, New York: Columbia University Press.

Rawls, W. A. (1987) 'The Interaction Oder Sui Generis', *Sociological Theory* 5:136–49.

—— (1984) 'Interaction as a Resource for Epistemological Critique', *Sociological Theory* 2:222–52.

Ray, L. J. (1996) *Social Theory and The Crisis of State Socialism*, Cheltenham: Edward Elgar.

Reich, R. B. (1994) 'The fracturing of the middle class', *New York Times*, August 13:19.

Reid, L. A. (1977) 'Comparing telephone with face-to-face contact', in: I. de Sola Pool (ed.) *The Social Impact of the Telephone*, Cambridge, MA,: MIT Press.

Reiman, J. H. (1988) 'Privacy, Intimacy, and personhood', in F. D. Schoeman (ed.) *Philosophical Dimensions of Privacy: An Anthology*, Cambridge: Cambridge University Press.

Reis, E. P. (1998) 'Banfield's Amoral Familism Revisited', in J. Alexander (ed.) *Real Civil Societies*, London: Sage.

Revel, J. (1989) 'The uses of civility', in R. Chartier (ed.) *Passions of the Renaissance*, (A History of Private Life vol. III), Cambridge, MA: The Belknap Press.

Rheingold, H. (1993) *The Virtual Community*, Reading, MA: Addison-Wesley.

Rice, F. (1991) 'Champions of communication', *Fortune*, 3 June: 111–20.

Ring, S. M. and Van de Ven, A. (1992) 'Structuring cooperative relationships between organizations', *Strategic Management Journal* 13:483–98.

Ritzer, G. (1993) *The McDonaldization of Society*, The Thousands Oaks: Pine Forge Press.

Roberts, J. (1996) 'From discipline to dialogue', in R. Munro and Mouritsen, J. (eds) *Accountability. Power, Ethos and The Technologies of Managing*, London: International Thompson Press.

Rock, P. (1978) *The Making of Symbolic Interactionism*, London: Macmillan.

Rogers, S. C. (1991) *Shaping Modern Times in Rural France*, Princeton: Princeton University Press.

Rohwer, J. (1996) *Asia Rising*, London: Nicolas Brealey Publishing.

Rona-Tas, A. (1994) 'The first shall be last; entrepreneurship and communist cadres in the transition from socialism', *American Journal of Sociology*, 100, 1:40–69.

Roniger, L. (1994) 'The comparative studies of clientelism', in L. Roniger and Gunes-Ayata, A. (eds) *Democracy, Clientelism, and Civil Society*, Boulder: Lynne Rienner.

—— (1990) *Hierarchy and Trust in Modern Mexico and Brazil*, Westport: Praeger.

Rose, A. (1962) 'A systematic summary of symbolic interaction theory', in A. Rose (ed.) *Human Behaviour and Social Processes*, London: Routledge and Kegan Paul.

Rushkoff, D. (1994) *Media Virus*, New York: Ballantine Books.

Rutenbeck, J. (1996) ' A victory of form over content', *The Australian*, 9 July: 12.

Ryan, A. (1983) 'Private selves and public parts', in S. I. Been and Gaus, G. F. (eds) *Public and Private Social Life*, London: Croom Hall.

Rychard, A. (1985) *Wladza i Interesy w Gospodarce*, Warszawa: Officyna Naukowa.

—— (1980) *Reforma Gospodarcza*, Wroclaw: Ossolineum.

—— (1993) *Reforms, Adaptation, and Breakthrough*, Warsaw: IFiS PAN.

Sabel, C. F. (1994) 'Flexible specialisation and the re-emergence of regional Economies', in A. Amin (ed.) *Post-Fordism*, Oxford: Blackwell.

—— (1993) 'Studied Trust: Building new forms of cooperation in a volatile economy', in R. Swedberg (ed.) *Explorations in Economic Sociology*, New York: Sage.

—— (1989) 'Flexible specialisation and the re-emergence of regional economies', in P. Hirst *et al* (eds) *Revising Industrial Decline*, Oxford: Berg.

Sabetti, F. (1996) 'Path dependency and civic culture', *Politics and Society* 24, 1:19–44.

Schama, S. (1988) *The Embarrassment of Riches*, Berkeley: University of California Press.

Scharpf, F. W. (1993a) 'Coordination in hierarchies and networks', in F. W. Scharpf (ed.) *Games in Hierarchies and Networks,* Campus Verlag: Westview Press.

—— (1993b) 'Games in hierarchies and networks: Introduction', in F. W. Scharpf. (ed.) *Games in Hierarchies and Networks,* Campus Verlag: Westview Press.

Scheff, T. J. (1990) *Microsociology Discourse, Emotion, and Social Structure,* Chicago: University of Chicago.

Scheibe, K. E. (1995) *Self-Studies. The Psychology of Self and Identity,* Westport: Praeger.

Schoeman, F. D. (1988) 'Privacy: Philosophical dimensions of the literature', in F. D. Schoeman (ed.) *Privacy and Social Freedom,* Cambridge: Cambridge University Press.

Schumpeter, J. (1991) *Essays on Entrepreneurs, Innovations, Business Cycles and Evolution of Capitalism,* edited by R. V. Clemance, with R. Swedberg's introduction, New Brunswick: Transaction Books.

Schutz, A. (1967) *The Phenomenology of the Social World,* trans. G. Walsh, London: Heinemann.

—— (1964) *Collected Papers. Studies in Social Theory. vol. II,* The Hague: Martins Nijhoff.

Schwartz, H. S. (1993) 'Narcissistic emotion and university', in S. Fineman (ed.) *Emotion in Organization,* London: Sage.

Scott, J. (1991) *Social Network Analysis,* London: Sage.

Seabrook, J. (1997) *Deeper. My Two-year Odyssey in Cyberspace,* New York: Simon and Schuster.

Secord, P. F. (1997) 'The mark of the social in the social science', in J. D. Greenwood (ed.) *The Mark of the Social,* Boulder: Rowman and Littlefield.

Seligman, A. B. (1998) 'Between public and private' *Society* 35, 3:30–6.

—— (1997) *The Problem of Trust,* Princeton: Princeton University Press.

—— (1992) *The Idea of Civil Society,* New York: Free Press.

Senker, J. and Faulkner, W. (1992) 'Industrial use of public sector research and advanced technologies', *R & D Management* 22, 2:157–75.

—— (1996) 'Networks, tacit knowledge and innovation', in R. Coombs *et al* (eds) *Technological Collaboration,* Cheltenham: Elgar.

Sennett, R. (1998) *The Corrosion of Character: The Personal Consequences of Work in the New Capitalism,* New York: Norton.

—— (1974) *The Fall of Public Man,* Cambridge: Cambridge University Press.

Shapin, S. (1994) *A Social History of Truth,* Chicago: University of Chicago Press.

Shardlow, N. (1996) 'The Internet and the I', *Time Literary Supplement,* 10 May: 14

Shelley, L. I. (1990) 'The second economy in the Soviet Union', in M. Los (ed.) *The Second Economy in Marxist States,* London: Macmillan.

Shils, E. (1992) 'Civility and civil society', in E. C. Banfield (ed.) *Civility and Citizenship in Liberal Democratic Societies,* New York: A PWPA Book.

Silver, A. (1997) 'Two different sorts of commerce', in J. Weintraub and Kumar, K. (eds) *Public and Private in Thought and Practice,* Chicago: University of Chicago Press.

Simmel, G. (1978) *The Philosophy of Money,* London: Routledge.

—— (1950) *The Sociology of Georg Simmel,* trans. and ed. by K. H. Wolff, New York: Free Press.

Simonton, D. K. (1997) *Genius and Creativity,* Greenwich: Ablex Publishing.

Smejdy, M. (1996) *Szara Strefa w Okresie Transformacji Gospodarki Polskiej,* Katowice: Wydawnictwo Uniwersytetu Slaskiego.

Smith, M. *et al* (eds) (1997) *The Creative Cognition Approach*, Cambridge, MA: Bradford Press.

Smolar, A. (1994) 'Komentarz', *Nowa ResPublica*, 70:26.

Spiewak, P. (1997) 'Cynicy i integrysci', *Tygodnik Powszechny* 19, 11 May: 3.

Sorensen, K. H. and Levold, N. (1992) 'Tacit networks, heterogeneous engineers, and embodied technology', *Science, Technology and Human Values* 17, 1:13–35.

Sproull, L. and Faraj, S. (1997) 'Atheism, sex, and database: the Net as a social technology', in S. Kiesler (ed.) *Culture of the Internet*, Mahawah, NJ: Lawrence Erbaum Associates.

Sproull, L. and Kiesler S. (1991) *Connections. New Ways of Working in the Networked Organization*, Cambridge, MA: MIT Press.

Stacey, J. (1993) *Brave New Families*, New York: Basic Books.

Stallabrass, J. (1995) 'Empowering technology: the exploration of cyberspace', *New Left Review* 211:3–33.

Staniszkis, J. (1995) 'Polityka postkomunistycznyej institucjonalizacji w perspektywie historycznej', in A. Sulek and Styk. J. (eds) *Instytucje i Ludzie. Stawanie sie Ladu Spolecznego*, Lublin: Wydawnictwo UMCS.

—— (1991) 'Political capitalism', *Eastern European Politics and Society* 5:17–31.

Stark, D. (1992) 'From system identity to organizational diversity: analyzing social change in Eastern Europe', *Sisyphus* 1, 8:77–89.

—— (1990) 'Privatization in Hungary', *Eastern European Politics and Societies*, Fall: 351–93.

—— (1989) 'Bending the bar of the iron cage,' *Sociological Forum* 4, 4:637–64.

Sterling, B. (1992) *The Hacker Crackdown: Law and Disorder on Electronic Frontier*, New York: Bantam.

Steward, F. and Conway, S. (1996) 'Informal networks in the origination of successful innovations', in R. Cooms *et al* (eds) *Technological Collaboration*, Cheltenham: Elgar.

Stichweb, R. (1997) 'The stranger – on the sociology of indifference', *Thesis Eleven* 51:1–16.

Stinchcombe, A. L. (1990) *Information and Organization*, Berkeley: University of California.

Szacki, J. (1979) *History of Sociological Thought*, Westport: Greenwood Press.

Szelenyi, S., Szelenyi, I. and Kovach, I. (1995) 'Sfragementaryzowane elity wegierskie; krazenie w politcyce, reproducja w gospodarce', in I. Szelenyi, Treiman, D. and Wnuk-Lipinski, E. (eds) *Elity w Polsce, w Rosji i na Wegrzech*, Warszawa: Instytut Studiow Politycznych PAN.

Szelenyi, I., Treiman, D. and Wnuk-Lipinski, E. (eds), (1995) *Elity w Polsce, w Rosji i na Wegrzech*, Warszawa: Instytut Studiow Politycznych PAN.

Sztompka, P. (1996) 'Trust in emerging democracy', *International Sociology* 11, 1:37–62.

Tarkowska, E. (1994) 'Awaiting society: the temporal dimension of transformation in Poland', in A. Flis and Seel, P. (eds) *Social Time and Temporality*, Krakow: Goethe Institut.

Tarkowski, J. (1995) 'Political patronage', *Politicus*, Special Issues, August, Bulletin of the Institute of Political Studies Polish Academcy of Sciences: 32–8.

—— (1994a) *Socjologia i Polityka, Volume 1: Wladza i Spoleczenstwo w Systemie Autorytarnym*, Warszawa: Instytut Studiow Politycznych PAN.

—— (1994b) *Socjologia i Polityka, Volume 2: Patroni I Klienci*, Warszawa: Instytut Studiow Politycznych PAN.

—— (1989) 'Old and new patterns of corruption in Poland and the USSR', *Telos* 80, Summer: 51–62.

Tatur, M. (1994) 'Corporatism as a paradigm of transformation', in J. Staniszkis (ed.) *W Poszukiwaniu Paradygmatu Transformacji*, Warszsawa: Instytut Studiow Politycznych PAN.

Taylor, C. (1985) *Philosophy Papers, Vol. 2: Philosophy and the Human Science*, Cambridge: Cambridge University Press.

Taylor, M. (1982) *Community, Anarchy and Liberty*, New York: Cambridge University Press.

Thompson, J. B. (1995) *The Media and Modernity*, Cambridge: Polity Press.

Thorngren, B. (1977) 'Silent actors', in I. de Sola Pool (ed.) *The Social Impact of the Telephone*, Cambridge, MA: MIT Press.

Touraine, A. (1998) 'Can we live together, equal and different?', *European Journal of Social Theory* 1, 2:165–79.

—— (1995) *Critique of Modernity*, Oxford: Blackwell.

Trilling, L. (1974) *Sincerity and Authenticity*, Oxford: Oxford University Press.

Turkle, S. (1996) *Life on the Screen*, New York: Simon and Schuster.

Turner, B. S. (1996) 'Introduction', in B. S. Turner (ed.) *The Blackwell Companion to Social Theory*, Oxford: Blackwell.

—— (1992) 'Introduction', in *K. Mannheim Essays on the Sociology of Culture*, London: Routledge.

Turner, J. H. (1988) *A Theory of Social Interaction*, Stanford: Stanford University Press.

—— (1987) 'Analytical Theorizing', in A. Giddens and Turner, J. H. (eds) *Social Theory Today*, Stanford: Stanford University Press.

—— (1982) *The Structure of Sociological Theory*, Hamewood , Ill.: The Dorsey Press.

Unger, A. (1994) 'The Economist Survey of Poland', *The Economist*, 16 April: 1–22.

Unger, R. M. (1987) *False Necessity*, Cambridge: Cambridge University Press.

Vetlesen, A. J. (1994) *Perception, Empathy, and Judgment*, University Park: The Pennsylvania State University.

Wagner, P. (1996) 'Crises of Modernity: Political Sociology in Historical Context', in S. P. Turner (ed.) *Social Theory and Sociology*, Oxford: Blackwell.

—— (1994) *A Sociology of Modernity*, London: Routledge.

Wallace, D. B. and Gruber, H. E. (eds) (1989) *Creative People at Work*, Oxford: Oxford University Press.

Walzer, M. (1983) *Spheres of Justice*, New York: Basic Books.

Wasilewski, J. (1995) 'Formowanie sie nowej elity', in A. Sulek. and Styk, J. (eds) *Ludzie i Instytucje*, Lublin: UMCS.

Weber, M. (1991) *The Protestant Ethic and the Spirit of Capitalism*, London: HarperCollins.

—— (1968) *Economy and Society, Vol. 2*, Berkeley: University of California Press.

Webster, F. (1995) *Theories of the Information Society*, London: Routledge.

Weigert, A. J. (1991) *Mixed Emotions. Certain Steps Toward Understanding Ambivalence*, Albany: State University of New York.

Weintraub, J. (1997) 'The theory and politics of the public and private distinction', in J. Weintraub and Kumar, K. (eds) *Public and Private in Thought and Practice*, Chicago: University of Chicago Press.

Weintraub, J. and Kumar, K. (eds) (1997) *Public and Private in Thought and Practice*, Chicago: University of Chicago Press.

Weisberg, R. W. (1986) *Creativity, Genius, and Other Myths*, New Yorks: W. H. Freeman.

Weiser, J. (1996) 'The tyranny of informality: denim downsize', *The New Republic*, 26 February: 7.

Wellman, B. (1997) 'An electronic group', in S. Kiesler (ed.) *Culture of the Internet*, Mahawah, NJ: Lawrence Erbaum Associates.

—— (1983) 'Network analysis: some basic principles', *Sociological Theory* 1:155–200.

—— (1979) 'The intimate networks of East Yorkers', *American Journal of Sociology* 84, 5: 1202–28.

Wellman, B. *et al* (1996) 'Computer networks as social networks: collaborative work, telework and virtual community', *Annual Review of Sociology* 22:213–38.

Wesolowski, W. (1996) 'The new beginnings of the entrepreneurial classes', *Polish Sociological Review* 1, 113:79–96.

—— (1994) 'Social bonds in post-communist societies', in M. Alestalo *et al* (eds) *The Transformation of Europe. Social Conditions and Consequences*, Warsaw: IFiS PAN.

Wichman, H. (1970) 'Effects of isolation and communication on cooperation in a two-person game', *Journal of Personality and Social Psychology* 16:114–20.

Wilde, O. (1970) 'Phrases and philosophies for the use of the young', in R. Ellman (ed.) *The Artist as Critic: Critical Writing of Oscar Wilde*, New York: W. H. Allen.

Williams, B. (1988) 'Formal structure and social reality' in D. G. Gambetta (ed.) *Trust. Making and Breaking Cooperative Relations*, Oxford: Blackwell.

Willmott, H. (1994) 'Bringing agency (back) into organisational analysis', in J. Hassard and Parker, M. (eds) *Towards a New Theory of Organisation*, London: Routledge.

Wilson, R. (1997) 'What the butler saw: a woman who lives for the camera', *The Australian*, 22 January: 9.

Wnuk-Lipinski, E. (1990) *Grupy i Wiezi Spoleczne w Systemie Monocentrycznym*, Warszawa: IFiS PAN.

Wnuk-Lipinski, E. and Wasilewski, J. (1995) 'How much communism is left with us?', *Politicus*, Special Issues, August Bulletin of the Institute of Political Studies PAN: 39–45.

Wolfe, A. (1997) 'Public and private in theory and practice', in J. Weintraub and Kumar, K. (eds) *Public and Private in Thought and Practice*, Chicago: University of Chicago Press.

—— (1992) 'Democracy versus Sociology. Boundaries and their Sociological Consequences', in M. Lamont and Fournier, M. (eds) *Cultivating Differences. Symbolic Boundaries and the Making of Inequality*, Chicago: Chicago University Press.

—— (ed.) (1991) *America at Century's End*, Berkeley: University of California Press.

Woolcock, M. (1998) 'Social capital and economic development', *Theory and Society* 27, 2: 151–207.

Wooley, S. (1998) 'Should we legislate for privacy?', *The Australian*, 5 March: 11.

Woollacott, M. (1998) 'Weighed down by an information overload', *Guardian Weekly*, 15 March: 7.

Woolley, B. (1992) *Virtual worlds: A Journey in Hype and Hyperreality*, Oxford: Blackwell.

Wouters, C. (1986) 'Formalization and Informalization', *Theory, Culture and Society* 3, 2:18.

Yamin, M. (1996) 'Understanding "strategic alliances": the limits of transaction cost of economics', in R. Cooms *et al* (eds) *Technological Collaboration*, Cheltenham: Elgar.

Young, K. (1998) *Caught in the Net*, London: Wiley.

Zaborowski, W. (1998) 'Starta I nowa struktura spoleczna', in. W. Adamski (ed.) *Polacy 95*, Warszawa: IfiS PAN.

Zakowski, J. (1995) 'Pochwala skandalu', *Gazeta Wyborcza*, 21 January: 8–9.

—— (1994) 'Tak gnije demokracja', *Gazeta Wyborcza*, 26 November: 8–11.

Zaltman, G., Duncan, R. and Holbeck, H. (1984) *Innovations and Organizations*, Malabar: Robert E. Krieger Publishing Company.

Zeldin, T. (1998) *Conversation*, London: Harvill Press.

—— (1994) *An Intimate History of Humanity*, London: Sinclair-Stevenson.

Zukowski, T. (1988) 'Fabryki-urzedy i ich ewolucja', in W. Morawski and Kozek, W. (eds) *Zalamanie sie Porzadku Etatstycznego*,Warszawa: IS Uniwersytet Warszawski.

Index